From Pit Boots to Green Wellies

From Pit Boots to Green Wellies

Margaret Foster

© Margaret Foster 2010

The moral right of the author has been asserted.

Published 2010 by Fruition Publishing Limited
www.fruition-publishing.co.uk

All Rights Reserved. No part of this book may be reproduced, adapted, stored in a retrieval system or transmitted by any means, electronic, mechanical, photocopying, or otherwise without the prior written permission of the author.

ISBN 978-0-9566524-0-9

Prepared and printed by:

York Publishing Services Ltd
64 Hallfield Road
Layerthorpe
York YO31 7ZQ
Tel: 01904 431213

Website: www.yps-publishing.co.uk

Dedicated to Mam and Dad

Contents

Acknowledgements	viii
Prologue	ix
Chapter One	1
Chapter Two	16
Chapter Three	41
Chapter Four	61
Chapter Five	77
Chapter Six	83
Chapter Seven	97
Chapter Eight	112
Chapter Nine	126
Chapter Ten	139
Chapter Eleven	151
Chapter Twelve	168
Chapter Thirteen	185
Chapter Fourteen	196
Chapter Fifteen	209
Chapter Sixteen	224
Chapter Seventeen	233
Chapter Eighteen	248
Glossary	256

Acknowledgements

About five years ago, I was talking to my Niece, Kelly, about my life as a landlady and the hilarious things that happened in those years. Kelly suggested that I should write a book about my life. I had thought about writing a book and knew that one day I would, speaking to Kelly made me realise that I should get on with it.

I wanted to be able to remember the wonderful people that I have met in my life, and those wonderful characters that have made this book possible. I would like to thank all these people, and remember the ones that have now sadly passed away. I would also like to say thank you to my sons, Adrian, and Christopher, who moved from one place to another in their young lives without one word of complaint.

Thanks to my brother, Patrick, and my niece, Kimberly, for being the first to read my script and for constantly ringing me, telling me how funny they thought it was, giving me the encouragement I needed.

To Nadio, for taking so much of his time to help get this book published and to my editor and sister-in-law Susan, for all the hours spent, correcting my grammar. Thank you.

Most of all I would like to thank my husband Geoff, for everything.

Prologue

Sitting in this recreation park knowing it was for the last time tore at my heart. Although I was looking forward to my new life, I wished that I could put the view that was all around me into a suitcase and take it with me. Steeton was such a lovely place to live, near enough to the main towns and yet one of the gateways to the Yorkshire Dales.

From the first day of moving into The Goat's Head, I had brought my dogs here with me, I loved to sit on the swings that were in the park, and look at the spectacular views in the daytime. Late at night after closing time, I would go back there again and stare out towards Ilkley Moor, and watch the headlights of cars flickering as they travelled up the hills. In the summer months, different sounds travelled from afar and then it would fall silent again; sometimes I could hear the sounds of animals coming from the woodland behind me. The winter was even nicer. When it was freezing cold I would wrap up well and watch the stars twinkling down on me in the dead of night. My feet would crunch in the frosty grass and the air would have a completely different feel to it.

I had come here twice a day, every day, for two years in all kinds of weather; if it rained or snowed I would wear my green wellies and a waterproof jacket. During the day you could see Ilkley Moor and all the surrounding hills and woodlands. Further up the road was a little village called Cross Hills and one of the locals told me this was named so because from there you could see all across the hills that surrounded the area and that if anyone asked where a certain place was, they would say;

Right ore yonder, cross hills.

This, however, was to be the last evening sitting here on this swing, looking up at the sky and the stars. It was January and bitter cold, I took some deep breaths and looked at Gyp my older dog, I was sure she sensed something was about to change. I felt so privileged to have lived here and wondered if I would ever get to live in such a perfect place again.

I made my way back to The Goat's Head for the last time and went to bed with all my bags packed ready for the move tomorrow. This was the end of being a landlady and my mind was drifting back to where it all began.

Chapter One

I was collecting glasses and trying my best to get the locals to drink up so that I could get finished off and go home. I had to be up early in the morning for work.

Can I have your glasses please; it's time to go home now. Have you no homes to go to or what?

I wandered around collecting as many glasses as I could from each table, ready to wash and put them away, and then empty the ashtrays and wipe the tables down. I was busy at one particular table when one of the customers commented on me having my own pub;

Have you ever thought of running your own pub Maggie? You would make a good landlady.

I have actually, I have thought about it a lot lately and Chris is really keen on the idea, but to get a pub in a nice place like this, is not going to happen.

My friends had a pub in a quiet little village on the outskirts of Barnsley, near enough to the towns and still with a feeling of being in the country. I helped behind the bar there occasionally and really enjoyed it. This particular pub had no taproom or juke box but it was always busy and as they were mostly local people, you got to know them well. There was always laughter around the bar and without sounding big headed I was well liked and popular amongst the customers. I had a good job, driving for the Social Services, transporting the elderly and mentally handicapped in a mini bus and was happy in my job. This was the only doubt I had; I knew we would have to sell the house to raise the large amount of money needed for the tenancy and the fixtures and fittings, but that didn't bother me.

The thought of a country pub sounded ideal and I would lay day dreaming and picturing the scene in my mind. A country pub with a nice setting, tables outside on a summer's day, the sounds of nature all around and me, standing there behind the bar chatting to the locals. But just as I thought, we were offered a pub in a council estate near to where I was brought up. At least we were offered one straight away, the area manager had said that there were no country pubs available at that time. Things happened pretty fast after our interview. One day we seemed to be discussing having a pub of our own and the next minute we were on a training course.

I found it hard to view property when people are still living there; it's like an infringement of their private life, which meant I didn't really remember much at all after viewing the living area. But we would go to the Woodmoor and have a drink often, to 'weigh' the clientele up, posing as customers, making plans as to what we would like to change. The first change would be a carpet as there was no carpet down in the lounge bar. The furniture was Olde Worlde and I thought it would look nicer with a carpet and some plants around the windows. The bar was one long bar that ran all the way through from the lounge to the taproom, it was divided by a small square room where the doors to the living quarters were and also the cellar door. The lounge and the taproom were also divided by a small corridor where the customers could go from one room to another; it also contained the ladies' toilet. Tucked in the corner of the right hand side entrance, was a small room called the snug which was a place that sold alcohol to the public without actually going into the bar. When I was young I remember women used to go with jugs to fill with ale for their husbands. My Grandfather was one of those men that had a jug of ale. When my grandmother brought it home he would put the poker in the fire until it was red hot and then stick it in his glass of ale, this was common practice then. He would sit in his chair with a pipe and his glass of ale like a king on his throne. The snug was also a shop that sold sweets and soft drinks and this is where we used to buy our sweets when we were children. In those days shops closed at teatime and supermarkets didn't exist.

It isn't easy moving from one place to another as anyone who has moved house knows, but moving into a pub is very hard. The previous tenants move out the same day you move in and then you're expected to work immediately. The place is in a mess upstairs with unpacked clothes, tempers flare, boxes need unpacking and there isn't enough room for everything. Everyone is hungry and asking what time dinner will be. You're unable to find anything and there just aren't enough electrical plugs for the kitchen appliances. All this and you're expected to look your best in the evening; after all you know that people are coming in to 'weigh' you up now.

The thing I remember the most now about the Woodmoor was the dowdy colours of brown. I suppose that was to mask the nicotine really, it certainly wasn't dirty, just dull and I could not wait to brighten it up, upstairs and downstairs. The living quarters of the 'Woody' had a very large lounge with patio doors leading to a balcony overlooking the back of the pub and the schools behind it. In fact one of those schools was the senior school I had attended until leaving school in 1963 and unlike my junior school, it was run by teachers and not nuns.

The bathroom was opposite a very tiny kitchen and there was a long dark passage way with four bedrooms leading off. The whole place, just like the downstairs, was dark, dingy and old fashioned. It didn't take long for me to realise that this was a pub and not a house and that as this was a drinker's pub, they were never bothered about what the place looked like. It had a really good atmosphere and the people felt comfortable popping in straight from work. The previous tenants were there a long time and Jack, the landlord, was quite a character and the customers were sorry to see him go into retirement. We got to really like him ourselves in the short time we knew him. He would sing behind the bar and sounded just like Bing Crosby.

The day after moving I got up early and had a good look around the place. Behind the bar was a door to the upstairs and a door that went downstairs into the cellar. Up to now I had not seen the cellar so that was my first call. I felt a little scared down there, which is unusual for me; it was huge, in fact the size of the whole building. It had passages with separate rooms and high ceilings. All the stock was kept down there; the spirits and bottled beer were locked in one of the smaller rooms. Some parts of the cellar were very chilly as one would expect but one room was exceptionally warm due to the boiler being there.

There was a room with big switches for the gas and electric and in this room I felt very uneasy and couldn't get out quick enough. For some strange reason I felt as if I was being watched.

The upstairs living quarters were very cold; in fact it was October when we moved in and so cold that you could see your own breath. We could not get this place warm other than by practically sitting by the fire. We bought extra fan heaters and it was still cold.

The help from my family was very much appreciated. My mother and Aunty Rene took the job of cleaning the pub each morning, my cousin

John helped behind the bar and he was brilliant with the customers and Billy, another of my cousins, helped us so much in getting things sorted upstairs. I felt so lucky now to be there with my family. There was still much to do and Teresa, my sister, came to see if I needed help. We rearranged the furniture and put the books on the book shelf, then sat down and had a cup of tea. I commented on the place being cold and said that I hoped it wasn't haunted. I had no sooner said it when a book seemed to throw itself off the shelf and landed on the table. Now this may be hard to believe, but the book was called 'The Haunted Sisters', a book I had bought years ago and had never read. Perhaps it was a coincidence, chances are it was and no more was said.

One of our first customers was an Irishman that I knew as a young girl. He was the rag and bone man. He came around our streets with a horse and cart shouting 'pots for rags' and we would take old clothes out to him and get cups in return. He came around regularly, which we all liked. Being a big family meant that crockery was constantly being broken, and we had to drink tea out of jam jars, just as most big families around these parts used to do and if the jams jars got broken, then we had to wait while a cup was free to use, which meant that by that time the tea in the pot was cold and 'stewed', as we called it. There was always a crowd of kids around him, as we were all in the same boat. We had very little in those days, although there was plenty of work. Dad worked very long hours on the building sites but the wages were very poor. Most people remember the poor days as the good old days and I believe they were in some ways. There was never any competition as to who had what, doors were never locked and, apart from my friend Nora, I didn't know anyone who had a phone and phone boxes were sparse in the estates but then the only time they were used was in an emergency. It was four pennies to stay on as long as you wanted and they had an A and a B button. The B button gave you your money back if no-one answered and often people would forget to do this so we went regularly to phone boxes pressing button B and getting money. Being without a phone meant writing letters or catching a bus and as it was a long ride to our grandparents' home in Kendrey and our uncle's house in Wombwell, usually two buses there and two buses back, this usually meant making a full day of it or even staying overnight. We always looked forward to these special days and also looked forward to our visitors coming to see us. The pace of life was much slower, no-one ever seemed to be in a rush then, we had such basic lives. It must be hard to believe to young ones today that we lived without hair dryers, showers, duvets, extra televisions, house phones and don't forget the mobile phone.

We lived on what was called the green, a large area of grass with houses all around it. The green was an ideal place for play, it was also the place where fights were held and I'm not just talking of children's fights. Parents often had arguments over children and some ended up in fights and they always seemed to be in the centre of the field. We thought that was funny, and once I went running into dad;

Dad, Dad, Mrs Myers is killing Mrs Hardy, hurry up;

Jaysus, Mary and Joseph, where?

On the green, she's nearly dead, hurry up, Mrs Myers is strangling her.

My father was having a shave at the time and he had just a towel wrapped around him and his face had shaving cream all over it. He ran outside (ok I might have exaggerated a little, the killing bit) but Mrs Myers was on the top of Mrs Hardy and belting away at her. He pulled Mrs Myers up as if she was a toy doll; he was very strong through his job of hod carrying, as this involved carrying a load of bricks up ladders for the builders. The whole street was watching my dad split this fight up in just a towel. Good job Mam was in town shopping.

I was always fighting with the boys on the street; I hated anyone pushing me around and I always fought back. After one fight that I had, which as usual was with a boy, I ended up much worse off than him and I went home crying. My mother was fuming because he was much bigger and older than me. She stormed across the green to the boy's house and brayed on the door; both my mother and his mother came out arguing like mad as they walked to the centre of the green. A crowd of kids soon came out of no-where waiting for a fight.

The shouting continued on the green;

Go on then, you strike me first.

You strike me first.

You started it.

Your bloody son started it.

Yeah, after your bloody daughter bit him on his hand. They were only fighting because she let down the tent pegs when they were camping arht in field last neet.

Me mam knew nothing of us letting their tent fall in on them. We had run like mad as they crawled out from the collapsed tent, putting their fists up and threatening to kill us. Me mam threw me a look and carried on arguing. We were all around them in a circle wondering when they were going to start fighting; I stood there and said to my friend Irene excitedly;

Me Mam'll kill her, just you wait.

We were let down because they both walked away and went home, and we stood there disappointed. This was not the end for me, however;

When are you going to bloody well grow up? Its time you acted your age, get them pots weshed up en dunt think yer laiking arht teneet.

Parents would fall out, all over the children, but within an hour or so the kids would be back playing together.

Through all the falling out and the fights we were still a very close community. Everyone chipped in to help if a mother was sent into hospital, usually by cooking and minding the children. In our case it was usually the maternity hospital for my mother, although our next door neighbour was the same, she had ten children. In those days if you didn't pay the electric bill, a man from the Electricity Board would come and 'cut you off'. This happened a lot on our street and even that wasn't moaned about. Me mam would cook on the fire and at night we would have candles burning and make shapes in the shadows as we played guessing games and we told stories. The electric man would have to catch you in first, to get inside, so we had look outs, the word would be passed up the street;

"Electric man is on his way, he's at number 33", and we would lock the doors and hide behind the couch. In fact we had to do this when any debt collectors came, they were known as 'callers'.

I must admit I felt a little embarrassed at first on seeing Johnny coming towards the bar and hoped he wouldn't recognise me, but immediately he asked how the 'auld fella' was in his strong Irish accent. This made me feel a little ashamed of my thoughts but I quickly put that behind me and told him Dad would be in later, asking if he remembered the little Labrador pup he once gave to me.

Oh Jaysus, de Labrador pup, course I remember Skipper; he was one of de pups frum me auld dog.

He had given me the pup free and I was glad I didn't have to find more rags in return. Had that been the case I would have taken clothes out from the wardrobes regardless. I was always in trouble for 'that dog' as Mam used to call it; she would wait while I got home from school and yell;

That bloody dog has shite in bedroom again; I'm telling you its bloody going.

My mother was not a dog lover in those days, but perhaps having a large family to look after had something to do with it. Besides having five surviving children, she had given birth to a still born, also a baby that died after a few weeks named John, and she also suffered five miscarriages. Both my grandmothers had a child late in life and my father's brother, Michael, who was two years older than me, lived with us for a while. On top of that my mother's sister, Val, was three years younger than I was and often slept at our house. These were happy days; the house was always full of laughter. However, a dog was not at all as welcome to me mam as it was to us.

Being the eldest, it seemed to me that my mother was always pregnant and when I reached my teens and understood more, I made up my mind that when I got married, no Pope, Church or Priest was going to tell me not to use contraception. I had seen my mother close to death more than once through pregnancies, on one occasion she was given the last rites by the priest and I went with Dad to see her in hospital. Although I wasn't allowed in the ward, I peeped through the glass door and saw her bed tipped up so that her legs were higher than her head. There were all sorts of tubes coming out of her and blood was being pumped into her body. Even after all this she went on to have yet another baby, Kevin, who was the last one. There came a time when she decided to go against the Catholic Church and have an operation to stop her having more children, as her life was greatly at risk with each one. The date was set then my brother had an accident with a dart and lost an eye. This according to Mam was God's anger at her and she cancelled the operation.

Skipper stayed and although she complained about him often enough, I believe there was a part of her that loved him. I caught her stroking him a couple of times. We had Skipper for some time and we loved him. He was a beautiful golden Labrador and I have very happy memories of him. Skipper was always in trouble for doing his business in the house. He was not very house trained and as me dad was usually the first up in a morning, he had the job of cleaning up after him and used to moan that there was always 'string' coming out of Skipper's bum. I suppose we knew little of dogs at that time and the 'string', as me dad called it, was probably worms and that must have been the reason he couldn't wait to go outside.

Then the worst possible thing happened to him. A neighbour's cat jumped on his back and clawed the poor dog's eyes and ears. They became infected a few days later and as he also had distemper by this time, I seemed to be forever cleaning up shit. It was horrible to clean up and made the place stink. We couldn't afford a vet and I think he was too far gone anyway, so I knew he would have to be put down, but no-one we knew had transport to take him to the RSPCA. Looking back now they probably would have come to take him.

"The lad across the street knows someone who will take it". Mam said to me while I stroked Skipper. He looked so ill and thin by now.

My heart was broken. I cried all the time, at home and in school. A few weeks went by and my mother was reading a book downstairs when we were all in bed. There was such a commotion that it woke the whole house up. My mother insists she heard the dog scratching behind the sofa where he used to lay, she was almost hysterical. I found out years later that it was guilt; she had asked the lad over the road to shoot the dog because she didn't want it to suffer and couldn't think of what else to do.

Thinking back to that time, I wondered where all the rags came from. In a family the size of ours, clothes were constantly passed down and apart from Whitsuntide, we never had new clothes, yet my Mother always managed to find clothes to get the pots.

I poured Johnny another drink and told him how nice it was to see him again and that he hadn't changed at all over the years, I told him that my dad would be in soon for the craic. The Irish always relate talk, beer and music as the craic (crack).

We were made to feel welcome right from the start. Barnsley folk are well known for their friendliness and hospitality, plus there were lots of my cousins there, my parents, aunties and uncles and people who I had grown up with. The locals in the 'Woody' were very down to earth and what you saw was what you got. They were like a huge family and everyone knew everyone. They would argue at times but never fell out; usually it would be an argument over pub games. For instance:-

When they were playing pool

Tha touched red ball with thi elbow when tha took that shot.

Aah dint.

Tha did, a saw thi, en it's a free shot, so shift thi sen aaht o'rooad.

Wat tha talking abaht, ah wah niva neer theear.

Or during a game of Dominos

Why did tha knock earlier when tha knew thad gorra five?

Ah dint know ah ed wun, what's up with thi.

Tha did.

Ah dint.

Tha did.

Darts seemed to be the game that they never disagreed about, except when someone didn't subtract the scores properly. I could add up the prices of a long list of drinks in my head, in no time at all, but never got into the hang of scoring darts. Cribbage seemed to be the most popular game during the daytime and it always caused some arguing during the game, but after the game it was back to normal and forgotten.

While collecting glasses in the taproom, you could hear different conversations going off at every table, usually to do with pub games. Everyone used to engage in some form of game or another and the taproom had a real old fashioned feel to it with both young and old mixing together. I never worked much on that side of the bar. The lads were gentlemen enough not to use bad language in front of ladies and if they slipped up they would always apologise, but it was best to leave them to feel comfortable instead of minding their Ps and Qs.

Trying to write in Barnsley slang is not easy, even with the book I bought for the spelling of the Yorkshire accent. It is never the same when you read it. Barnsley slang is spoken very fast but on reading it sounds much slower, even to me. I would have a guess that only Barnsley people can fully understand the old Barnsley slang. Unfortunately it's fading fast now in many parts of Barnsley. Children today tend say Mum and not Mam anymore, a word that only 'posh' children used when we were young. Words such as coit, (coat) coil, (coal) and laiking arht (playing out) are not heard much now. Thee and tha was used all the time in our pub, although it was never used at home, if me mam heard someone say thee or tha she would say;

Thee tha thee sen, afooar tha tha's me; en see arh tha likes it.

She then finished with "so theear".

Now more people are speaking in the 'proper manner' so to speak, it seems that the only ones today who use this dialect are the older generation. As the locals in the Woodmoor spoke this way, it shows their characters as they were and this is the reason I have written it as I have.

During the week the taproom was usually busy, both in the daytime and the evenings; the lounge was a sort of a weekend place apart from the odd few that came in most evenings. Two of the lounge regulars were Jim and Arthur. They sat in the same seats every night and Jim would sit and smoke his pipe. They were a very popular pair with the locals and they were always smartly dressed. Without any disrespect to these gentlemen, they reminded me so much of the two men that sat in the balcony on the Muppet Show. Statler and Waldorf would sit in the balcony and heckle the performances. Well, Jim and Arthur didn't quite heckle, but you could see them nodding or shaking their heads and facing each other to discuss the changes being made and they did see the funny side when I told them this.

Do you know who you two remind me of?

Go on, who?

Statler and Waldorf

The Muppet Show was very popular at the time and they knew immediately who they were. They simply turned their faces to one another in an astonished look and I creased myself with laughing. One day while rearranging the glasses on the shelf, a glass flew across the room, just missing my head. This was witnessed by three people besides 'Statler' and 'Waldorf', who looked to face each other and I knew they were thinking I should leave things as they were.

Obviously there are some people who simply don't like change and have no intention of welcoming new licensees, and sadly we had a one or two like that, but the others were so welcoming toward us.

Before long Eric McDonald walked to the bar. Another familiar face from my youth, all the locals called him Ez for short. He was a really good looking man who was considered quite a catch in the sixties. Although he had put a lot of weight on, he hadn't really changed that much over the years. We all used to say that he looked like Rock Hudson, but I believe that Eric was unaware of his good looks. He was never big headed and always treated women with respect.

Hey up Lass, ah ent sin thee fo years, ah tha or reight? Your Bill told me that yer war gerring this pub.

I'm ok. It's nice to see you again Eric, must be twenty years since I last saw you.

He was still tall and good looking, but with a 'beer belly' now. His personality hadn't changed, he was such a likeable person and he still looked like Rock Hudson.

Thall bi reight ere lass, it's a good bunch in Woody; your Bill said tha laiked poo'il, dus that still laik it.

I still enjoy a game but I'm not in a team now. It's too much of a commitment.

I was in the local papers a lot in the 70s through playing pool. Once I was on the front page of the Sheffield Star. I was the only female player out of 350 men and I was in a man's team and I had won countless trophies. Women were getting more interested in pool in the 1970s and we later had a ladies' league. I was the captain of our team and pool was something I enjoyed, plus I liked the social side of it and the competition.

Al gi thee a game later en see arh tha laikes.

Yeah, can't wait,

Ez was a loyal, loving family man and was adored by his wife and children as much as he adored them; his family were everything to him and so were his mates. Ez was referred to as the gentle giant; he had the strength to knock someone out with one punch, but preferred to keep the peace unless he was pushed which did happened once while we were there.

A customer said something to his attractive daughter which had upset her. Ez knocked the customer down with one hit; the man was so stunned he wet himself. Ez immediately helped him up and asked 'ah tha or reight lad', because that's the personality he had. No-one ever had a bad word to say about Ez, he was loved by all. He used to drink beer that came in a bottle called Gold Label, when we were there, but he always referred to it as 'a quick gold' whatever time it was, as if he was in a rush, but a rush was something that the laid back Ez was never in.

Ah lass'll be in later. Tha remembers her dunt tha? Arh Barbara.

I didn't really know Barbara, but she soon introduced herself and she was just as popular as her husband and very soon she was helping us behind the bar.

Ez loved the old Beatles songs and every time the Beatles were played on the jukebox, or brought up in conversation, he would start this debate off;

Arh can the bi eight days in a week, wen the's ony seven, arh can the bi?

He always had his palms out as if trying to stress the fact that it just wasn't right and this discussion went on regularly. Most of the year Eric McDonald only wore vests or short sleeved T shirts, his tattooed arms bulging out like Popeye's after eating his spinach. He was always warm and I can't remember seeing him in a coat or 'coit' as he called it.

It would always be the same group of customers that stayed behind after closing time for a drink, my cousin Billy and Cousin John and the regulars. They always stood at the bar, leaning on their elbows. One particular evening, they stood or should I say leaned up at the bar all in a line with big Ez at the end. They were all chatting away until Ez decided he needed the toilet. As he stood up straight and moved away from the bar, everyone fell down like a pack of Dominos and the drinks went flying off the bar. They had been leaning on each other slightly due to the consumption of drink and the fact that it was late, so when one lost his balance, so did the rest. That sight was so funny, seeing them go down like that and trying not to fall. I laughed so much that I was choking and spilled lager all down myself.

Well I think it's time you should be going home now lads,

This was repeated several drinks later and Ez always had the last word

Just giz a quick gold lass en then we'll all goo hoo'am.

Sadly, just before I started writing this book, Eric died suddenly and I feel honoured to have known this lovely man, he will be well missed in the community.

The opening night party at Halloween went really well and everyone in the pub had made an effort to dress up, even if only by wearing a mask. Angie, a regular, and someone I had known for years, came dressed as a dustbin man, with a dustbin on her back and her head inside the bin; hard to explain that one on paper. A relation of hers came as Quasimodo, that too was fantastic. Chris and I came as cave man/cave woman. Luckily I have photos of this night. This was the first buffet I had ever made and everyone commented on how good it was and there was even a welcoming speech at the end of the night.

It was a typical mining pub and the men liked the pub games and, of course, the beer, but at the weekends the men would come with their wives or girlfriends and the women would sit down at a table and the men would order at the bar. Some of the men would order a pint and order say a gin and tonic or some kind of drink for their partner and while I put the ice and lemon in the lady's drink, the beer had been drunk and they would order another to carry to the table. This happened quite a lot and their partners never saw that as they had drunk it so fast. I have seen many locals there drink a full pint straight off, but my cousin Billy could drink a pint without swallowing. He simply poured it down his throat without a swallow. The lads used to say after the first drink;

Ah, a wah ready fo that.

Although my son Christopher who was nine at the time seemed happy enough in his new home. I was quite worried about him; almost straight away he was having very traumatic nightmares. Christopher would shout out, "it's a bomb, a bomb has gone off" and then start to cry. Another time he would run out of the bedroom shouting; "it's an explosion, run, there's been an explosion". He had started to sleep with the light on, which he had never done before. I put this down to moving to a new place, that he had started a new school recently and also that Christopher was very shy.

The dreams went on a while and they were always about an explosion that caused him to feel as if he was suffocating. I decided to give it a few weeks and then take him to the doctor's, but they gradually stopped being nightmares although he still had vivid dreams about explosions. There was something very strange about the dreams that he and I had sometimes. I also had dreams where I was sheltering from bombs with my family. I was only a child in my dreams, and this was something that I never told anyone about because it was just a dream. Christopher, one day out of the blue, told me that he had had a dream where he was in an air raid shelter with his children when they were hit by a bomb; it was strange that he was a father in his dream and I was a child.

From the moment that we moved into the Woodmoor, much of the conversation between the locals was a fervent discussion about the miners' strike which had already been running for some seven months. Most of our customers were miners, some working on the coal face and some above ground and as the strike had started at a local Barnsley pit named Cortonwood, feelings ran very high.

A strike had been on the cards for some time before the announcement of the pit closure at Cortonwood. Previous miners' strikes were usually short lived, but one had eventually brought down the Conservative Government of which Ted Heath was the Prime Minister. When Margaret Thatcher came into power, she made it very clear that she was prepared to take on the miners' trade union; there was understandably much bitterness amongst the miners and Margaret Thatcher was public enemy number one in their eyes and referred to as the 'Iron Lady'.

She's determined to crush us.

Scargill's a match for 'er, 'es beaten 'em afooar, en 'e'll beat 'em ageean

Ah but what's going to 'appen to us if it carries on? Ah lass is on me back all the bloody time en then thus bloody scabs letting us dahn.

Scab was a word for someone that didn't support the strike by going back to work. The longer the strike lasted the more people were drifting back and this caused bad feelings in the Woodmoor. There were fathers not speaking to sons and brothers not speaking to each other. People were becoming segregated and there was, as yet, no end in sight.

The nationalised industry that was the Coal Board was costing the Government millions of pounds in subsidies to keep the pits open. Many of them were not viable but the miners' union was a powerful force and had forced many earlier governments to safeguard mine workers' jobs and keep the pits open.

The National Union of Mineworkers was very strong in Yorkshire and it was here that Arthur Scargill built his base along with strong support from the Kent coal fields and also Scotland. In 1981 the sixty six thousand members of the Yorkshire branch voted for strike action to be taken if any pit was to be closed, unless the coal in that pit had run out. They had heard rumours that a list of pits to be closed had been drawn up by Margaret Thatcher's government and they were prepared to fight tooth and nail to keep their jobs.

They saw the closure of the mines as a threat to the future of their families and generations to come. Miners saw their sons go down the pits as their fathers had watched them go down and their fathers before them. They were convinced that if the Government had its way then all the pits would be closed and Scargill used this fear to fuel the determination to keep the strike going as long as possible

She's got all coil piled up in power stations, so shis not bothered if we go back or not.

Eye, she knows what shis doing, the waint be any three day week this time.

The Government worked out that to beat the miners, they had to make sure that the country was unaffected by a strike and this was to render the union's power impotent.

So it had been since the fifth of March 1984 when the men at Cortonwood had walked out because the pit was to close. All the Yorkshire miners joined them because they now knew that twenty pits were to close and twenty thousand miners were going to lose their jobs.

The strike soon spread, with the Scottish miners quickly joining in; by the twelfth of March the strike force had risen to approximately sixty five thousand men. The miners marshalled themselves on one front and the Government retaliated by organising police barricades as the flying pickets travelled around the silent pits in an attempt to keep the strike solid.

Each evening the national news, on television, would show the pitched battles between miners and the police, many of whom had been issued with riot gear. When the situation turned more violent, police were drafted in from all over the country in an attempt to control the situation. Throughout the summer these running battles between pickets and police continued with lines of mounted police wielding batons at the charging miners. I had watched these news bulletins on several occasions but had never recognised or thought about our future customers as being involved. No-one ever said they had been there, but I was sure that more than a few of our locals would have many a tale to tell.

Not all the miners in the country agreed with the strike and in certain areas many tried to continue working as normal. This was particularly the case in the Nottinghamshire coalfields where the future of the pits was more secure and where pit closures were to have less of an impact. The miners here broke away from Arthur Scargill and the National Union of Mineworkers and eventually formed their own Union of Democratic Mineworkers. It was here that some of the worst fighting occurred as the Government continued to hold out against the strike.

All over the country there was both condemnation and support for the striking miners. Many local businesses and communities suffered because the miners only had strike pay to live on and no one knew how long it was going to last. As their savings dwindled, many miners were faced with financial hardship and this in turn was reflected in the local shops and businesses who were also hard hit.

By the time we had moved into the Woodmoor, they had been on strike for just over six months and many of the miners' families had had no real income since the strike began. All over the country people donated to the strike fund and the money was used to fund food parcels and soup kitchens, often run by women's support groups. We knew that the strike was going to affect our takings at the Woody but we were prepared to sit it out and hoped that a resolution would soon present itself. After all we were a part of the community now and though we would have to remain impartial we could not help but be acutely aware of the situation. I was sure that in the future the strike would play an important part in our lives.

Chapter Two

After the first few days I was able to relax and have a little time on my own for the first time. I stood drinking my morning coffee out on the balcony and found myself staring across to where the old pit stacks were. Memories of my childhood were flooding back, things I had completely forgotten about, almost as if my life was being rewound on a video recorder. Over the years, I had not really been in this area much, apart from driving through occasionally and whether it was seeing people from my past that made me think of these forgotten times, I'm not sure.

The Woodmoor was built at the edge of a council estate in the early 1950s. It was very close to a pit called the Wharncliffe Colliery where a lot of men from the council estate worked, and when we were children we would run up the pit stacks which looked liked black mountains. We always seemed to end up there and we were only young. Looking back I realise how dangerous that was. One time my friend Nora and I reached the top from one side and started to run back down the other side, but once we started running we couldn't stop and at the bottom there was a murky pond, where we fell in. As it happened, it was shallow enough to climb out near the edge, but just a little further in the pond was very deep and being unable to swim at the time we would never have got out. There was no-one else around and we could have ended up at the bottom of the sludgy pond for days before our bodies were found. In those days children went out to play for hours on end and the old saying was 'they'll come home when they're hungry.'

Of course both of us got a clip round the head off our mothers for coming home in such a state. Neither of us was prepared to tell the truth, as the consequences of that would be to have to play out 'on the front' and the thought of playing in front of the house was a boring one. We liked adventure. You would have thought that incident would have deterred us from venturing there again, but not long after that we were there again getting our shoes mucked up and due to the fact we only ever had one pair of shoes, until they wore out, we decided to clean them in a puddle of water.

Nora never wore glasses, but I think if she had ever been taken to have her eyes tested she would have had to wear them. There were many times when Nora had to squint to see something.

We were on to cleaning the second shoe when Nora shouted,

What's he doing up there Marg?

Nora always shortened my name by only using the first half of it.

"Who," I answered without even looking up. I was more concerned with getting my shoes clean. I daren't go home with my shoes in that state again.

Him with the big long coat. He's pointing something at us; I think it's a gun Marg.

This worried me because the week before someone was firing pellet guns nearby and fired one our way. I stopped cleaning my shoe and stood up and then I saw him, a man in a long coat and his trousers were down to his ankles. At first I wasn't sure what he was holding in his hand, it took a few seconds to realise it wasn't a gun, it was his tail, (tail was the only word we knew for a penis in our childhood days). Apart from seeing babies' tails we had never seen a 'real' one, not even in pictures, plus the fact we were both brought up in a strict catholic home, went to Mass every Sunday and also went to a school run by very strict nuns; having said that, at that time a person didn't have to be Catholic, sex simply wasn't a word in our vocabulary or that of most of our non Catholic friends either. In the 1950s television was new, children always went to bed early in the evening and the only books or comics we read were ones such as the Beano, Dandy and Bunty. I shouted loudly to Nora;

Run, Nora, grab your shoe and run.

I shouted again with panic rising in my voice;

Nora, run.

I was way ahead while she was still looking at him and trying to figure out what he was doing.

NORA, come on, COME ON, hurry up, he's holding his tail.

His tail?

It suddenly hit her and what was happening; she grabbed her shoe and ran like mad trying to catch me up.

Marg. Wait for me.

We ran for our lives with one shoe on and one held in our hand until we got onto the road. We were in a state of shock and my mother would have known straight away that I was hiding something from her especially after the last near drowning episode. We thought it would be best to go to Nora's house instead of mine. Her parents had a business and no-one would be in at this time. Unfortunately her family didn't like the idea of me being a friend of Nora's and I always had to wait outside of the house when her family was at home. We were very close friends, but her family lived in a huge detached house and had cars and holidays abroad, which in those days was just unheard of where I was brought up. I was once waiting in the porch while Nora went to get changed for Mass and it was freezing cold, and I heard her brother yell to their mother;

'She's got 'that lass' outside again, the one from the council estate;

"Tell her to bugger off home", was the reply, but it wasn't Nora's fault and she was my closest friend. This was in total contrast to all my family who adored Nora and Nora loved to be at our house. We reached Nora's house completely out of breath, from running all the way there and thankfully no one was at home.

Marg what we gonna do, it's a sin.

Dunt know Nora. Me mam'll kill me if she finds out; she'll blame me for being there in first place.

En me mam'll blame me anall and then she'll stop me coming to yours altogether. What we gonna do Marg? I can still see his face in my head, he was laughing at us.

I can still see his thingy, it wah massive, that's first time 'av seen a real un.

It wah 'orrible Nora.

We sat quiet for a few minutes Nora was still going on about it being a sin;

It's a sin Marg, what we gonna do? Miss Parkin said that God can see everything we do.

We'll go to confession,

Father McNamara will come out of the box and take us straight home.

We'll go to Mass on Sunday.

"We always go to Mass on Sunday"; Nora was looking at me in a puzzled way as if I'd gone mad.

"Yeah, ah know that Nora, but we'll pray to 'Our Lady' for forgiveness".

Both Nora and I always pictured 'Our Lady' as being a sweet, motherly, kind and loving figure because that's how the statues of her looked at school and in the church and we liked her better than God.

We jumped as we heard the door open. Nora's older sister walked in and put a record on the record player; the record was Buddy Holly's 'Rave on'. She twirled around to face us in her lovely yellow dress that flared out from the waist, her hair piled high up into a bee hive. She looked at Nora then looked at me. I looked at Nora, Nora's nose started to run and it was green snot and I wanted to laugh, which set me off in giggles, which set Nora off giggling.

What you two been doing?

"Nowt", Nora replied, trying to wipe her nose on her sleeve that was already shiny from previous nose wipes.

Her sister gave her a clip round the head and told her not to be cheeky and muttered that she wasn't born yesterday and I was glad I didn't have an older sister.

Weeave yea been, yer shoes a filthy.

Wiv just been for a walk.

Well, why is yer face red?

Cos yer just hit mi.

She cuffed Nora on the head again and said,

You two are up to somat, am not daft. Yev been darn to that pit field ent yeah, me mam said you ent to go theear any moore.

We ent, wiv been te rec.

She looked at us both for the last time and then informed us she was going to get a bath;

It looks like you two scruffs could do wi a bath.

As soon as we heard the bathroom door close, we fell into a fit of laughter.

I was the eldest in our family and Nora was the youngest of nine in hers and in all our growing years I only ever saw her mother just the once. She was what was considered old in those days and she seemed to spend a lot of time in bed, but whatever it was that made her ill was never spoken about, but then people didn't talk much of illnesses, not in front of children anyway. In fact I knew a few of the neighbours over the years that had what I know now as a hysterectomy. The word hysterectomy was never spoken but whispered, mouthed or referred to it as the 'major'. It was also known as a 'woman's complaint'. Les Dawson did a really good impression of this in the seventies and he really got it right.

We decided the best thing to do was to make a promise to each other to never talk about it again or tell anyone else at school. We went to Mass twice in one day the following Sunday and prayed for forgiveness.

Usually we would go to the evening Mass and sit at the back where the priest couldn't see us chewing gum. When it came to Holy Communion we would hide the chewing gum down our socks until the body of Christ had melted on our tongue.

This Sunday, however, we sat at the front (without chewing gum) and I was sure the priest knew something because he kept looking at us all the time. It never occurred to us at our innocent age that he was looking at us because we looked guilty and that for the first time we were sat at the front. During the service a few weeks earlier he had brought up the subject of empty seats at the front and people sitting at the back during the service. No names were mentioned but he meant us for sure.

The Mass began, which in those days was always said in Latin.

In nomine Patris, et Filii et Spiritus Sancti: – (In the name of the father and of his son and the Holy Ghost) to which we all chanted back; 'amen'. It continued on

Kyri Eleison–: Lord have mercy

Christi Eleison –: Christ have mercy

Dominus Vobiscum –: May the lord be with you

Et cum spiritu tuo–: And with you and your spirit

Oremus–: let us pray. And we did.

The confessional continued;

I confess to almighty God, to the blessed ever Virgin, to blessed Michael the archangel, to blessed John the Baptist, to the holy apostles Peter and Paul, to all angels and saints and to you my brothers and sisters that I have sinned exceedingly in thought, words and deeds.

Here we strike the breastbone three times and say; through my fault, through my fault, through my most grievous fault.

We did go to confession but we never told him of that incident. We did the act of contrition and were told to do three Our Fathers and six Hail Marys.

After sitting there rushing them off quickly, holding the rosary beads in our hand whilst muttering the prayers, we went outside and commented how many Our Fathers and Hail Marys we would have had to do if we had told the truth, that we had seen a real tail. I only admitted to missing Mass once, which was a mortal sin, cheeking my mother and telling a few lies, name calling, they were venial sins, oh and chewing gum in class, which was another lie there and then because I didn't tell him I chewed gum in church. We linked arms and called at the shop for a packet of Beechnut chewing gum and decided not to go down the stacks.

I can't remember telling anyone about that day until now and we never did go down there again. I suppose I blanked it from my memory. It may seem hard to believe in today's society that we really thought we were to blame for this perverted flasher. We were never given sex education in school or at home and although we were taught religion at school and often heard the term, 'Immaculate Conception', we had no idea what that meant, 'Our Lady' was sometimes referred to as the 'Virgin Mary', but we didn't know what a virgin was either and after hearing this term once again, Nora asked me on our way out to play;

What's Immaculate Conception mean Marg?

Well, ah know that immaculate means clean cos ah heard me mam say sometimes that when she's cleaned up it always looks immaculate, so ah suppose it means spotlessly clean, but ah dunt know why the call Our Lady the Virgin Mary. You would have thought they called her Sister Mary or Mother Mary.

We walked up to Janet McCartney in the playground, who knew everything, and asked why they called Our Lady the Virgin Mary;

Because she was a virgin, idiots, dunt you two know owt.

We looked at each other and asked what a virgin was;

it's sumdy that's never kissed a man, cos they'll get a baby if they do that, en then it comes arht o yer belly button, dint yea know that?

I remember seeing me dad kiss me mam once and sure enough the week after she had a baby.

So Our Lady was kissed.

No, an Angel looked down at her and gave her Jesus without kissing her. That's why she's called the Virgin Mary cos she dint ev to kiss' im.

We linked arms and walked away discussing the information we had just heard, hoping that an angel wouldn't look down on us and give us a baby. Later that same week, Nora had asked one of her older sisters what conception meant, to which Nora received a clip round the head and was told that she was disgusting and should wash her mouth out with soap.

I used to spend a lot of my young childhood days not far from the stacks. It was a sort of recreational place near to where I lived and there were some swings and an old steam roller left there for us to play on. Now of course, the pit stacks are no longer grey or black. They have been grassed over and look like green hillsides and now it's a little beauty spot. The murky looking pond is no longer dirty, but a popular place for fishing.

A few weeks after the pit field drama, Nora came down to our house and indicated that she needed to speak to me in private; we went out into the garden and she took some squashed up money out of her pocket. There were loads. I had not been used to seeing paper money, only copper and silver and apart from an occasional ten shilling note when sent for errands, I had never seen this amount of money before.

Nora, where've ya got that frum?

Table. We can go to fair; it's darn near pit field.

Being market traders meant that Nora's family took an awful lot of cash and I remember Nora telling me that they poured all the cash out on the table to count it and apparently, as they walked out of the room, Nora had grabbed a fistful of notes, completely unaware of how much there was. We were so excited at being able to go to the fair that nothing concerned us about it being a sin or that it was theft, even though it was from her own family.

We went to the fair and went on the rides that were the most expensive, usually sixpence. We would go round and round on the big wheel, time and time again, without getting off. Then we would go on a ride known as the cocks and hens, a ride that went round and round and up and down. After a few times, we were very dizzy, so we walked around and then bought ice creams and candy floss and we played on the slot machines. After eating hot dogs and drinking pop, we had several sessions on the Waltzers, finishing off on the bumping cars. Nora slept at my house that night and we were both really poorly. Apart from feeling sick when we lay down it felt like we were still on the rides; it felt as though the bed was spinning.

The next morning we still felt ill and came to the conclusion it must be God's punishment. We were still left with money and we didn't know what to do with it, we only knew it had to go. There was no way it could go back to her house and at that young age it was hard to spend more than a couple of pounds at the fair. We decided to bury the half a crowns and all the silver in the garden and as it was a windy day we held the paper money up while the wind took it. Then the guilt set in. We had to confess to stealing, although we made an agreement not tell the amount, but just to say it was sixpence out of our mother's purse. At least we were admitting to stealing, even though we didn't quite tell the whole truth.

My mother was always struggling to feed us all in the winter months when working hours were less for dad. At times we couldn't afford coal and she would say;

I don't know whether to buy a sack o spuds or a sack o coil.

You can imagine the guilt I felt knowing I threw all that money away and then hearing her say something like that, but then she would have gone mad with the idea of stealing money. While Dad worked long hours in the summer, it was difficult to work regular hours in the winter. He was working outside on the building sites and at certain times of the year, when it snowed heavily and in the winters then, it did snow quite often, Dad would have to go on 'National Assistance' and although. I'm not sure of this, I remember me mam saying, he had to sign on every day and they gave them jobs to do such as clearing the snow from old people's paths. Most of the families on our road were miners and had free coal and in the winter, the snow on their roofs melted pretty quickly because the houses were warm whereas on our house and the few that weren't miners', the snow turned to ice. We were always short of coal, but we survived. Dad would go down to the pit stacks with an old coach built pram and pinch coal from the train wagons. I went with him myself sometimes and we had to climb up the embankment and get the coal piece by piece, throw it down to the ground and then put it in the pram. There were usually other people doing the same and once me dad picked up a great big piece of slag and threw it away. Because it was pitch black on the stacks it hit his mate on the head and nearly knocked him down.

When Dad was working, me mam would 'Barrow Coil' for the neighbours. This was when a ton of coal was dropped on the pavement of a miner's house and me mam would shovel it in the barrow and put it in their coal shed. In return, you were given a barrow of coal or if they felt generous two barrow loads. This was hard work but my mother, a petite woman, used to shovel the coal and push that heavy barrow on her own and after that, she would struggle across the green with her reward. More often than not we would help her as much as we could. I remember me mam and dad falling out over this. He tried to stop Mam from asking them if she could barrow the coal, but that's the way it was in those days and me mam was a survivor. It was years later when I told her about the stolen money and how we got rid of it, expecting a telling off and lecture about stealing money. However, she immediately went for a shovel and started digging the area where we had buried the money, looking for the half crowns buried there. But the years of ashes from the fire being thrown on the garden must have buried it deep down and, as usual, she saw the funny side.

Only very recently I was telling my sister about this and I couldn't believe what she told me;

Oh my God is that where that ten bob note came from? Me en ar Val wah walking through snicket en we found a ten bob note on path. We went to fair darn on pit field and spent it all.

I was still deep in thought, as I drank my coffee on the balcony and I wanted to stay there thinking of those innocent days. I could hear the children playing in the schools, laughing and shouting and my mind wandered to a time before the schools, a time when there was a wood there where we would go blackberry picking in the summer, and in the winter we would collect wood for Bonfire Night. We locals called this 'bunny wooding'. Bunny wooding was a serious business back in the fifties. All the kids battled to see who could get the biggest fire. Fires burned in almost every garden and our next door neighbours usually had the biggest fire because there were eleven kids there.

We had to hide the wood in the wash house; the wash house was a brick building with a room that was meant to be for washing clothes and had a copper boiler. The washer used to stand in the centre with a mangle for wringing clothes and a big sink in the corner for wash days. This room always smelled of wet clothes, even when there were no clothes there. After me mam was able to buy a washing machine for inside the house, the wash house was never used for anything. This was the place where we stored the wood, because if the wood was left outside someone would set it alight or steal it on Mischievous Night. Mischievous Night was the night before Bonfire Night and you were mischievous with the neighbours and, I'm ashamed to say, I was one of those that put boot polish on windows and knocked at doors, then ran away.

We were still full of mischief on Bonfire Night. It was a big event and other parents and their children came, if they didn't have a fire of their own. We once put a jumping cracker under a neighbour's chair that she was sitting on. She jumped up from the chair and ran and the jumping cracker seemed to follow her everywhere, as she went running and screaming. We laughed our heads off until we were 'sent in', where we had to watch everyone enjoy the roast potatoes and bonfire toffee from the bedroom window.

On a serious note, there were many people who were seriously harmed by this silly behaviour. My friend Irene had a penny banger thrown at her which landed in her wellington. Due to her trousers being tucked down her wellies, she didn't suffer from any serious burns, in fact she was back out in no time with a toffee apple in her hand and we were laughing at the funny way she went running up the path before the banger went off.

It was time to go in now and sort more things out before getting ready to go down to the bar later that evening. This place had brought so many childhood memories back and of course meeting people once again from those times made the memories so clear.

Chris was my second husband, and he was brought up in a 'posh' area of town; his father had his own business for all or at least most of his working life, so in comparison to us Chris spoke pretty 'posh'. My cousin Billy was listening to him and I knew straight away what he was going to say.

Weears tha from then Chris? Tha speyks different to us. Tha's not from raand ere, a tha?

Chris told him where he grew up. Those two were like chalk and cheese, but hit it off straight away because Billy and my other cousin John made Chris laugh with their infectious laughter and broad Yorkshire accents. It was Billy who introduced Chris to fishing.

Why dunt tha cum fishing wi mi? Am off early 'ours in morning, if tha wants te cum.

I haven't got any tackle.

Well, tha can watch en if tha likes it, al get thee a rod.

Chris was up early in the morning to sit with Bill and watch him fish. He came back and told me how calming fishing appeared to be and how therapeutic it was. He told me how Billy would sit chatting away, while putting a few maggots in his mouth 'To keep em warm' before holding them between his teeth ready to hook one to his fishing rod.

It was really calming, sitting there, watching the sun rise and hearing the sound of birds twittering away. It's really therapeutic and great for stress; I think I could get right into this.

Therapeutic? I would have run a mile at the sight of a live maggot wriggling in his mouth. I hope you don't start doing that, or bringing them home to put in the fridge like some people do.

Chris now had two hobbies, clay pigeon shooting and fishing. He had bought a gun for shooting, which was a .22 or something; I didn't like the idea of having a gun in the place, especially as he kept it stood in the corner of the bedroom, fully loaded, but Chris insisted it was there for protection.

Look what they did with the kids' tents in broad daylight and what about the garden furniture? We have to be prepared. We have to protect our property.

The kids had put up a tent in the back garden, with the intention of sleeping there with friends. It was only behind the back door on the grass, but two hours after erecting it, it was stolen including the sleeping bags and everything else that was in it. Later on, during the same week, someone was walking past the lounge window carrying the outside table and chairs. There were six of them, in the afternoon, carrying the furniture as if they'd been on a shopping spree. Chris ran outside and they dropped the table and fled, so he chased after them and gave them an earful. The next news was the police were on the door step accusing Chris of threatening behaviour!

One Sunday morning he went fishing at about 4am and someone broke into our pub. After that he slept with his gun at the side of the bed instead of in the corner, loaded of course, so all he had to do was 'fire it' to 'save time'. I was more frightened of this gun than the thought of being burgled. I don't know to this day if he would have used it or if it was all for bravado and to make things worse, one evening a hardened criminal who came in the pub, was talking to Chris and the conversation got around to clay pigeon shooting and guns.

If somebody breks in, tha better off shooting 'em dead, instead o just injuring 'em, then the police dunt 'ev any evidence. Tha gets a leeter sentence that way.

I couldn't believe I was hearing this conversation and later I told Chris he had to get rid of the gun;

That gun is going to have to go before you end up in prison for murder.

He was only kidding, take no notice of him.

He wasn't, I'm not stupid.

Well, I'm not going to shoot anybody, just frighten them off.

Either that gun goes or I do Chris.

It cost a lot of money, this gun; I'll have to think about this one.

A few weeks went by and we heard a noise outside in the middle of the night. He jumped out of bed for the gun and it banged down on the floor. Had it gone off one of us might have been killed. He ran out to the balcony at the back of the upstairs lounge and fired a shot, I nearly died of shock. We heard the shouts of some men below and could just make out in the darkness that they were running for their lives. We had the biggest row that was probably louder than the gunshot.

What the bloody hell are you playing at Chris, are you mad?

I was only scaring them off; I could see where they were.

It might have been just a courting couple in the long grass, you idiot.

This is private property and I wasn't aiming at them.

How many times have you been on private property?

It's the middle of the night, they shouldn't be there.

But you could have killed them Chris, have you no consideration for others?

Not for thieves, no.

You don't know if they were stealing anything, you didn't give them a chance.

The argument went on and on but the gun remained in the bedroom.

The next morning we had a look outside the back and found he had shot the tree. Beneath the tree was some copper piping which was obviously stolen; they had tried to hide it in the long grass until later. The locals started talking about the shooting at the bar the following evening;

Did tha ere that shot goo off last neet?

Eye aah did. Dus tha think sumdy got shot? Aah gorrata bed en ed a look but aah dint see nowt.

Everyone in the pub was talking of a gunshot going off in the night. One of the locals lived in a house lower down from the Woodmoor and said;

That sounded like a 2-2, tha knows which 'am on abart Chris.

Chris just listen to them all talking and said nothing. I just thank God it was the tree and not one of those poor men. It must have scared the life out of them, although Chris being Chris thought it funny by this time and the gun incident quietened down after a couple of days.

One particular morning, while hanging out the washing, I noticed the grass was very long and looked a complete mess. I trooped down into the cellar where Chris was sorting the barrels out, in readiness for the draymen;

Chris,

Whaaat?

Sooner or later we are going to have to cut that grass; it's a jungle out there;

The front and sides were almost as bad as the back and that was not good for business. His reply to that was;

I do but it keeps coming back.

He could be so infuriating sometimes. Chris was never one for D I Y and he hated gardening altogether, but he was very good on the computer and also at fixing cars, and of course 'thinking'. He really didn't have that much time, to be fair. He ran the bar every afternoon and night besides bottling the shelves and checking stock, then there was re-ordering and cellar work. Every morning he would do the book keeping; he used to say;

While it's fresh in my mind.

I was also kept busy with everyday chores and cooking during the day and then working every night, and really for the size of the land that came with the pub I suppose the most logical thing to do would have been to hire a gardener. Chris was not a logical person; very clever but not logical.

I knew that he was trying to tell me something, I knew him only too well.

I was thinking about the grass earlier on, we could buy a goat.

I noticed he kept his head down when telling me this and avoided looking at me face to face.

You are joking Chris, a goat! A goat, in the middle of a council estate, they were made for farms and the country. What would we feed it on?

Grass. It would eat all that grass.

Where would it sleep and who would clean the shit up after it?

They're vegetarians, they just eat grass.

So, what's eating grass got to do with crap?

Because they don't make the same shit as humans and dogs do. It's like pellets and goes in the ground, plus it's a good fertiliser.

He didn't stop there;

If we got a nanny goat then we could sell the milk to the locals.

A pub that sells milk you mean?

It's supposed to be good for you, goat's milk.

We are definitely NOT having a goat Chris and that's the end of this conversation, NO.

The goat arrived the next day and I named her Sherry.

She soon became a family pet. She was very stubborn and strong and sometimes she would escape from the chain that was anchored in the garden and the neighbours would ring and complain of her eating their flowers. In the summer, children would feed her grass and she was very friendly towards them. She was very placid really, for the little I knew of goats, even when dogs barked at her she carried on eating grass and ignored them. One sunny afternoon a little noisy dog went too far and kept nipping at her legs. Sherry quite calmly turned round and butted the dog way up into the air. The next day the dog sat quietly with its head resting on its legs and its head down with eyes looking up watching the goat. The only time she made a fuss was when it rained; that goat hated the slightest rain and made such a funny noise, if we didn't put her inside the garage. As for milking, Chris decided it wasn't natural for a man to do it and so I got the job of milking her and I hated it. Chris walked over to me once while I was milking and I turned her teat as he knelt down beside me and squirted it in his face. No-one was interested in the milk anyway and it was thrown away, so I refused to do it anymore and she eventually 'dried up'.

Sometimes after a busy night, it could be hard to sleep, the body may be exhausted but the mind is still active. On one particular night, I was wide awake and could not sleep at all. I tossed and turned for ages and eventually closed my eyes and then I had a strange feeling of someone being in the room and the room turned freezing cold. I opened my eyes and a young man stood there looking at me in such a sad way. I started to shake Chris to wake him up and as I turned to look at the boy again he seemed to drift slowly backwards into the wall. Chris finally woke up and muttered something, turned over and went back to sleep, which was just as well really or he might have shot him.

I loved the pub life, especially late on in the evening when everyone had gone home and then you could relax yourself with just the company of friends and family, a time to relax and have a drink. We were talking about the area surrounding the Woodmoor one night and we were talking of times when we were kids and of course the pit stacks. Conversations always started with 'As I remember' and people always liked to talk about their 'ghostly experiences' after a drink or two. This was a good time to tell them of the 'young man' that I had seen and after listening to my experience, I was told of a burial site around the Woody;

This pub is built very near to a Quaker burial site.

What, in these parts, a Quaker burial site, are you serious?

Yeah, Monkbretton was the first place to have a Quaker burial ground going right back to the 1600s, but I'm not sure how far it stretched. Monkbretton covered a large area at one time; the place was full of monks and Quakers then. Places were nearer then, than now, because you could walk over the fields and through the woods before the estates were divided up by buildings.

A voice perked up

As the crow flies you mean.

Yeah, as the crow flies. There's also talk of underground tunnels going through here that were used by the monks to travel from one village church to another, you know, the monks from Monkbretton Priory. They used to hide their valuables in the tunnels during the time when religious persecution was rife.

By lad tha knows thi stuff, although I remember talk o tunnels, going from Monkbretton through to Carlton.

Everyone was listening, the phone rang and we all jumped. Two of the lads immediately said;

If it's wife, am not 'ere, av just gone, tell 'er.

And off they would go, but they would always have another quick pint before going home.

The customer carried on;

I read a lot of local books. I also read a book once about a Quaker haunting, in a ghost book, and it said that the Monkbretton Social Club was haunted. A few locals have seen 'ghosts' in that club.

The man telling the tale was cut short by someone trying to be funny.

Tha dunt mean spirits dus tha? Cos all pubs hev spirits behind bar.

He was the only one to laugh and the tale carried on.

The club was built right on top of some of the land of the burial site, but it was the only burial site there was around these parts so it stretched for a few miles and there's always been a lot of talk of pubs being haunted in these parts, including the Woody.

Brilliant, so now we had a ghost, not only a ghost, but an unhappy ghost. If there was a Quaker burial ground around here, they wouldn't have liked the idea of pubs and clubs being built nearby or on top of them and that's for sure.

Our conversations turned to the pit;

I remember it was always classed as being a spooky place around here when we were children, due to the pit explosion in 1936; there were tales of ghosts roaming round looking to find their families,

Aye, I remember that...well... I remember hearing about it. Fifty eight men were killed in a huge dust explosion, the wah bodies all ore place, en they took em to that school ore yonder.

"You mean the school opposite the Woodmoor?" Not giving him time to finish;

I remember me and my friend Irene climbing the wall there to see the children that played in the school yard.

Some of them also remembered the school;

It was a really dark dingy place; I suppose it was a Victorian building. There were kids stood in the playground looking at us outside of the wall, it must have seemed like a prison.

"You should have seen our school" I spoke out, "that WAS like a prison. It had high walls with broken glass concreted into the wall. I don't know whether it was there to keep us all in or others out".

Thinking about my old school, I remember that the school had tunnels underneath the building which led to the convent where the nuns lived. Once me and Nora went behind a curtain that was on the stage and we found a door with stairs, and you couldn't see the bottom because of the dark, so we went down. It was a tunnel and we started to walk down and see where it led to. We knew it was wrong and if we got caught we'd be in big trouble and thought the best thing was to be careful and not to get caught. We held on to each other tightly, it wasn't completely dark but dimly lit, and we heard a noise and stopped dead in our tracks, Nora said;

What wah that Marg? Did yeah 'ere that noise, it sounds like somebody walking en it's gerring nearer.

It came from up theear; we ought to go back, en it's too dark and scary to go any further.

Come on then, let's go back Marg.

We heard footsteps getting closer to us and assumed it would be a nun, but it wasn't a nun, it was a man coming towards us and do you know I can still see his eyes after all these years, he had the most evil looking eyes I have ever seen. We started to walk at first, but his pace speeded up, so we ran like hell and he started running then. We ran back up the stairs but he stayed at the bottom. We opened the door and Sister Mary Teresa grabbed each of us and marched us off to the office. The office was quite small and had statues of the Blessed Mary who we only knew, at that time, as 'Our Lady' and Jesus Christ, who was known to us as 'Our Lord'. I wanted to ask why Our Lady always looked sad when looking down on baby Jesus, but thought this was probably not a good time.

We were expecting a good hiding but instead she gave us a right telling off and she was adamant that we should never go down there again. We stood there with our faces looking down at the floor, shuffling our feet and every so often we would look up. Nora's nose always seemed to run in these situations and in those days the only handkerchiefs we knew were our sleeves. Nora wiped her nose and although there were no words said about this, the look on the Sister's face was of sheer disgust, which made me want to laugh. It seemed such a long time to be stood there and we instinctively knew not to look at each other, as this would set us off giggling and to show disrespect to her would have resulted in slapped legs. She sent us off and told us to pray for our sins. On reflection the strange looking man was probably a caretaker.

I briefly mentioned the 'tunnel' at my old school to them and our experience of it.

What did you ev a tunnel under a school fo?

The school, the convent and the church were all joined together. It was a very old, large building and the tunnel probably went to the Church as well as the convent. The Church itself was huge with little alcoves down both sides with beautiful statues and this is where we made the 'Stations of the Cross'.

What the bleeding hell's a 'Station of the Cross'?

I tried my best to picture the scene and remember and wished there was someone here that was a Catholic to help me explain.

There are fourteen 'Stations of the Cross' and each had a statue and each statue tells a story. I'm not sure if they are all in order, but here goes;

1. Jesus is condemned to death
2. Jesus is given his cross

3. Jesus falls the first time
4. Jesus meets his mother
5. Simon of Cyrene carries the cross
6. Veronica wipes the face of Jesus
7. Jesus falls a second time
8. Jesus meets the daughters of Jerusalem
9, Jesus falls the third time
10. Jesus is stripped of his garments
11. Jesus is nailed to the cross
12. Jesus dies on the cross
13. Jesus' body is removed from the cross
14. Jesus is laid in the tomb and covered in incense

There was silence for a moment and then someone said;
JEEE-SUS, what wah point o that?
I thought for a minute and said;

I ent a clue, I did as I was told. I do remember a time once though in Ireland, doing the Stations of the Cross with a relation of Dad. The 'Stations' were outside, it was Christmas and very frosty which made the Christmas lights twinkle over the city and there were the sounds of Christmas carols floating about in the evening air. My uncle, or whoever he was, would kneel on a pad and say a prayer at each one while I stood and watched. I was very young then, but I will always remember that evening.

Gis quick gold, lass.

I passed Ez his 'gold' and pulled a few more pints and continued to explain;

It is also the church where we made our first confession, I was seven at the time, and the girls were all sat on one bench to the right of the church and the boys to the left side. As young as we were, we were all nervous and some of the girls came out of the confessional box crying. We did not speak to each other in church so until it was your turn you didn't know why they came out crying.

What did you say, when you warrin box?

Bless me Father for I have sinned and this is my first confession. I was looking around the box at the same time. It was small with a little window that was covered so the priest couldn't see who he was talking to. After I confessed my 'sins', he spoke very softly to me and told me what penance I had to do and he made me feel so guilty even though he sounded really nice. I started to cry just as some of the others had.

Med yer feel guilty at seven?

I carried on talking;

The priest had made us feel ashamed of our 'sins' and we sat there holding the rosary beads with our hands in prayer and heads down.

Bleeding 'ell, I'd be theear all day me.

Aye, me annall lad.

We all laughed at this and then I continued.

This was followed later by our first communion which was a special day. We all wore white dresses, white gloves with a little white Bible in our hands and a white veil with new shoes and socks. Money was always found for this occasion. We sat at the front of the church waiting for 'Our Lords' body to be placed on the tongue. We were told that this had to stay in place until it melted and under no circumstances were we to bite or chew it, but if it stuck on the roof of your mouth then you could use the tongue to get it off provided it didn't go near the teeth. The priest was five children away from me when I realised I had chewing gum in my mouth. Mary was one of my best friends at that age; I turned to her in panic;

Mary, what will I do with my chewing gum?

Swallow it.

But every time I tried it just came back up and I knew I would be in serious trouble, one of the nuns was already scowling at us for whispering.

Mary it won't stay down.

She slipped her glove off quickly and said;

Give it to me.

I took off my glove and gave it to her and she swallowed it for me.

They laughed at this and I told them about sleeping in the playground to shock them more.

When I was first at that convent school the nuns would put camp beds out with an army blanket and we were made to have an afternoon nap in the playground when it was warm. If it was cold we slept in the hall.

Yer kidding, afternoon naps?

I'm not kidding; bear in mind we had to travel what was considered a long way for a young child, it seemed to take forever on that bus. Your schools were all in the housing estate and that's where me mam wanted us to go because the school was at the back of our house. God, I remember that day. The priest came, almost running, down the street. He went mad and persuaded Mam to let us go to the Catholic school on the other side of town. I hated it and missed me mam.

They all laughed at that and in unison said, "Aw", but it was true. I was the eldest and helped my mother a lot with looking after my younger sister and baby brother, plus she was having another baby. I thought something might happen to her if I wasn't there to look after her, even as young as I was. I missed the radio and my mother singing along to the songs as she swept away the dust from the red painted concrete floor. If I hear the song; 'She Wears Red Feathers' by Guy Mitchell, it reminds me of the second day at school. Dad was singing this song in the bathroom while having a shave on that second morning, the second day at school was far worse than the first day, because you knew what to expect.

Dad took me to school the first morning and the nuns were so nice to me, talking all sweet and nice until he'd gone home and then they seemed bossy and frightening and I felt so lost in this big old school that I cried all the time. The nuns were all stood there that first morning in the hall, dressed from head to foot in black with rosary beads hanging from their gowns. The only part that showed was the face, and you couldn't see a neck. There were one or two really nice nuns there as well; there was one in particular who would always comfort you when you cried. That nun is still alive to the day of writing this and as far as I know, just as well loved and respected.

After the first week a lady who lived up the road used to take me to the bus stop where the school bus picked us up. Her daughter was a little older than me and went to the same school. I would scream and kick her mother as she held my hand dragging me down the road. I hated school and I hated the nuns; they would smack you on the legs if you were naughty, even from a very young age. With their big hands and with our little thin legs it always stung. Sometimes it would be on the back of the hand and I was smacked on the hand on my second day of school at five years old.

The nuns wore a wedding ring on their right hand, as they were 'married' to God and it was this ring that would leave weal marks on our legs each time we were smacked. They would often grab us by the shoulders and shake the life out of us. It must be because they wore long black gowns that made them seem so tall; I used to think they had skates on because they walked so fast and you never saw their feet.

Before our lunch we had to stand on our chair and say, 'grace' and after we had finished we had to say a little prayer of thanks. Once, after being smacked in the dinner hall, I threw a potato across the room, in a fit of temper, and Sister Mary Assumpta told me to go to her office at 4.0 clock. I did so but she wasn't there, so I waited a while and I missed the school bus home. I seemed to be in that little room for ages and thinking about it now I realise the nun must have forgotten about me. It was a long bus ride to where I lived and I think I must have only been six years old because my sister is two years younger than me and she hadn't yet started school.

After sitting there scared to death, swinging my legs under the chair for what seemed a long time, I wandered off to see if the bus was waiting for me, but it wasn't. I decided to find my way home and a woman stopped me and asked why I was crying, I told her my name and said I was lost because I had missed the school bus. She asked me where I lived, but I only remembered the name of the street, I didn't remember the estate.

"I know where that is", she said as she knelt down beside me.

We walked down to the bus station and that kind woman held my hand, gave me a toffee and took me home on the bus. The lady was very pretty and looked posh for those times. She didn't come up to the house, but stroked my hair and walked away as I ran up the path crying. I was too young at the time to think that this was a strange thing to do, but I was reading a book about 'Earth Angels' a few years ago and I am convinced that the lovely kind lady that just appeared to me, only a few yards from the school, was an Earth Angel.

My Aunty Ann was there when I finally got home. She was only eight years older than me, but seemed really grown up. She was so angry that she was going to go to the convent and pull the nun's hair out.

My mother looked at her and told her to calm down;

Anyway, you'll be lucky Ann.

Why?

They don't have hair.

Don't have hair, what do you mean?

The nuns' cut it off for the habit.

I never understood what they were laughing at, until I got older.

Don't worry Ann, I'll be up there first thing in the morning and I'll sort her out.

But she wasn't.

In those days mothers very rarely went to the school to complain. Those of the Holy Cloth were held in high respect in a catholic family, in fact if we saw a priest coming down the road we would scarper, but if we saw a policeman we would run up to him and follow him. My brother Tony made me laugh when the priest came to the house. He would slide down near the sideboard and close his eyes tight shut. He had this idea that if he couldn't see the Priest then the Priest couldn't see him.

The incident was forgotten and I never threw another potato.

I've often wondered what would have happened, if the nice lady hadn't taken me home. I had no idea where I was going but remember that day well.

When I have looked back on my life at a Catholic school, I'm puzzled as to why the girls and boys had separate playgrounds, the girls were in the front of the building and the boys were at the back. Yet when it was P.E day, we all had to undress together in the class room, the boys undressed to their vests and underpants and the girls to their vest and knickers. There weren't any changing rooms. We had to play out in the cold all the time in harsh weather apart from heavy rain and the 'dinner ladies' would wrap you up in their big coats to keep you warm and when we got older we would congregate in the toilet block which was an outside building.

One day a friend came in late and she was crying. I asked if it was because her Dad had died. It was, but I don't know how I knew because he had only died the night before and she had only just walked into the playground, I was only about seven years old then.

My mind was snapped back to the here and now as a voice perked up;

I wonder why priests have to wear frocks.

I don't know, but they always reminded me of Wee Willie Winkie. When I was young, me mam used to say if we didn't go to bed that Wee Willie Winkie would come and get us and seeing as, at that time, I didn't know what Wee Willie Winkie looked like, I assumed he looked like a priest because he was a man and wore a nightgown. We all laughed and then everyone started to sing;

'Wee Willie Winkie runs through the town,

Upstairs and downstairs in his nightgown,

Tapping at windows and crying through the lock,

Are all the children in their beds, its past eight o'clock?

We laughed and talked about all the things that scared us as children.

Ah wah scared to death to cum hoo'am late frum me mates, cos o green lady.

Ah can remember her, she used to wear green en carry 'er 'eead under 'er arm.

We all laughed and it went quiet for a while as we had another drink. Then the conversation went back to the pit disaster and the school; there seemed to be a debate as to which school it was.

Yeah, it wah that school near pit shaft. They used it as a mortuary, all bodies wah took theear. Old Green Lane School a think they call it, in fact a thinks its weear them Jehovah witnesses ev a church.

It wan't that wun, it wah tuther wun, that wun on't corner. Not tharren near pit.

Ez spoke up;

Giz a quick gold lass, followed by a few more empty glasses that needed refilling.

I remember ghostly tales of that pit; I can remember the 'Monkey Tunnel' I said as I poured another drink for Ez,

There were tales of some people seeing pitmen carrying their Davy lamps. In fact one of the locals, who had seen this, was our Billy, who, braver than the average, almost shit himself once when running through the tunnel for a 'dare' in the dark. He was only a youngster then, but he still swears today at over sixty years old that he saw a man carrying a Davy lamp.

The Davy lamp was designed by Sir Humphrey Davy in 1815. A safety lamp containing a candle, it was created for use in coal mines, allowing deep seams to be mined despite the presence of methane and other inflammatory gases called firedamp or mine damp.

Davy had discovered that a flame enclosed inside a mesh of certain fineness cannot ignite firedamp, the screen acts as a flame arrester. Air can pass through the mesh freely enough to support combustion, but the holes are too fine to allow a flame to pass through them and ignite any firedamp outside the mesh.

Canaries were used for years in the pit. Any sign of distress to the canary or if it died meant that the miners knew there was gas in the area. Terrible really to think that something a human being can't see, can't hear, can't smell or can't feel could just end your life in a flash.

Come on, its bedtime, it's time to go home, we'll talk about this tomorrow.

I went to bed and the same thing happened again. I saw a young boy that looked sad, this time it was clearer, he didn't look like a Quaker, he looked more like a miner this time and he was gone in an instant rather than drifting backwards like before. I decided not to tell anyone this time and I even convinced myself into thinking that I might have dreamt it through talking about the disaster.

There was something about the tragedy that made me want to know more and I didn't know why. I went to the local library without telling anyone and got a copy of The Chronicle from the archives. I read the article in the afternoon while Chris was sleeping. It was so sad. Mothers would be preparing meals, waiting for their sons to come home, wives preparing their husbands' meals. Most of the men were local men and so the deaths affected a lot of the community, brothers, nephews and grandsons, uncles as well as husbands and sons.

A crowd of about a thousand men and women began to gather around the pit yard, their anxious faces waiting for news of loved ones, faces showing shock and disbelief. They huddled together, many of them with protective arms around their young, in total silence, apart from the sounds of quiet sobbing.

The air was filled with fog and smoke, hovering around them like a black shadow. Cold rain falling on their skin made it even more miserable, it was also a cold day for August. Four or five of the men had left only half an hour before and had just got home when they heard the news; they had finished their tasks and left early.

Due to the noise of the engines down in the mine many of the men did not hear the explosion but knew something was wrong when a terrific gust of wind swept past the engine house. One young lad that died, named Earnest Dalby from Lundwood, had a promising career in football and was due to have a trial with Manchester United the following week.

There was one survivor, Alfred Brown of Smithies, who was amazingly over a mile away from the explosion and he was very badly burnt and battered. People commented on how much of a heavy blast it was, to have blown back one thousand and eight hundred yards before catching Alfred Brown. His mother was at home getting his meal ready when she heard the news. Sadly, he died the next day of his injuries.

I looked at all the names of the men and caught sight of a little article. A man who had died called Lewis Boyd from Carlton Road, the street on which the Woodmoor is situated, had a son that died in the pit six months earlier. The boy was William Boyd and he was sixteen years old. Was this the young lad that came to me? Was this why it was important to find out more about an accident that happened so long ago? Was he looking for his dad? Later that day, I laid flowers in the back garden and told the young boy that I hoped he would find his Dad now.

I was on my own one day when I suddenly thought of something that made my blood run cold; was it the explosion at the pit that my son Christopher was somehow 'picking up'. He has always been a sensitive person. I decided it would be best not to mention anything about the disaster to him.

A lot of people don't believe there are such things as ghosts and everyone has a right to their own beliefs, but there are too many unexplained things that have happened in my life. I have seen many spirits from being a very young child, beside just 'knowing things' such as I knew my friend's Dad had died that morning at school. I believe there are spirits, although most of the time they are neither seen nor heard. I also believe there is a difference between a ghost and a spirit.

A ghost is a personality or soul of a person who has died and is stuck between this life and the afterlife. Some researchers believe that they do not know they are dead. They may have had a traumatic death or have unfinished business here on earth and can't move on. Ghosts may have a certain odour or scent and a sensitive person may 'feel' their presence or even 'see' them. A ghost stays in the same place because they have an attachment to that place, or perhaps something terrible happened in their life, such as a murder or accident and they feel very sad; perhaps they loved the place and couldn't leave it behind because they were very happy there. Ghosts haunt places whereas spirits do not. Sometimes a ghost will only be seen at a certain time of the year and constantly relive the events that led to their death.

Spirits on the other hand are different; they are not bound to this earth and can move anywhere. Usually, they are seen by a loved one in times of sorrow or to let their loved ones know they are safe and happy. There are many books on the subject of 'near death experiences' and the person who 'died' spoke of a loved one waiting, or then there are times when you may have been with a loved one who was dying when just before they passed away they spoke to a 'person,' smiled and in some cases, held their arms out and called out a name.

Chapter Three

We never had any problems regarding drunks in the Woodmoor, although just one or two didn't know when enough was enough and one particular customer who was quite young used to drink Bacardi and lemonade at the weekends. He would get paid and spent loads of money on drink. When it was late in the evening the young man's eyes would become glazed over and his speech became slurred as he ordered yet another drink. What I'm going to say next is not what you could call ethical, but it proved a point. With one of the barmaids as a witness I poured the lemonade with ice and lemon in the glass, leaving out the Bacardi and when he paid me I put the money to one side. He still seemed to get drunker with every glass and ordered more drink as the night wore on. The next day when he came in he looked worse for wear and miserable. He ordered a soft drink, and I served him one and took his money and handed him his change. Beside the change, I gave him the full amount of money from the night before.

What's this? There's a pile of money here.

It's your money.

"What for?" he said with a puzzled look on his face.

I explained what I had done and hoped he forgave me and I promised not to do it again, but believed I had done the right thing because I was worried.

What time did you start doing that then?

It was late on, but you were knocking em back in two sups. Anyway you were still getting drunk just from lemonade.

Strong stuff that lemonade.

Drinking shorts as fast as he did was not only a dangerous thing to do, but very expensive and he didn't have that good a job. I know that people could say that I should have refused to serve him, but all that would have happened was that he would have wandered off to the next pub. Chris on the other hand was annoyed at me and said if he wanted to spend his money in our pub then it was up to him. The young lad's face lit up and he thanked me time and time again because he thought he was skint. It was only a few weeks before this happened that a body was found on what the locals called the 'pit field'. As it happened the man had had an epileptic fit and died, but at the time a body was mentioned we had thought it was this particular person because he could hardly stand up when he left the Woody that same night.

We had been there a couple of weeks when a couple came in; they were both in smart suits and had a distinct look of disgust as they walked to the bar. We had put a carpet down, but the place still looked old and tired. Angie, one of our bar maids, went to greet them and the man asked;

Could you tell me where the lounge is please?

"Yer init," she replied.

They looked a little disgusted but ordered two gin and tonics anyway and stood at the bar, rather than sitting down, as if they were just going to have the one drink. The inner doors opened from the taproom to the lounge and my cousin came in, selling raffle tickets for the darts team. He walked up to the bar and the couple standing there and said to the man;

Dus tha want any raffle tickets?

Excuse me?

Billy replied;

"Why wats ta dun?" He said with a mischievous look on his face;

I beg your pardon.

Dus tha want a raffle ticket?

I was at the other end of the bar cringing, but within a short space of time, the couple were talking and laughing with my cousin. They ordered more drinks and went into the taproom at his request to have a game of pool.

Mam and Dad used to come in at the weekends. We were quite close to where they lived and all this talk of the pits brought up conversations of how Dad came to live here from Dublin. We would sit drinking Jamieson's whiskey around the bar and listen as he spoke in his soft Irish voice. Strange to say when Dad was speaking of Ireland his accent was stronger than usual.

To get the full extent of the conversation with my Irish family, it's important to write as it sounds but unfortunately this is not an easy task. As an example the letters Th were never used at the beginning of a word;

Words beginning with Th;

This, that. There and them sounds like – Dis, Dat, Dere and Dem; for example; 'Over dere'.

My father left his homeland of Ireland at the age of twenty to work down the mines after leaving the Irish army. He was telling a few of the locals about his new life here;

What pit did you work in then Pat?

I worked at Askern main colliery for me training. After leaving de Irish army there was no work over in Dublin and I saw dis advert for workers in the coal mines over in England.

Wah that in 1947 when mines wah nationalised Pat?

Yes it was, 1947. It broke me ma's heart when I left, but I says to her I would be back when I'd made me money.

What wah Askern like then?

Lovely. I could have lived dere, where we were staying. Dere was a big Victorian lake and around de lake, dere were houses, hotels and a picture house. It was grand and I was sad to leave de place.

He had been brought up in Dublin and had just finished serving in the army. He told me he had done his square bashing in the Curragh camp, County Kildare. Very recently, at the age of eighty two, he surprised me when he started calling out marching orders in Gallic after all those years. I suppose he remembered the words because they had been drilled into him for so long. I do remember seeing a photograph of him in an army uniform taken in 1945, and he was a very handsome man. During his time in training, he had worked in the officers' mess, laying out tables for their formal dinners and he knew the layout of table setting well. In fact all his life he had used a tea towel as a napkin that he always placed on his lap at the table. Good table manners and cleanliness were important to him and even if we only had bread and jam for tea, we were brought up to sit down at the table to eat. He taught us to place the knife and fork together when we had finished a meal;

Sometimes de people eating would rest de knife and fork down for a few minutes, but when dey had finished you would know de right time to move the plate because de knife and fork would be placed together and not apart. We were taught to look out fer dis.

A lot of Dad's Irish friends worked with him in Askern and when they were allocated to a pit in Barnsley, quite a lot went home to Ireland.

He lived in the Bevin huts with many of the lads that had come over here to work in the pits and this is where he met my mother.

I saw dis beautiful girl in front of me serving me dinner in the canteen and I knew dat dis was the girl I was going to marry.

There were Polish men living in the Bevin huts beside the Irish and there was a lot of fighting between the Irish and the Polish. Dad had arrived back at the hut after walking my mother home and an Irish man was fighting outside with a Polish man, so Dad broke the fight up. He went to his bed and never gave it another thought. As he was dozing off into a sleep, a crowd of Polish men gathered around his bed and beat him up. According to my mother he was nearly dead. He had no defence, because he was lying on the bed, and they administered blows one after the other. Dad was rushed to hospital where he had serious throat and facial injuries. The word got around that he had died. My mother, who was pregnant with me by this time, was hysterical when she heard the news. The men were arrested and sent to prison and I think they were also sent back home to Poland.

Not long after that happened, Dad had a telegram to say his Uncle Jamie had died. His uncle had helped to bring him up and lived in the same house as my dad and his mother. Dad was very close to his uncle and, on hearing this news, he wanted to go back to Ireland in time for the funeral. My mother begged him to stay because she thought he wouldn't come back. He stayed, much to my mother's relief.

In 1948 my parents married in a hurry due to my mother's pregnancy. Times were very hard for them and, like most people after the war, they had nowhere to live. There were still a lot of Irish coming into the country to work down the mines in Barnsley and many of the lodging houses would have signs that read;

NO BLACKS, NO DOGS, NO IRISH.

My parents lived with my grandparents, but because of overcrowding, tensions were soon raised. According to my Mother, there were constant rows between her step-father and my father.

After one particular argument, Dad walked out of the house when my mother's step-father threw my bottle of milk across the room during their argument. My grandmother sent the police after him, saying he had deserted his wife and child. Dad told me;

The policeman was very sympathetic and advised me to get away from dere before it ruined me marriage. I was only reading a letter from me ma and yer Mam's dad stood up and went mad saying "we don't read at the table in dis country". I told him that I was only reading a letter from me ma, but he ordered me to leave the table. We had a row and he snatched the bottle from yer mam's hand while she was feeding you and threw it across the room, shattering the glass and frightening yer mam and her mam to death. He walked towards me and told me to get back to where I came from; he hated the Irish and didn't try to hide de fact.

My mother was born in Littleborough, Lancashire, after her parents had moved there from Barnsley to work in the mills, along with her sister Rene and her brother Tom who were both born in Barnsley. Although my mother was only young, she remembers this as a happy time in her life, but this was to be shattered when she was four years old. Her father died, at the age of thirty one, but she didn't know how he had died until she was much older. Much later in life she was told that her father had been kicked in the head by a horse, at the mill where he worked and he later died as a result of this. My grandmother was beside herself after her loss and decided to move back to Barnsley with the children. She found work in the local hospital, which had been the Barnsley Workhouse up to 1931, when it's named changed to the Municipal Hospital, eventually becoming St. Helen's Hospital in 1935. This was a very hard time for a widow who had young children. My mother remembers the journey over the moors from Lancashire to Yorkshire. They came by horse and cart with all their worldly goods, I suppose just like the 'Railway Children'. Shortly after arriving in Barnsley, my mother was hospitalised with diphtheria and later, my aunty Rene was in hospital suffering from rickets. My grandmother met a man who worked at the hospital; he was a porter and they later married. Eventually they were offered a council house in a tree lined street, which was very modern for its time and they lived there for many years raising three more children.

After endless searching all over Barnsley for somewhere else to live, me mam and dad decided they would go and live in Ireland with plans of a job and hopefully a council house. He had heard from his ma that new council houses were being built in Dublin and that they should go back home to put their names on the waiting list as soon as possible and although my mother was only a young girl, she decided that they had to leave now, even with a young baby, rather than carry on as they were, there were just too many people living in one house.

The journey to Ireland was to start with a train journey to Liverpool. The train was drawn by a steam engine which belched out smoke and soot, as its wheels gripped the steel tracks that rose up into the Pennine Mountains that divided Yorkshire from Lancashire. The carriages of the train had corridors which led to the next carriage and a single toilet which catered for the sixty or more passengers who travelled in each carriage. My parents had been lucky to get a seat; people were standing in the compartments and in the corridors, hanging by a hand to the leather straps that hung from the ceiling. My mother was carrying me in her arms and a kind couple had moved sideways to make room for her. Everywhere smelt of smoke and grime and the dimly lit compartments were uncomfortable and noisy, especially when the train passed through the many tunnels on the route through the Pennines.

Eventually, the train arrived in Manchester and all the passengers piled out of the crowded train to change platforms and board the new train that would carry them to Liverpool and the docks. The run from Manchester to Liverpool was flat and level, compared with the climb from Penistone and the steep descent through Hyde into Manchester. On arriving in Liverpool the street lights of this vast city were a reassuring sight to my mother, who was beginning to become uneasy, thinking of the boat crossing to Ireland. She had never been on the sea before and had little idea of what lay in store for her. The steam train pulled into the station and me mam and dad carried what little luggage they had, making their way towards the bus which would take them to the docks, along with all the other passengers who were bound for the ten hour passage to Dublin. It was dark when they finally reached the docks and she had her first glimpse at the cattle boat that would take her to Ireland.

We recently went over to Ireland and the crossing was so calm it was hard to believe that you were actually on a boat, but it wasn't always like this before the stabilisers were introduced to counteract the pitch and roll of the boat. I remember as a child the crossings were always rough as the boat went over the waves.

My mam and dad queued for such a long time on the gangway, out in the cold and rain. They would cram as many passengers as possible onto the boats. Once on board everyone barged through trying to find a seat and at this point a lot of children became separated from their parents, which was terrifying for both parent and child. There was very little seating on the cattle boats at that time and what few cabins there were, were only for the rich and fortunate. Once the few seats were taken, women huddled together sitting on the floor with their children, holding crying babies in their arms. Once the indoor floor space had been taken, people had to make the best of sitting outside on the deck, trying to shelter from the wind and rain. Most of the men headed towards the bar, holding on tightly to their bottles as the boat moved away from the quay. The boat soon left the calm of the harbour and entered the Irish Sea. Suddenly the pitching and rolling started. The boat would roll over waves and the people would lean to the left and then to the right, holding on to anything in their reach. The worst time was when the boat hit a wave full head on and then crashed down again with an almighty splash, leaning and rolling into the giant waves. This would send tables and chairs flying, people would lose their balance and fall. Mam remembered the first journey to Ireland very clearly;

The crossing was awful. People were being sick everywhere and the men got drunker at the bar, including yer Dad.

Dad looked up and smiled his cheeky grin;

Me Guinness bottle would go sliding down the end o de bar, every time I let go, so I had to hold on to it tight.

Mum scuttled him across the head, laughing and said;

It was noisy and full of children crying. You could hear the accordions being played and people singing. I cried and wanted to go home. I was sick as a dog and the thought of the ten hours were in my mind and I wished I could sleep through it all.

She stopped awhile as if picturing the scene in her mind;

A steward took pity on me because you were a tiny baby wrapped in a shawl and he went and brought you another bottle up from the kitchen and a cup of tea for me. Every time I put the bloody cup to my lips the boat rocked and I had to give up.

She lit up another cigarette and sucked hard and then blew out again;

That crossing was mild compared to one a few years later. It was the worst Irish crossing on record, not one person was able to stand up. The waves would throw people across the room and there was a lot of screaming. The seas were so high that when the boat went into the bottom of the hollow, there was a wall of water on both sides of the boat. This wall was as high as you could see and everyone including the crew was terrified, even though they were used to bad storms on the Irish Sea. No-one was allowed on deck, life jackets were provided and blankets were passed round. I thought we were going to die. People were doing the rosary and others were praying, the sight of that alone scared the bloody life out of me. Furniture turned upside down and there was sick all over the place. I was covered in it and had to wear the same clothes until we arrived home.

Eventually Mam and Dad docked at Dublin and made their way to Dad's family. They were so glad to reach shore after the gruelling journey. Dad had a brother who was born the year before he came to England so as you can imagine, he was thrilled to see his new little brother Michael. Mam said that everyone was very welcoming when they arrived in Dublin;

I always remember a lot of people coming and going and I think they were all family, aunts and uncles, cousins of yer dad. There was only one room, one bed with a mattress underneath the bed, for pulling out at night and a bucket in the corner. There was an altar above the bed with an oil lamp with a red shade. At the back of the lamp was a picture of the Sacred Heart; the shade gave the picture a red glow.

She stopped to light up a cigarette and have a drink, and then carried on;

It was just the one room with a sideboard, a table and chairs and this is where we would all sit. The lighting was a gas mantle which had to be replaced and we often ran out of gas. There was only one sink to share between everyone in the whole building. It stood outside on the landing that we were on and had to be used by all the families that lived on all four floors. The stairs didn't have any lights or windows so it was pitch black, both day and night. It was that dark on the stairs that you couldn't see anything at all, it was a case of feeling your way around.

A few coughs from the cigarette and then;

The toilet was outside and as we were next to the top floor, going to the outside toilet was out of the question. All those stairs for each landing and only the one sink. It was easy for us, but the ones on the other floors must have found it difficult, having to carry buckets of water up and down the stairs in the dark. We had the job of carrying the slop buckets down all those flights of stairs every morning. Molly was on the top floor and she had to pass our door with her bucket, you could smell it for ages, God knows what the woman ate.

Dad piped up laughing;

I remember de one time when she had the chimney on fire. Molly trew de bucket of slops on the fire and it came down all de chimneys smelling. All yis could hear, was; Jesus, Mary and Joseph where de hell is dat smell cuming from? Jaysus.

My mother told me,

It was one big open house where you helped each other out, especially when it was overcrowded, by offering mattresses for the floor, and there was always a kettle on the open fire for a sup o 'tay'. The place was always full of company and laughter. We would play cards in the evening with light from the fire and candles. There were gas lights but, as I said, we were forever running out of gas during the winter time. The Irish are natural story tellers and I remember Molly Sheridan sitting with us and telling tales of Dublin in her black shawl and long black dress and black shoes.

Molly was the lady who lived on the top floor just above us and she was related through marriage. She was nearly blind, but she managed to get by with the stairs all right. She was often referred to as Mad Molly because she would say such funny things that had everyone laughing. She was also extremely religious and she had statues of the Sacred Heart and the Virgin Mary in her room along with other holy statues. Oil lamps glowed in the dark beneath pictures of the Sacred Heart and holy water fonts were everywhere and it was custom to bless yourself before entering the room and leaving it.

Holy water in a font was normal practice in all Catholic homes then. We had it just inside our door when we were children and had to bless ourselves before entering the house. The holy water had to have a Priest to bless it or else you had to take the water to the church and the Priest would bless it there instead of coming to the house. I always remembered a strange church smell in Molly's room, when I was young, that now I recognise as incense. It was very dark and scary in her room, but she was always very pleased when you paid her a visit as were all the rest of the residents in the house on Dominick Street.

There was never a dull moment in these houses; residents would gather for a 'Hooley', singing and dancing on the street, and in the summer people would bring out the penny whistles, fiddles and spoons while someone played the accordion. They were certainly never short of entertainment in the tenement houses. Sometimes there would be a 'rugger up' where differences were solved by a punch up.

My mother told me how they would hear the door creak open as they sat round the fire in the evenings and Mad Molly would pop her head round;

A yis making a sup o tay, if so I'll join yis? I might as well be sittin here as on me own fer God's sakes. Jaysus, Joseph and Mary, those stairs, sure to God I'll be breaking me neck one o dease days, fer God's sakes, yis wouldn't be able te see yer hand in front of yis face.

Molly would shuffle herself up towards the fire;

How are yis all?

My mother told me that Molly was Irish history itself and that she must have swallowed the Blarney Stone instead of kissing it, as she talked so much. Strange to say me mam always said the same about me, but I was talkative before kissing the stone.

As me mam always said, the Irish are natural born story tellers. I suppose in those days there wouldn't be much else to do, but there appears to be a lot of truth in these tales, thousands of people can't be wrong. They were very superstitious people and these superstitions were passed down from generation to generation, including me dad, who then passed them down to us.

Molly shivered, wrapping her shawl around herself;

It's very cold out dere dear God. Tis me poor auld feet dat are freezing, sure dey are.

My Grandmother laughed at her and said;

Well den, get nearer to the fire missus and sup yer tay.

Molly supped her 'tay' and she started to tell me Mam and Dad tales of olden times, ghost stories and the famous tale of the cry of the banshee. According to legend every family in Ireland has its own banshee that warns of impending death. Molly went on to describe her to my mother;

Now dere has been many descriptions over de years of how de banshee looked, but I have seen her me self, sure I have. De banshee is a small woman with long grey hair and a silver comb in her hand, not dat her hair was combed mind, it was long and wild. Now she could be dressed in grey or red, but usually wears a dirty white dress and tis me self that saw her dressed like dis. Most of de people only hear her wailing, rather den seeing her. Some have told me of her flying on a grey horse trew the sky, others say dey have seen her floating on a wisp of air. Will there be another sup o tay now Peggy Ryan?

She passed over her cup and my Grandmother poured her another cup of tea from the teapot that stood warming on the fire. She passed one to my mother and lit another candle.

In de quietness of de night you will hear her wailing, some mistake the wailing for de wind trying to get trew de chimney pots. De banshee waits outside o de winda and often dere's de sound of her comb scraping on de glass. If you were to open de winda she will trow de comb at de person who is about to die. She is ugly wid a hook nose and she looks like a witch.

My mother was terrified now as Molly went on;

Never pick a comb up, if you see one in de garden now, she may come back for it and dats been known; de banshee leaves it dere to lure people, she throws de comb back at you and den you die, I know this happened to old Mrs O'Brian, God rest her soul. Tis true as God's word. If yis were to hear the awful wail of the banshee, yis wouldn't want to hear it again. It'll frighten the life out o yis, worse than a cat or an animal, tis an unearthly sound.

I remember once, when I was out with my mother when I was young, seeing a comb laying on the path. She snatched my hand tight and told me not to pick it up. I never knew why she had made such a fuss over a comb, but then me mam was a very superstitious person all her life. She would blame someone or other if things went wrong saying they had cursed her. If she had done something that she considered to be wrong and later had an illness, she would say it was God's punishment. This was a lady that knew nothing of catholic life until she went to a convent to learn the catechism and take her first confession and communion before marrying Dad. After that she was then christened in a Catholic church. She spent many weeks converting to Catholicism and knew more about the subject than me.

The catechism that she had to learn was a question and answer format that you had to know and remember and it went like this;

Question

Who made you?

Answer

God made me.

Question

Why did God make you?

Answer

God made me to love him…and so on…and so on.

It was also taught in our school. From an early age, we repeated it every morning as the teachers asked the questions and we would answer in unison like robots.

The Irish believe in the banshee and many a person who has had a loved one that died has sworn they heard the wailing a few nights before. My grandmother said to me Mam;

Now some are said to hear moans from de banshee. She'll sit on de winda moaning all night until de person dies. Now I never heard her moaning, no, I heard her wailing, though. I never saw her in me life but dear God, I heard her wailing.

Molly asked for another refill of tea and looked around the room as if someone, that shouldn't be listening, might hear her talking and as she whispered low, everyone leaned in closer. Molly had a sup of her tea and started to speak in a low voice again;

I heard the banshee wailings, carried by de wind dat was piercing trew de night. Within tree days a boy of the O'Connell's was killed by a cart, sure he was. Tis I heard it me self, as God is my witness.

Molly sniffed a little and looked up towards the ceiling making the sign of the cross and whispered;

May God rest his dear soul and let de choild rest in peace. I heard it again me self only de day before yesterday, so I did, but I have heard of no deaths since den, may God forbid...as yet.

My mother said that all this was said in a matter of fact way, even though this indicated that there was to be a death. Mam leaned back on her chair and shivered again as she listened to Molly.

Dogs are very sensitive to de wail of de banshee and yis can hear it coming. De dogs will howl in de night, and de longer de howls are, de nearer de death. Oh and another ting here, if a person has just died recently far away from here, de banshee will come back to the house dey were reared in.

My mother's skin started to crawl and her hair felt prickly on her head. Dad already knew of these tales and sat quietly beside mam and she pulled her chair up closer to be near Dad as the tale went on.

My grandmother spoke up and said;

Oh, Jaysus and de knocks, tree knocks on de door, knocking fer de ones dat was going to die. I heard de tree knocks when missus O'Brian was dying, dear God, and twas terrible, terrible. Tree loud knocks.

Molly suddenly jumped up from the chair, making everyone jump, including me dad.

I'll be going now to me bed, God bless yis all and have a good sleep, mind.

Molly blessed herself on the way out and the room was silent.

When families ran out of coal, turf would be burned instead, which in turn brought fleas that hopped and bit on your skin; they were called hoppers and drove a person mad with the itching. The bed was full of them at night and it was hard to sleep. When we were children we were constantly covered with Calamine lotion.

After a while in bed Mam was unable to sleep for the itching that the fleas were causing and lay awake listening for noises. At first, she thought that she could hear someone moaning, but then she was sure there was a faint cry from outside.

Paddy, Paddy did you hear that, Paddiee?

Hear what? I can't hear anything. Go to sleep, it's only de wind coming down de chimney.

Another ten minutes passed and the same faint sound of a wailing could be heard coming from a distance which could have been the wind she supposed. My mother never did like the sound of the wind. One of Dad's cousins had told her it was the lost souls that hadn't known they were dead.

Paddy, wake up, it's the banshee, Paddy, Paddy, I heard it coming from the window.

Joyce you're dreaming. De silly auld woman has scared de living daylights outa yer and I'll be talking to her in the morning.

It went quiet, and then all of a sudden there was a scratching at the window. My mother dove under the blankets, terrified and crying by this time.

Paddy, tell her we're not going. Tell her to go away, Paddy. Paddy tell it to go, she's not taking me bairns.

Dad jumped out of the bed and me mam screamed at him to keep away from the window. I was only a baby at this time and she was pregnant with my sister. This was 1950 and infants were dying all the time from diseases such as Dysentery, TB and Diphtheria. Hundreds of babies died in the first two years of life.

Jaysus, Mary and Joseph. I'll kill that owld wan wid me bare hands.

My mother screamed as Dad went toward the window, waking up my grandmother.

What in Jaysus name? What's going on here? Have yis all gone mad er what? You've woke the choild up now.

He opened the old sash window and there was a comb attached to a string. He grabbed hold of the string, pulling hard on it and a shout from upstairs came down in the wind.

Jaysus, Paddy Millar, for de love of God what're doing to me? Trying to kill me er what? You ideut, I'll nearly fell out de bloody window, I did. May God fergive yis fer trying te kill me.

You'll fall out de bloody window tomorrow, I'll push you out me self, you auld wan.

That tale was told so many times in our house and we still laughed as if it was told for the first time.

Premature deaths were very common through various diseases, but one of the most common of diseases was Tuberculosis. Deaths were estimated as being fifty per cent higher in Ireland than England and Scotland.

There were tales of wakes, told on those winter evenings around the fire;

Oh we had some great wakes. Remember de one dat went on for tree days Peggy?

A wake is preparing a body for the funeral by cleaning and shaving, if a man, putting on the shroud and placing rosary beads with a crucifix in the hands. There would be candles around the coffin, the mourners would gather around and, if this was an intense and sad time, the mourners would wail and cry. The clocks would be stopped and mirrors turned to the wall. The window would be left open for the soul to depart and no-one stood between the corpse and the window in case they blocked the passage.

Wakes are held at home and could even last for three or four days and I remember my grandmother telling us of these occasions. The women loved a wake especially as it meant that they could have a day off from doing the usual chores, socialise and go to the pub drinking with the men instead of going home. There would be singing and dancing and 'acting out', and my grandmother told me of the woman in the coffin, who when she was alive enjoyed her drink so much that they sat the corpse up and poured stout down her and put ribbons in her hair.

There was always lots of food and stout. The money for the food and beer came from money that they received from the wake collections, and people scoured the papers for news of a death, knowing there would be free food and alcohol. They would turn up pretending they knew the dead person. Often someone would slip up by saying "May God rest his soul", when in fact it was a woman. These people were called 'Moochers'. An Irish wake was common place right up to the 1970s. It was more like a party or 'Hooley' than a funeral. The people would talk about the life of the deceased, remembering the good times and the laughs. It was almost a celebration of the deceased's life if they were old. Sometimes they would play cards and deal a hand for the deceased. Though it is a time of sadness, the presence of friends and family makes it more bearable and there is generally great joviality, as the deceased is fondly remembered. The Church tried several times to ban alcohol at funerals without success. The Irish wake, in the sense of celebrating at a death, originated with the ancient Celts. In their belief system, once someone died in this world, they moved on to the afterlife, which was a better world, and thus a cause for celebration. Of course things were different when it was a child or someone young who had died.

Dad was laughing at the old tales and he told my mother;

Jaysus when we were young, we were scared to death of walking down the stairs after someone had died. The stairs were so dark and we have often seen a white cloud when looking up from the bottom. The Nan used to say;

Sure it is de dear souls passing on dere way to heaven. May God bless de dear souls on dere way.

Dad has told this tale many times;

We would always whistle or sing going up de stairs and run up two steps at time until we reached de landing. I was on my way back home on a dark winter's night. I was about to start singing before I climbed the stairs, when something caught me eye at de top of de landing. I saw two glowing eyes glaring at me in de darkness; I screamed the bloody place down. The whole house come out to see what de commotion was and when de candles lit the stairs, I saw me cousin standing dere, laughing his head off, holding a turnip in his hand wid two holes in it and a candle burning inside de turnip. Me ma shouted;

Fer God's sake, what are yis playing at. Yis could have killed the choild wit fright, waking the bloody place up, yis scared us all half to death.

Dad also remembered his little sister dying at the age of six months. He was about nine years old at the time his mother married a man from Tipperary and they had a girl named Mary. Mary died at the age of six months, of dysentery, and Dad carried the coffin with his stepfather through the streets of Dublin. There was a white sheet over the coffin which represented purity. Everyone they passed stood still and made the sign of the cross and the traffic came to a halt in respect, as people saw the coffin. Mothers weren't allowed to go to a child's funeral in those days and their babies didn't have a formal funeral as adults did; they were buried very quietly in a place especially for babies while friends and family stayed and consoled the grieving mother.

Dad told me in a very quiet voice;

When we returned from the burial, all the family was there and everyone was crying. Me ma's sisters and her brother were consoling her. Me ma's sister, Sissy, held me and told me;

Sure, yis will always have yer own guardian angel now Paddy Miller, God rest her dear little soul.

Being unable to get a council house in Dublin meant pressure was building up there now. As there was little money, even though Dad had a job, it was hard to find a home of their own. They moved from pillar to post, living in already crowded rooms and, according to my uncle, my father and my grandfather were constantly falling out. A pattern was now repeating itself and they were feeling really down again. There was no choice for them other than going back to England, where they started looking for lodgings again, but now they had two children.

I have a memory of one of these lodging houses where we lived. I would be three and a half and my sister was one and a half years old. The toilet was out in the back yard. It was a box with a big hole in the middle and you could see the excrement at the bottom of the hole. There was old newspaper cut into squares hanging on a nail, just the same as the old tenement house in Dublin, but then most old houses were like that in the 1940s and early 50s. Teresa and I were pushing little prams with dolls in and I was holding her hand as we walked up and down in front of the house. Suddenly a river of excrement started running down the street and ran over our feet. My mother came rushing out and picked both of us up at the same time, one under each arm, even though she was pregnant at the time, and rushed us inside. It was something to do with the cesspit or something overflowing.

Later, I heard Dad, yelling at the man that lived there for something, but I didn't know what it was about then. They were using words I didn't understand, but the next day we were living at Aunty Rene's house. Apparently Dad was annoyed because my mother had told him that the man brought prostitutes home during the day and Dad was concerned about my sister and me, besides being worried about my mother.

When me mam told my Aunty Rene, she asked her husband if we could stay there and even though she had her own family she made us welcome. I was talking to my aunty one night after my mother died and she remembered the day we all turned up with suitcases.

Yer mam was so happy and grateful; she never stopped cleaning the house and trying to please me. She would be washing the windows and singing at the top of her voice.

Of course it was overcrowded, with four adults and four children, and this time it was me mam and me Aunty Rene that were falling out over us kids fighting, although they never fell out for long and my aunty and uncle were very good to us all. There were lots of happy times at my aunties; my cousin Billy was very funny. Once we had a party and my aunty said the first to finish their jelly and ice cream would get a prize, so Billy said his younger brother;

Do you want to win that prize Dave?

To which David nodded and Billy said;

Reight then, al help thi.

Billy started eating David's jelly and ice cream with him and when that was finished off Billy went about eating his own. That's not all, the prize was a penny arrow (a toffee bar) and Billy said that David should share it with him seeing as he helped him to win.

One Christmas I cried my eyes out because I didn't get a cowboy outfit that I had asked for, instead I got another doll and pram. David who was about three years old at the time, swapped with me and he proudly pushed that pram up and down the street while I kept shooting him

Fortunately, when I was five years old my parents were offered a council house in Barnsley, only a few streets from my aunty's house. That same week, a letter came from Dad's mother to say they had been offered a new council house in Cabra, Dublin. It was a difficult decision to make, because Dad missed his mother and his home land, while Mam wanted to stay in Barnsley with her family. The house that we were offered in England was huge. It had large gardens and the biggest bedrooms I had ever seen. Me mam was singing all the time, as she went along flicking dust that wasn't there. Dad went around the house kissing the walls and saying;

Jaysus, Mary and Joseph, we have our own home.

Then he sprinkled holy water everywhere and went to the Catholic Church up the road to ask the priest to come down and bless the house.

There was singing in the house all the time. Dad would lay in the bath singing, he would sing while he was shaving and Mam just sang everywhere with a smile on her face. She was so beautiful, dressed in nice bright clothes, with a pretty apron on. She was very happy.

At first, we all slept in the same bed with Mam and Dad, before being able to buy furniture, and as soon as we moved into the bedroom I started hearing voices. In fact the voices continued for years. They seemed far away and sounded muffled and I couldn't hear what they were saying. I never mentioned this to anyone, but years later Mam mentioned that she and Dad had also heard them in their room and never mentioned it in front of any of us.

It was very hard to build a home up from nothing and we had to make do with what was given to us. Because we had to have a second hand flock mattress, we acquired bugs. It's strange how you adapt to things in childhood that would drive you mad as an adult. I used to lie in bed and watch them crawl up the wall and guess which one would be the winner. This would go on for ages. One time something made me lift the corner of the mattress and there was a nest of them there, so I assume they must have been bed bugs. I find it hard to believe now that I just turned over and went back to sleep. My mother bought a tin of DDT, from which you puffed this powder out like a pump action. It was very effective, and she got rid of them all and told me to keep my mouth shut. After Dad had been working a while we got rid of the old flock mattress. I didn't tell my sister or anyone else about the bugs even though I didn't realise what they were.

Every time we went to Ireland to see our grandparents, the fleas would come back with us, travelling in the cases. Mam would laugh and say they were 'on holiday'. I used to have this picture in my mind of little fleas holding suitcases and wearing sun hats. Our next door neighbours to one side were what we called 'posh' because they had new furniture and carpets in the bedrooms, but the fleas went through the skirting boards into their house. Me mam kept quiet while the neighbour complained of the kids coming out in a 'rash'. She took them to the doctors and was appalled when the doctor told her they were bites from fleas;

"Well, I'm sorry to hear that Edith, have they been playing near straw or somat like that"? Mam asked, passing her a cup of tea for the shock.

When we were younger, we often went to Ireland to see Dad's family. The fleas didn't seem to bother me much as I got a little older. I was probably immune to them after being half eaten as a baby, but Teresa and Patrick caught chicken pox while we were there and the fleas had a field day infecting the spots so badly, that they both were taken into hospital and bandaged up everywhere and placed in cots. I remember the doctor at the hospital asking me Mam if I had any spots, lifting my skirt up to look at my legs and I kicked him really hard and ran out on to the corridor. I was terrified of being put in bandages like them.

Michael, my uncle who was only two years older than I was, would tease me and my sister about the way we spoke. He would ask us to say something in front of his mates and they would all fall about laughing. When it was time to go home, Michael was to come to England with us and go to my school. I was so excited because, apart from having an older brother, I could now tease him about his accent in front of my friends and get my own back. Unfortunately everyone at school loved him, he was very popular. Although we regularly fell out and constantly fought, I missed him when he went home to Ireland and I felt guilty for drawing all over his Elvis Presley posters the week before, and the house seemed very quiet without him.

Dad's cousin Alice came from Ireland to visit for a few days with her father and her son. We had to make special sleeping arrangements which often meant the women and girls slept in a double bed, the boys in another bed and the men on the sofa or on two chairs pushed together. They would always do that even though the chairs separated in the night as your bum fell through the gap. Having three, four or even more in a bed was common in those days; you made the most of what you had. In fact, the children were all crammed in one bed whether girl or boy if need be, and this was often the case in the cold winter months to keep warm. We didn't have enough pillows for everyone at first and used coats as pillows, all rolled up, and we covered ourselves with Dads army coats to keep us warm. Mam and Alice were laid in bed talking on this particular night when the subject got round to ghosts and, of course, the banshee. They laughed at the old tales that Molly used to tell. Mam told Alice about the voices in the bedroom late at night; this made Alice laugh, that is, until she heard them during the night. She immediately jumped out of bed and with her hands over her ears she yelled;

Oh Jaysus, Mother of God, I won't be sleeping in dere again.

She slept on the couch that night and the next night. Whether she heard them downstairs or not I don't know, I was so used to it by now.

One afternoon, I was talking about the subsidence caused by the pit workings, to one of our locals in the Woodmoor, and mentioned how it was to be expected, living in a mining town.

The roads around here are shocking even though they are not anywhere near the pits.

Yeah, there is a lot of subsidence around here and another thing, you can hear men's voices travelling up te houses, yeah know, if they're tunnelling beneath you. Sometimes you can hear them swearing and shouting down the shaft. Voices carry up frum the pits and.....

I never did hear him finish the sentence;

Oh my God.

What's up, what did I say?

That was what it was. For all those years, there was I believing there were spirits in the walls of the house and I also believed for all those years that our house was haunted by a young girl. Years earlier a young girl was murdered in Barnsley, she was in her teens and the girl had lived in our house with her family when the houses were first built, before we moved to England. I used to think that she didn't like me being in her room or something like that, although I did hear the voices long before she was killed.

I'll have to go and ring me Mam.

I rang her number and told her what I had just heard.

It never occurred to me that they worked underneath the houses; I assumed that they kept digging downhill.

Me mam laughed and said at that rate they would have ended up in Australia.

Chapter Four

Since Christmas the striking miners had been finding it very hard to make ends meet and what had been a trickle of men, that slowly crossed the picket line to go back to work, began to increase as families found the going harder. Their decisions were not easily made. If you went back and crossed the line you were a scab and would become an outcast among the striking ranks. Feelings ran very high and it was a brave man who renounced his friends and colleagues and ran the gauntlet at the pit gates. Brothers fell out with brothers and fathers refused to speak to sons, as the return to work gathered momentum. Work buses had to be protected by lines of riot police and wire mesh was fitted to stop windscreens and windows from shattering as rocks and missiles were thrown by the chanting pickets. Every evening these scenes would be seen on the television news and support for the striking miners was slowly beginning to wane. January progressed into February and the trickle of returning miners quickly became a flood. Feelings grew ever more intense as the hardliners tried to convince their returning colleagues that they should still support the strike. But even though the picket lines became ever more violent, the number of men who needed to go back to work increased until even the most militant of union members realised that they would have to call the strike off, before more miners were working than were striking and the whole thing collapsed.

On the third of March, two days less than a year from the start of the strike the National Union of Mineworkers called a specially convened conference to decide what action to take. Ninety one delegates voted to continue the strike, but ninety eight delegates insisted that the strike be called off. A majority of just seven votes heralded the end of the longest miners' strike in history and two days later many of the pits resumed normal working. The men gathered and lined up proudly behind their union banners, huge square sheets of embroidered material depicting the struggle for mineworkers' rights, each with the name of the colliery it came from written on the top. Colliery brass bands played as the men marched over what had once been a fiercely fought picket line and returned to work.

The strike had ended in failure; many of the families had lost all of their savings and much more. Margaret Thatcher had taken on the might of the miners and had beaten them. We knew that it would take time for things to return to normal and for some time the pub was quiet and subdued, as many of our customers came to terms with the cost of the strike.

I usually came down early doors on a Saturday night and we hadn't been open long when a local came through the door;

Have yer heard news? There's been a big fire in Bradford. The wah bodies on fire from head to foot running across football field, it happened during a football match, loads dead.

We immediately switched on the television and were shocked at what we saw. The television cameras were filming the match, to be shown later, and so they were able to show it as it really happened.

Fifty six people were killed in the fire which started when a spectator dropped either a match or cigarette which fell through the holes in the stand, on to rubbish accumulated below; this was seen by a witness who reported paper on fire below the floorboards. It took only four minutes for the entire stand to be engulfed in flame. Strong winds on the day made the flames spread, creating what looked like a fireball, and the smoke could be seen for miles. Even though the fire brigade was there only four minutes after being called, it was difficult for the firemen because they were faced with huge flames and dense smoke. Men at the front threw children over the wall and saved their lives, but many were crushed to death as they tried to find an exit and one man on fire from head to foot, ran on to the pitch. People fought to extinguish the flames, but he died in hospital.

This was terrible enough for the people and their families and of course those who had witnessed this tragedy, yet within literally a few hours, young people were collecting money for the victims' families in the pub. It wasn't until I asked a young girl for identification, because I was suspicious, that I realised they were collecting it for their own pockets. A few days later, I was informed that there was a team of them, moving from one pub to another and even though it been hard times for our customers due to the strike, everyone had been happy to put money in the tin for the Bradford fire victims. The youngsters had already been found out by the other pubs around the area and the police were involved.

It was Dad's birthday and my Uncle Tom, Mam's brother, and Aunt Silvia came up without realising it was his birthday, so we made the most of it by having a night upstairs while the staff ran the bar. We took a bottle of whisky up and some wine and Chris would go down for the beer as needed. I made a meal for us all and we sat and talked about the old days because Uncle Tom was always fascinated by this.

My Dad was born in the Rotunda Hospital in Dublin City in 1927, in fact, only a stone's throw away from Parnell Square where there is a monument to Charles Parnell. Dad was raised in one of the Georgian tenement houses at 61 Upper Dominick Street; his mother was also born in Dominick Street in 1905, and her mother before her. The tenement houses were known then as the slum lands of Dublin.

The tenement houses were very overcrowded. In those days families were big, a family with twenty children was not unusual and, in fact, my grandmother's sister had twenty three children, though I'm not sure if they all survived. There were very few families that were lucky enough not to lose a child. Children died all the time from poor sanitation, TB, diphtheria and other deadly diseases and obviously poor diets. Sometimes TB could wipe a whole family out.

People were so desperate for money in the 1930s and 1940s that many had lodgers sleeping on the floor, even though the place was full already. They were so frightened of being evicted; the rent was the most important thing. If the rent wasn't paid, you were out on the street. The landlords were said to be greedy and heartless and eviction was still in the minds of the Irish, after all, between 1846 and 1854, during the famine, as many as five hundred thousand people were evicted from their homes.

The tenements housed up to eighty people in most cases. This may seem incredible, but when you realise that these buildings had four storeys with two single rooms on each floor and each room held an average sized family of eight to twelve, the numbers soon added up. Many had more than twelve children, Most people lived in very cramped conditions where there could be up to eight or more children in one bed and the rest slept on straw mattresses on the floor which were then placed under the bed during the day.

Dad's mother gave birth to him out of wedlock and the priests tried talking her into giving him up to put him in a home. I remember once talking to my grandmother about this.

The priest came to see me after the birth and tried taking the choild from me arms and dear God I held on to the child widt all me strength. He wanted to put him in an orphanage width de Christian Brother's fer me own good, says he. It was very hard times and I was given just half a crown for me and Paddy to last a week, dear God.

Years later when Dad needed a passport, we sent to Ireland for a full birth certificate and on his birth certificate, my grandmother had put down her mother's maiden name as being her own maiden name and her mother's married name which she used as being that of the father. This was confusing as we knew she had never married when dad was a baby. It wasn't until searching for the history of my grandmother that I realised she had probably done this to stop the Priest from realising she was unmarried. The church did find out and tried taking Dad away, as they had done with so many other children of unmarried girls. That was how powerful the Church was then and for many years later.

There has been much written recently about the Christian Brother homes. There are court cases pending with men who were brought up in these places and also the notorious 'Magdalena Laundries' where young girls were sent.

For years many organisations have been looking into Ireland's Catholic-run institutions such as Catholic industrial schools, reformatories, orphanages and hostels that housed more than thirty thousand orphaned or unwanted children. Often they were no more than petty thieves, truants or they came from dysfunctional families and these included unmarried mothers.

A report that I read in an Irish newspaper recently, found that molestation and rape were "endemic" in boys' facilities, chiefly run by the Christian Brothers' order. The Christian Brothers industrial school in Artane is probably the place where my father would have been sent to as a child, a place where children were regularly beaten and sexually abused by staff members and also older boys. Reports have said that sexual abuse was at epidemic levels in boys' institutions and that the children would be moved from place to place in an attempt to cover up what was happening. For a young, innocent child to see older boys being beaten must have had a terrifying psychological impact, knowing that eventually this would almost certainly happen to them. Quite a lot of people who suffered abuse in the industrial schools are understandably unwilling to speak of it and just want to get on with their lives.

I read an article a while ago that stated that while there was only one elderly Christian Brother and a few boys that prepared meals for seven hundred to eight hundred inmates, in contrast to this, two trained cooks and female maids catered for just twenty four Christian Brothers.

I was speaking to Michael, my uncle, recently and he was telling me of the time when he was up in court for truancy. Michael was such a lively lad and was very mischievous. He was always in trouble for something and nothing he did surprised anyone. He told me how he would hide his school bag on the stairs in a corner. The stairs in the tenement buildings were always very dark because there were no windows or lights and the school bag could not be seen. He would walk in through one door of the school and out through a door at the other side and go off for the day. Because of his behaviour at school he told me that he changed schools often, but carried on with his truancy. However, one time he went to court, the judges decided he should be sent to an industrial school which was also run by the Christian Brothers. Luckily, after much discussion, because he was almost fourteen years old when the date of the hearing came around, they decided not to send him there. Going into a place like that would have broken my uncle's spirit and changed his whole life as it had for so many others. A customer of ours went to an industrial school in Dublin, but had settled over here now as a singer in pubs and clubs. He told me that it had ruined his life and believes the reason he is gay now is because of the abuse he suffered for all those years.

A shiver went down my spine, knowing both my father and uncle could have spent time in there.

Girls supervised by orders of nuns, chiefly the Sisters of Mercy, suffered much less sexual abuse than the boys, but they still suffered frequent assaults, humiliation and cruelty, designed to make them feel worthless. They were often struck on all parts of their body with implements that maximized the pain. As far as young orphans were concerned, it has been documented that girls as young as eight years old were repeatedly raped by care workers or laymen in institutions which were run by nuns. If the girls complained of being assaulted, they were often sent to lunatic asylums where some remained all their lives. People that were brought up in orphanages run by the 'Good Sisters of Charity' claim that they were beaten as young as six years old, kicked and even tortured. Their names were taken from them and they were given another name or a number to take away their true identity.

Since the early 1900s, Ireland has had a system of convent laundries where they took in laundry from prisons, orphanages and even local butchers. It's easy to imagine the state of the laundry coming from places such as these. Girls were sent to work in these places at very early ages. The girls would have to go to Mass at five in the morning and then work until seven at night. They were slaves, hand scrubbing bedding and clothes with their knuckles and ironing whilst praying out loud for their 'sins'. The Magdalena Laundry was a place where girls were sent for various reasons, sometimes for just being too pretty and being too much of a temptation for the men in the village. It is the place they were sent to for being pregnant, sometimes for twelve months while the child was adopted, but some spent the rest of their lives there if their family wouldn't have them back. Even if the child was that of the girl's father or brother, or whether she had been raped in the street, it was always classed as the girl's sin only. If you were an illegitimate child then you were to carry the sin of the mother and a child would suffer greatly because of this sin. There was no escape from these places. The girls were completely cut off from their families, letters were held back, many losing touch with them forever. There were high walls, with glass embedded on the top, surrounding the premises and if you did try to escape, then you would be put in solitary confinement or shipped off to an asylum.

I would imagine now, through all the publicity of late and the fact that a film has been made of the Magdalena Laundries that most people have heard of the nun run laundries. Until the film was released, most people were unaware of the terrible atrocities that went on in those awful places. This was highlighted in 1993, when the Sisters of Charity sold some of their land. It came to light that there were one hundred and thirty three graves belonging to women who had worked in the convent. Many graves were unmarked and it is not known who these poor women and young girls were and what they had died from. They had no names and identities in life and no names and identities in death. They were simply invisible.

Babies were taken away for adoption, as the girls screamed to keep their children after having breastfed them. Sometimes it could be up to two years before they were cruelly taken away from their mothers. There have been recent allegations of abuse at an orphanage in Dublin where newly discovered archives show that as many as two thousand children were exported to the US and other places. The Magdalena Laundry is one of the places my grandmother could have gone to, especially in 1927, had she not had a supporting family, but this didn't stop the priest coming after the birth to try to take her son away.

Girls could be sent to places such as these by parish priests, catholic curates and even family members and once a person went into the Laundries they could be there for the rest of their lives as innocent as they were. Even if a girl's family wanted to take her home, the Church still had the power to retain her. Girls could still spend the rest of their lives there as they were moved around and many, as I said earlier, ended up in asylums and were 'lost'. Letters weren't passed on and some were never to see their families again. The girls were often innocent, as sex was never discussed; some young girls had no idea of how they became pregnant in the first place and thought they were just fat. How could it be that a man could 'have his way', through gentle persuasion and promises of love to a young girl, and then go on living as if it had never happened? Yet, a young girl could be locked away for life in some institution, beaten, tortured and abused physically and sexually by 'lay-men'. How many men have no idea as to the number of girls they have made pregnant? How many have not bothered to be 'careful' because they knew they would never see them again? After all, it was not considered a sin for a man.

I remember Dad telling me once about Thursday nights being skivvy nights. Skivvy was the term used for girls that were in service as domestics and they used to work in large houses as parlour maids and kitchen staff. These young girls worked and lived in the houses; their bedrooms were often in the attics which were reached by a separate staircase that was at the back of the house. The occupants of the house would never use this staircase, which meant that the comings and goings of the staff were hidden. It was as if they were out of sight and out of mind. These girls worked very long hours and looked forward to going out on Thursdays, hoping to meet a young man. A lot of girls were to meet their future husbands this way. Dad was a very good looking man in his teens and he and his friends would go out on a Thursday ready to meet up with a few of the girls. Dad told me a little of his girlfriends of that time;

Dere was one who I called 'ten-o- clocker' because she had to be in by ten and she came and told me one day she wasn't a 'ten-o- clocker' now but a 'half past tenner'.

He told me of a young girlfriend called Fiona who died at sixteen from tuberculosis and how it broke his heart. He also went on to tell me about when he woke up in the 'dead house'; he was only young at the time and remembers waking up in a room with a sheet over his face. When he sat up he saw the room was full of trolleys with dead people covered in white sheets. He remembers it being the Mater Hospital in Dublin, but can't remember much more than that, although he has a really bad scar on the front of his neck and never knew where it came from. Mam said he looked as though he had had a tracheotomy at some time. Perhaps he was luckier than Fiona. We will never know, but he had that scar from a young age.

It was not uncommon for a young girl working as a domestic to be made pregnant by the master or a son of the house, resulting in them being turned out onto the street. Some of the girls would obviously end up in the Laundries but quite a few turned to prostitution as a last resort and people were sympathetic. These girls were never frowned upon by the Irish, in fact, they were known as the 'unfortunate girls' rather than being called prostitutes and they were respected by everyone, including women and children. The red light district was known as the Monto because it was on Montgomery Street and the girls were looked after by Madams who ran the brothels and the girls were kept clean and well dressed. The girls were respected because they had very little choice; many desperate young girls threw themselves in the river Liffy when they were turned out by their families through being pregnant.

Dad told us about the Nan, the reason she was 'The' Nan was because she had so many grandchildren. The Nan was a 'fortune teller'.

Dad was always talking about the Nan when he got older and although I have no memory of her myself, it seemed she lived to quite an age because Michael, my uncle, remembers her in his growing years. He told me;

Although the Nan was really old, she managed very well and still did her own sewing. She would come down the stairs shouting me name out to thread the needle for her. She used snuff all the time and one time gave me self some. It nearly blew me head off.

The Nan lived on the floor above, next to Molly; she dressed in the same way as Queen Victoria, including her hairstyle, my dad once told me. She used to read the cards and had a crystal ball; people sat on a bench outside her door where they would wait their turn wrapped in the shawls that were worn in those days. Dad would sit and read comics while the clients were having a 'reading'. If a client objected to Dad being there, the Nan would say to the client;

De choild stays where he is. He'd be doing no harm dere, fer God's sake.

When he was playing out on the front the Nan would always yell out the window;

"Here Paddy catch"; and it would be sixpence.

I have seen a lot of photographs of children in the 1930s while researching for this book and I noticed that the children in old photographs from the area that dad lived in had no shoes on their feet, even in winter months. I asked Dad if he had shoes when he was a child and he replied indignantly;

Of course I had shoes. Me ma always made sure I had shoes and boots in de winter and I had clean clothes.

Dad remembers always having money as a child and made sure he would go to Tara Street Baths once a week where he could hire a bath to soak in and he always used his own money. Nearby was another public baths where the women would take the washing. It was called the Iveagh Wash House. The wash house had big iron sinks where the women could boil the clothes and this was a place to get together and have a sing song and gossip. The women liked their clothes to be whiter than white and they talked about the ones who had dirty linen. It was not only the washing they took a pride in. The tenement houses may have been in very poor, dilapidated condition, but the rooms were kept clean. Floors and stairs were scrubbed clean by the tenants. In fact, a lot of photographs I have seen of the 1930s are of women with white crisp aprons on and a bucket and scrubbing brush in their hands. My grandmother used to say;

Deres no needing fer anyone to be dirty. Soap and water is cheap enough, fer God's sake.

Often the Nan would be invited to the city to read the cards for the gentry. They would send a horse and carriage for her and she would sometimes take me dad with her. He remembers going to a really posh restaurant a few times and, while the Nan was doing her 'readings', me dad was able to eat as many cakes as he wanted. The Nan once read me mam's cards and told her;

You will have lots of children, suffer ill health and never have much money.

Unfortunately, the Nan was right and that was, sure enough my mother's fate. She used to say;

I think she put a bloody curse on me for taking Paddy away from his mother.

Dad was an only child for eighteen years and the first part of his life was spent with just him and his ma, I think myself that there was a little jealous competition between my mother and grandmother, I remember Mam teasing Dad by singing Vera Lynn's; 'My Son My Son' when they arrived back in England. My Mother could be quite cruel at times and always thought of it as funny.

I have been reading the cards myself for about thirty years and I also had a crystal ball long before I knew of the Nan and amazingly enough, my grandchildren call me Nan. Children who are brought up in West Yorkshire usually call their grandmother Nana and it is shortened to Nan as they get older. What is even more strange is that their friends who often come to stay here with us when my grandchildren visit, refer to me as 'the Nan'.

Molly, my grandmother and the Nan, would tell my mother of those earlier days;

Ah, dey'd be rats the size of cats in dose days, dear God, out searching fer food and drawn by the scent of a nursing mothers milk. I heard many tales of a mother waking up to find a rat in the bed after the breast milk and people had a hammer close by to hit them on the head, or we would pour boiling water on dem as dey ran away on de floor and dey would scream like a choild. I heard a story one time of a woman who taught it was her baby suckling at her breast and woke to find dat t'was a rat.

This really concerned me mam and she told me how she tucked the blankets into the mattress so tight that Dad couldn't get out for a pee and fell head first onto the floor when he tried to get out of bed.

The Nan talked about the 1916 Irish uprising and the noise of the guns going off in Sackville Street, which, of course, became O'Connell Street, named after Daniel O'Connell who was the most famous Irish Politician of all time, and also the first Roman Catholic to become Mayor of Dublin.

It was a terrible time. We were so frightened by de sound of guns being fired and no-one dare leave the house. We didn't know what was happening out dere, fer God's sake.

My grandmother told me mam;

I was only a choild den, ten years old, and I was hiding under de bed wid me hands over me ears.

The Nan explained to my mother that it was Easter Monday when hundreds of people started a rebellion and took over quite a few buildings from the British. They took over the General Post Office and men like Patrick Pearse and Michael Collins declared that Ireland was now a republic and set up their own government.

The Nan continued;

De rebels managed to capture quite a few buildings and held on to dem for a few days, but de British sent fer thousands of troops and dey landed in Dun Laighaire.

Molly joined in and said;

De British soldiers marched trew the streets and into de city. Jaysus it was terrible. It didn't take long fer dem to take de buildings back again and arrest de rebels.

Everyone was now talking at once to my mother and telling her about the uprising;

Although it only lasted a week, hundreds of troops were killed and also hundreds of ordinary people were killed too, may God rest their souls. Of course den we all taught it was a waste of time, we didn't know what was really going on.

Dats right the British soldiers marched the rebels across the city and put dem in prison. People were shouting abuse at de rebels and everyone was glad it was all over, but Jaysus the whole of Sackville Street was demolished in so short o time.

Oh and dere was looting, shops had windows blown out and dere was glass everywhere.

What de Irish didn't know at de time was dat de British held a secret military trial and sentenced the rebel leaders to death. De rest of dem were sent to a British prison. Dey say that one of de leaders was so badly wounded that dey had to tie him to a chair so dey could shoot him. Sure none of dose men got a fair trial, even though it was held in a court house. Jaysus we just heard they had shot dem all.

Nearly everyone began to support de cause now and decided de rebels were heroes. Oh, Jayus Peggy, what was de name of the general dat de British government sacked?

Maxwell

Yes dats du one. Dey released the rebels who had been arrested and brought dem back from the English prison.

The 1916 uprising is well remembered in Dublin, as many people such as the Nan and Molly were there when it happened and so was my grandmother. They went through the struggle for independence and the formation of a republic. They spoke regularly about the period between 1916 and 1922.

The Nan looked at my mother and casually said;

Jaysus I nearly forgot to tell yis Joyce, Arthur Griffith was born in dis very house, 61, Upper Dominic Street.

Who's Arthur Griffith?

He was the President of de whole of Ireland, and he was born right here in this very house, a great man, God rest his soul.

Molly backed her up with this;

Lovely man, and he was born here, fer God's sake. He was a friend of Michael Collins and very well taught of in Ireland.

Many years later I looked for more information concerning Arthur Griffith and found out that he was indeed a great man. Apart from being a President, Griffith became very important to the Republic when, in 1921, President de Valera asked him to head the Irish delegation in London which produced the Anglo-Irish treaty of 1921. This allowed Ireland to have its own government, but still be under the rule of the British monarchy. The Earl of Birkenhead, the British negotiator at the treaty, was quoted as saying, "A braver man than Arthur Griffith I have never met". Sadly, he died on the twelfth of August 1922 only months after taking up the office of President.

Once Dublin City had streets lined with spacious Georgian mansions that were built during the reigns of George I to George V, (1714-1830). Beautiful rooms that contained marbled fireplaces and fine decor, a far cry from what they were soon to become. They were built mostly for the Anglo-Irish gentry, who purchased them for eight thousand pounds in 1791; this was a great deal of money, and the area was very affluent and much sought after. In the 1840s the same houses were sold for a mere five hundred pound, as the rich and wealthy moved away from the city centre which was being overrun by the hoards of incoming, poverty stricken former country dwellers.

As the population of the city grew, so did crime and poverty, leaving the well heeled gentry frightened for their safety. They were eager to leave, moving to safer areas on the outskirts of the city, handing over the management and sale of their properties to unscrupulous agents. The new purchasers of the properties had no intention of living there themselves, they were simply landlords who were only interested in profit. To this end, they divided the buildings into many, barely habitable, rooms and rented them off, packing as many people as possible into the small spaces. Throughout this era the face of Dublin was to change dramatically, when the mass exodus of farm workers from the country moved into the city and more and more of the wealthy left. Street after street of what were once high class houses rapidly became the expanding slums, as people were forced to live in whatever accommodation was available.

The British Census Commissioners in 1841 had declared the population of Ireland to be eight million, one hundred and seventy five thousand, one hundred and twenty four and growing rapidly. During the Famine years, 1845-1850, this figure declined by millions because of the people who died from starvation and those who emigrated. By 1851 the population was reduced to six million, five hundred and fifty two thousand, and three hundred and eighty five. It was estimated that had there not been a famine, the population was likely to have risen to just over nine million.

During and after the famine, Dublin became the principal destination for the people who fled the countryside and begged their way to the city where they hoped food and shelter would be available. Many died on the road side and were left there, as families did not have the strength to bury their loved ones. The population of Dublin now rose from two hundred and thirty six thousand to two hundred and ninety thousand and the landlords took advantage of this situation by shoving as many people as possible into these single rooms, making them unfit for habitation with as many as eighty people sharing one outside tap and one toilet.

The Irish Famine started suddenly in 1845 and lasted for six years, during which time the leaves on the potato plants turned black and then rotted away. The cause of this was an airborne fungus (phytophthora infestans). The blight was carried by the cool winds and spread rapidly leaving all the potato plants blackened and withered until they eventually died, leaving a nauseating smell in its wake. Potatoes were the main source of food for the families and as potatoes are rich in carbohydrates, protein, vitamins and minerals, such as, riboflavin, niacin and vitamin C, a person could survive on a diet of potatoes alone, along with salt for seasoning and cabbage water and buttermilk as a drink. The starving people tried to survive the famine by living on berries, nettles, turnips and grass; this caused a terrible onset of stomach disorders which led to dysentery and other serious complaints.

Potato crops were also a way of bringing in an income, enabling the farmers to pay the rent to their landlords. At that time most of the Irish countryside was owned by the English and Anglo Irish hereditary ruling classes. These landlords, who were mainly protestant, hardly ever set foot on their properties, using agents to manage the estates while they lived lavishly like kings. They lived off the rents that were paid mostly by the Catholic farmers, whose own ancestors had once owned the land.

The agents were known as Middlemen. They would buy large amounts of land, then sub divide it into smaller holdings which were then rented out to the poor catholic families. As their land decreased, the rent became higher and this was known as rack-renting. Any alterations made to improve their tiny cottages would only serve to make more monies for the landlords and because they could be given short notice for eviction, there was no incentive to make their lives more comfortable.

Although potatoes were the main food in the Irish countryside, the potato plants were said to have originated in the Andes Mountains of Peru, South America in the sixteenth century, when Spanish conquistadors found the Incas eating a vegetable that was called Patata. They were taken to Europe and found to thrive in Ireland's cool, moist soil, with little work involved in the cultivation of the crop,

The blight continued for six years and was made worse in 1846 and 1847 by the worst blizzards in living memory, when snow blizzards buried houses up to their roofs. The Irish climate is usually mild and snow is a rare sight but during those two winters there was a change in the prevailing winds, bringing in bitter, cold gales of snow, sleet and hail.

Having no crops meant that people were unable to pay their rents and unscrupulous landlords evicted them out on to the road. Thousands of homeless people died of the cold harsh weather. The landlords now wanted the land to graze cattle on and grow wheat, but were unable to do so until they rid themselves of the potato plots and dilapidated huts that belonged to the penniless tenants who had not paid rent for months.

The third potato crop in 1848 was blight free, but not enough potatoes had been planted back in the spring and they were in short supply. The people were too ill or simply discouraged knowing the landlords wanted their back rents, leaving them with nothing. Between 1849 and 1854, fifty thousand families were evicted out of their homes by the uncaring landlords and as a result of having neither food nor shelter many died. The dead were buried where they fell, without coffins, just inches below the surface of the ground and in time, the bodies were gnawed by dogs and rats.

Government efforts to help the starving in Ireland were both slow and ineffectual and were soon to come under the control of Charles Edward Trevelyan who, though he only ever visited Ireland once, became immortalised in the Irish folk song 'The Fields of Athenry', which tells of a young man who was torn from his wife and child then transported to Botany Bay in Australia, a fate that many of the starving families must have suffered.

Free passages were offered to many for emigration, as a cheap way for landlords to move tenants off the land. They were made promises of money and a new life overseas, only to find that they were packed into unseaworthy and dangerous ships, to make a crossing over the Atlantic Ocean which could last for anything up to three months. Quebec, Canada is a journey of three thousand miles; during the voyage people who died were thrown overboard in an attempt to stop diseases from spreading. Unfortunately, this was not to be the end of the emigrants' suffering as they received the roughest of welcomes when they arrived in Canada. Early in 1847 the disease ridden ships sailed up the Saint Lawrence River and a long queue of forty vessels carrying over fourteen thousand Irish immigrants formed, as the authorities checked for passengers who were showing signs of typhus and other contagious diseases. All those showing any signs were moved to Grosse Island, some thirty miles from Quebec. It was here that the doctors who were sent to treat them were overwhelmed, many of them succumbing to typhus themselves.

Eventually the line of ships grew to several miles in length and a fifteen day general quarantine was put in force. The passengers had to remain on the lice infected ships and the death toll rose so quickly that bodies were dumped overboard and many who were seriously ill were put aboard small boats and taken to the shore, where they were left at the mercy of the elements. Many were to die in the makeshift hospitals and along the roadside; there was now little difference to the plight they had left behind.

The situation became so extreme that all attempts to quarantine people were abandoned; people were given free passage on to Montreal, Kingston and Toronto just to get rid of them. The journey in the open barges was gruelling. It was sweltering in the daytime and extremely cold at night and when they arrived they found that the promises of money, food and clothing were false. The Canadian people were afraid of the immigrants and the diseases and fever they carried and the homeless Irish were forced to live wherever they could and brave the Canadian winter.

Over one hundred thousand Irish citizens sailed to Canada in 1847 and twenty per cent, over twenty thousand people, died from hunger and disease. Many of them walked into the United States, leaving behind them all ties with British rule, hoping for a new start in the newly expanded cities of the eastern seaboard and the vast expanses of the west. There was not always a warm welcome and in some areas of the United States, the sudden influx of large numbers of Irish immigrants caused much hardship.

Boston, Massachusetts, with a population of approximately one hundred and fifteen thousand was to be swamped by the sudden arrival of thirty seven thousand Irish refugees, fleeing their own famine stricken shores. At first the locals were amused, as the refugees came ashore dressed in clothes that were years out of fashion. Settling in the poorest sections of Boston and taking any skilled or unskilled work that they could find, the city soon became unable to support the vast numbers that were arriving and the 'Old Bostonians' were terrified of losing their own jobs to workers who might work for less than the going rate. In Boston the wages were ten times more than they had been in Ireland and to stop any undercutting, signs began to appear stating 'No Irish need apply'.

The situation in New York was much different; in 1847 its population was three hundred and seventy two thousand and growing rapidly. Immigrants from all over Europe were arriving and although fifty two thousand Irish arrived, fifty three thousand Germans also arrived that year along with immigrants from many other nations. Obviously competition for jobs and accommodation was substantial. This fuelled the rise of con artists and villains who greeted people as they left the ships. Speaking in Gaelic, these 'runners' as they were called, offered to help the new arrivals find housing and work, but as they were only preying on their vulnerability, many people ended up in overcrowded boarding houses, until their money ran out. Between 1847 and 1850 approximately six hundred and fifty thousand Irish people sailed into New York Harbour and those that stayed made up forty three per cent of the foreign born population. New York now had more Irish born citizens than lived in Dublin.

Even after the famine, back in Ireland, hunger was still a problem for years and matters were to worsen as the Encumbered Estates Act of 1849 allowed estates that were in severe debt to be auctioned off, at bargain prices, to British speculators only interested in future profits by starting up cattle grazing farms.

In 1879 the blight returned in force, but by this time, farmers and labourers were politically organised. They were now represented by a national alliance known as the Land League, led by Charles Stewart Parnell. The league, funded by donations from America, organised boycotts against the notorious landlords by encouraging the tenants to burn their leases and they had members that would physically block eviction. Parnell's, 'Land War' agitations were to bring about the beginning of British political reforms to help Ireland's small tenants and farmers. The Land Act 1881 granted rent reductions, and the Wyndham Act 1903 allowed a lot of Irish to purchase their holdings from their landlords with British Government assistance. Landlords received a generous price which was set by the government and the tenants repaid the government loan over a period of time. The suffering of the Irish farmers and tenants was finally at an end.

It's hard to believe now that John F. Kennedy was the great grandson of Patrick Kennedy, a farmer from County Wexford, who left Ireland during the famine and immigrated to America. Although there had been other Presidents who had Irish roots, John F. Kennedy was the first Roman Catholic.

Chapter Five

Chris had the weirdest sense of humour and most people thought he was really funny, but sometimes he would laugh uncontrollably at certain things that weren't funny. Once our dog Gyp was so excited to see him arriving at the back door with Adrian and Christopher, that she jumped up onto the wall of the balcony, to see them more clearly, but unfortunately she lost her balance and fell off the balcony, to everyone's horror. Everyone's horror that is but Chris. He thought it was so funny because she landed like a cat, on all four legs, and carried on greeting them as if nothing had happened, Chris was hysterical.

Another time he shouted to say he was letting the dog out the back before going to bed. I heard him open the door and then the sound of a girl screaming, followed by the dog barking. Chris walked back inside and was unable to tell me anything because he was laughing so much.

What are you laughing at?

Chris. Tell me.

Chris, for God's sake will you please tell me what has happened?

I was getting really angry with him and demanded to know why a girl had screamed. He eventually managed to get the words out. Apparently, a young couple were having sex behind the pub stood against the wall. The dog made them jump, she screamed and they both tried to run away from the dog. The young man's trouser legs were around his ankles and he fell flat on the gravel.

Well, is he all right? Did he hurt himself? It's all gravel out there, he might have done himself a right injury.

To this he popped his head out of the door to have a look, came back in and said;

No they've gone, but I bet his dick is a lot more swollen now than it was five minutes ago with the way he fell on it.

I gave him a dirty look and went to bed.

Another time, when we were in a dress shop, a mother and her daughter went into a temporary changing room. We were aware that the tent like changing room was moving a bit, as there couldn't have been very much room inside. All of a sudden, there was an almighty crash as the changing room, along with the two people in it, came crashing down. The woman had obviously got her leg stuck in her trousers and lost her balance. I felt so sorry for them; they were very embarrassed, the woman lay there, one leg in her trousers and one out. Chris was practically rolling on the floor with laughter and all the way home he was still laughing and was baffled as to how I didn't think it was funny. There have been many times that I have also lost my balance in a changing room, but luckily they have always been solid enough to hold my weight. Most women will be familiar with struggling to take off boots or trousers in a tight space.

Chris used to sit at the bar in the morning, after bottling up, to have a cup of coffee and read the newspaper. I was upstairs in the kitchen when I heard him laughing his heart out. I knew there was no one in the bar with him, so I went down to see what he was laughing at. He was shaking with laughter as he held the newspaper in his hands. Apparently, someone had thrown an old television from the top floor of a block of flats. The television hit a dog that was below and killed the dog. The owner of the dog that was holding the lead suffered a heart attack and died. I ask you? How funny is that?

In October 1995 Rock Hudson died of AIDS. He was the first major United States celebrity to die of complications from AIDS. All of a sudden Aids seemed to be in the spotlight and rumours of how a person could catch it were all the talk at that time. It was especially a bad time for gay men, because people were unaware of the facts. We did have a couple of gays that came into our pub on a regular basis and some of our customers complained about using the same glasses as a gay person. It was blown out of all proportion.

A customer that we knew very well came up to the bar and asked how things were in the pub. It was the way he said it, rather than what he had said, that made me prick up my ears.

OK, why?

Ave you bin a bit quiet in 'ere lately?

I replied 'no, in fact we've been quite busy actually, why?'

Coming nearer to me he began to whisper, while looking around at the same time, all very cloak and dagger. I couldn't wait to hear what he had to say.

The's rumours abaht Chris

"What sort of rumours?" I asked, dreading what I was about to hear now.

Evin AIDS, they're all on abaht AIDS at Woody and that Chris ez aids.

I was fuming. How could anyone say something like that?

Having AIDS? Chris? AIDS? Who's putting a stupid thing like that about? I'll kill em.

Well, let's face it Maggie; he has got Lemon-aides, Lime-aides en Lucoz-aides ent 'e?

He started walking away very quickly, laughing his head off, before I had chance to hit him.

At about this time we started to have entertainment, to encourage the locals to come in during the week. This worked well, although when the costs were worked out, such as extra bar staff and the payment to the entertainers, it was easy to either just break even or make a loss. Jack (the previous tenant) had given us advice on this and he was right, there was certainly more custom but not necessarily more money. However, you have to try things your own way and we had some very good entertainers, artists or 'turns' as they were called in Barnsley. They were solo singers and duos mostly, but on one night of the week we had a piano player that the older generation liked to sing along to. In fact, this was the busiest night of all during the week. One of the turns that we had booked for a night, was a young woman from out of town and as well as being very pretty; she was also a good solo singer. Chris suggested that we should book her for the week after and I readily agreed to this; however, when everyone had gone home, apart from the usual people that stayed, the woman came across to the bar for a drink. She ordered a drink for herself and immediately she started to flirt with Chris. I didn't mind at first, it's something that you get used to in a pub, but when the woman later asked Chris if he would like a drink, with a sultry smile on her face, without asking me if I would like one, I was annoyed. The woman continued to praise and flatter Chris, telling him that he did really well running the pub, as if it he ran it on his own, and even though I was standing with Chris, trying to take part in the conversation, she still continued to ignore me and I was fuming inside, but decided to keep my dignity for now. When the woman left the Woodmoor she shouted goodbye to Chris, only after leaving some large posters of herself for us to advertise that she was here again the following week.

The next morning Chris asked if I would like to put the posters up in the lounge, taproom and the two entrances. I unrolled the posters to see her smiling and pinned them to the walls. I stood back and looked at her, then went to get a black pen and put a dot under one of her nostrils on each of the posters. It looked as though she had a bogie up her nose. Perfect. When Angie came in and saw the posters, she commented on her having a bogie up her nose, which she said looked disgusting. She doubled up with laughter when I told her what I had done and admitted that she had noticed how the singer had laid it on a bit with Chris. The singer didn't come back after the second session, I think that she had sussed it was me and she didn't even stay for a drink.

We did make some good friends that sang for us; we had some really good nights, after hours, with the turns. Two of the singers were a duo called Derek and Jill that lived nearby. Jill listened to me one night as I confided in her about the young boy I had seen and she suggested we had a séance after closing time.

The last couple went home leaving us with the usual group including my cousins Bill and John. We lit candles and put the tables together in the taproom. I felt a little unsure at this stage and hoped we wouldn't bring any evil spirits into the place.

It was nearly midnight when we started the séance and lit the candles. Immediately the candle flames were leaning towards me, or so I thought, and this put me completely off the idea, I didn't like it and instead sat out of the circle and watched. The atmosphere was changing, I could feel it and because I didn't want to disappoint the others I sat there and said nothing. Adrian, my eldest son, walked in at that time and sat next to me watching.

Everyone had settled down with a drink at the side of them when Jill asked if anyone was there. All of a sudden we heard the door of the men's toilet bang. It was more than a bang, it sounded like someone had fallen through the door and we all assumed that someone was hiding in there. All the doors in this building were very heavy, but it did sound as if they'd been flung open or something like that.

Everyone jumped up and someone screamed out;

There's someone in the toilet.

We all ran into the toilet, but there was no one there. We all seemed to be talking at once, then it went quiet and everyone sat back down again. This time the middle door, which was a fire door, suddenly flung open and then shut again and the door opposite to that one banged shut, as if someone had walked through both doors. We jumped up again and looked around but again, no-one. The outer doors were all locked so no-one could have escaped. The doors to the cellar and to upstairs were in our view so that was out of the question.

Making our way back to the taproom, we saw that all the drinks had gone, not the glasses but the drinks from the glasses. Of course, we all blamed Billy who drank like a fish, but he denied it and was annoyed anyway because his drink had gone, although it had probably gone before. I still believed him, as I felt sure he never would have been able to drink so much in that short time; anyway I could tell by his face, he was as confused as us. I was scared now and worried. Of course, they would go home, but we would be here with whatever it was, so I decided enough was enough and ended it there and then. I was scared to go to bed that night and I knew that I would never mess with anything like that again. During the days after the séance the electric switch, that was down in the cellar, behind locked doors, kept turning itself off. The lights would flicker and then go off altogether. The following day, Angie told me that in the past a man had died in the gents' toilet of a heart attack.

We had a day out at Holmfirth, our first day off since moving into the pub. It was cold, but the fresh air was like a tonic. I looked at the hills and green fields and wished that I lived in a place like this; I would love to live in the country. When I want something I always picture it in my mind and make it real. When we arrived back our place, it seemed so grey looking and I suddenly felt unhappy. I suppose it was that time of year and when we were inside we found that the electric switch had gone to off again.

It was starting to turn even colder now as winter was approaching; we were drinking late as usual when suddenly I had this feeling that I had to go and check on the boys. I opened my son's door and the lack of air overwhelmed me, I could hardly breath. Christopher had got so cold that he had put the fan heater on full heat in this tiny room. He had placed it on his bedside cabinet blowing straight into his face. I had trouble wakening him and I'm sure he would have died had I not gone up to check on him when I did.

Although I liked the pub and the people there, I knew it was time to move. I never felt comfortable after the séance and deeply regretted ever having had one. Even though I read the Tarot cards, I never did like things like séances and wondered why I had agreed to it. The dream of having a country pub was also still on my list and to my surprise Chris was all for moving to another pub.

We informed the brewery we would like a change and very soon, in fact within days, a pub came up, out of the blue, in Oxenhope, a village right in the heart of the countryside near where the famous Brontë sisters had lived. Someone had listened to me up there and answered my prayers. We went out to view the place that we would be moving to and went in for a drink, once again to 'weigh' things up and we loved it; the countryside, the quietness, and, of course, the fresh air. It was opposite a large reservoir, surrounded by hills, and I knew the boys would love it here.

When we got home, we rang the brewery to arrange a meeting and, as soon as we knew for certain it was ours, we told the boys and my parents. It wasn't easy telling the locals and we hoped they would understand and not take it personally. It was time to pack again.

Chapter Six

Apart from going to visit our grandparents in Ireland once in a while, like many other families during the 1950s and early 60s, we didn't have holidays. We did, however, have day trips to the seaside which were fun, especially the old club trips and we enjoyed the coach ride itself, as it was all part of the day trip. The trips were only available to the families of fully paid up members of a working men's club. The yearly trips were something that all the families of club members looked forward to.

Getting up early on the morning of the club trip, my sister Teresa, along with me mam's younger sister Val, who was a few years younger than me, and more like a sister than an aunty, and my best friend Nora and I, would rush down to the club car park, as we had to be the first there, very early in the morning, to get the long back seat. The four of us would sleep in a double bed the night before, two at the top and two at the bottom. We talked all through the night sometimes, and one particular time we were hungry, so we crept downstairs for some toast, being careful to close all the doors behind us. Dad woke up to go to the toilet, but obviously heard a noise. We could hear him moving about and then we heard him coming down the stairs. We hid behind the kitchen door, in the dark, holding our breath with hands over our mouths to stop us from giggling. We were lucky really because Dad had thought that there were burglars in the house and was about to put his fist down on us. I don't know who was more surprised, him or us. We were soon marched back upstairs to the sound of me mam yelling;

Do you know what bloody time it is? We've to be up in morning. Gerrin that bloody bed will yeah?

We were up bright and early in the morning. We dressed in our best clothes and our hair was backcombed up at the top and loose at the bottom Nora, managed to get her hair like the Supremes, with a ringlet down one side. It took her ages to do. Everyone was talking all at once or rushing around; the conversations went as follows;

Hurry up befooar sumdy gets back seat.

A can't find me comb.

Will you 'urry up in that bathroom am peeing me sen.

It's my turn first, av been waiting ages.

Put kettle on sumdy, will ya? I'm dying for a cup o tea.

Where's me toothbrush? Somdy's nicked me toothbrush. Mam! Somdy's nicked me toothbrush!

There were voices coming from all over the house and although the house was usually full of people, it seemed to be even busier than ever as everyone was trying to get in the bathroom.

We only had a little mirror in our bedroom, so we had to stand on the bed to see the bottom half of how we looked and sometimes we would end up losing our balance and toppling over each other;

What's this frock look like? Does it look or reight?

Yeah, just 'urry up will yeah or we'll end up at front o bus.

We argued about who was next in the bathroom. Although we had another toilet downstairs, there wasn't a sink in that one. However, with nine people all trying to get ready, the downstairs toilet came in handy. There were never enough towels in our house and when you finally got one, it was usually wet through and so you had to dry yourself on a flannelette sheet. There were no radiators or tumble dryers then.

My young brothers were so excited getting ready and Dad would be shouting up to them;

Be sure to brush yer teeth now an make sure you have a pee.

The men wore suits in those days when they were going somewhere and so we were all dressed up to the nines and ready to set off to the club car park.

We really hoped it wouldn't rain because it was quite a walk to the club and our hair would be ruined. It didn't matter when we reached the seaside because it was usually windy anyway, but it was important to look good getting onto the bus. We rushed past the trippers on their way to the bus, some of the little ones had buckets and spades, and we managed to get the back seat, as usual. These club trips were such an exciting event and they were good days. After a little sing song, a committee man would come around with the pop and crisps and after a while they would give everyone pocket money. I can't remember just how much, but it was well appreciated. You would have thought we were going on a world cruise. Mam would make sandwiches to save money. It was always egg sandwiches or potted meat and we would eat them when we arrived there, to get them out of the way, as it was usually near lunch time anyway. It always took ages to get there on club trips and we always stopped at the 'Half Way House' for a cup of tea and a pee, then the men would have a pint' cos as they said;

Eeh am ready for this pint.

I am annall lad,

Norra bad pint this.

There was always a discussion on the quality of the beer, as they held it up to the light and turned the glass around.

There used to be a miniature jukebox control on the wall next to all the tables and we eagerly fed it with money, even grownups liked pop music in those days. If we went to Blackpool for the day trip, it would be a race to see who would be the first to see the Tower. Such excitement over such a small thing and many times there would be falling out and tears over this. The kids would watch out eagerly hoping, to be the first to spot it. The first child to see it would get a threepenny bit. On the way into Blackpool, by the side of the road, was the famous Windmill and when we saw this, everyone would start to put their coats on and fasten bags up, eager to be first off the bus.

We were always the first off the bus, even though we were sitting at the back, and coming home we would be the last on the bus, but no one sat in our seats, you had the same seat going and the same seat coming back. We had 'kiss me quick' hats on and sun glasses even if the sun wasn't shining and my brothers wore cowboys hats and had a silver gun in a holster and the gun would fire 'caps' to the annoyance of some.

On the way home there wasn't the same excitement at the Half Way House because we had spent up. Sometimes someone on the bus would start a sing song up and then there was always someone who wanted a pee. The bus would stop near to some hedges and the 'one' would end up being a dozen, especially the ones who had been drinking beer. People would go down behind the hedges trying to find a private spot. When we finally reached the club, the women would take the children home and the men would go into the club because 'they were ready for a pint'.

There was one trip to Bridlington that we went on and unknown to me and my sister, my little brother was lost for a good few hours. Mam and Dad were frantic. The police were involved in the search and cars with loudspeakers were asking people to watch out for a little boy on his own. Eventually he was found sitting on a kerb, unperturbed by the panic all around him; it was only about twenty minutes before the bus was due to leave when they found him. We knew nothing of my brother being lost, because after leaving the bus we could go all day without seeing anyone from Barnsley although at other times we were forever bumping into them. There were no mobile phones then, so we were unaware of his disappearance and because Mam was so upset, she yelled at us as soon as she saw us.

Where the bloody hell, have you been? Our Kev's been lost all afternoon and we couldn't find you anywhere to help look for him.

The size of Bridlington and she was having a go at us because she couldn't find us, so that we could look for him. Besides, we walked up and down the front all day and I think I would have recognised my brother if I had seen him. But I suppose it was a dreadful day for her and, to make things even worse, we had all come back laughing and we were late. Everyone was on the bus waiting to set off which didn't help. Mam said she would never go to Bridlington again as long as she lived and, in fact, it was to be thirty years before she went back there again.

Apart from that, we had so much fun, even with little money, but what you never have you never miss and this was the case with us. We were a very happy bunch.

Other than the day trips, our only other option was to catch a bus to visit parks or similar places. During the holidays we would go to my uncle's house in Wombwell. The journey would take quite a long time because the bus travelled to so many places before reaching its destination. Sometimes we had to go on two buses to get there and it seemed such a long way to get to Uncle Tom's. A car journey now would take about fifteen minutes. Going to my uncle's house was always a special treat when we were very young. He lived with his family, my Aunt Silvia and two boys at that time, Tommy and Alan, who were roughly the same age as my sister and I. They lived in a terrace house at the bottom of a lane and at the end of the lane was a canal that had an arched bridge going over it to where the pit was. The other side of the bridge looked bleak and scary to us as children and we never ventured much further than the canal, which in itself was a danger. I would probably have been between five and eight when they left that house, to live in a newer house and my cousins Tommy and Alan, my sister Teresa and I were very good friends and we were constantly getting up to mischief. We were playing under the bridge one day trying to catch a duck, when a swan jumped out of the water and chased us to the top of the bridge, trying to smack us over the head with its wing. We ran into the house and got a good telling off from my uncle who told us that they had been known to kill to protect their young. The warning lasted only a few hours before we were down there again throwing stones into the water. The arched bridge had walls on either side and I remember walking on that wall as my mother came out. When she saw what I was doing she yelled at me to get down because it was such a drop to the bottom of the canal. The yelling made me lose my balance and almost made me fall in. Going to my uncle's was like an adventure and Teresa and I looked forward to being there for a few days. The row of terraces had no electricity, but instead used gas mantles. There was no back garden, other than a large area that was shared with the rest of the terrace and in the summer people used to sit on the steps and peel potatoes. At the bottom of the yard was a row of toilets that were shared between the houses and we would climb on the roofs and jump from one to another.

About eight houses up from where my uncle lived, there was a house that had been burned. The windows were blackened and it smelled of smoke. Apparently, a man had tied his wife to a chair and set fire to her because he had found her with another man. He was accused of murder and hanged for the crime; me mam told me later that he was the last man to be hanged from Barnsley. My cousin used to scare me to death with tales of hearing the woman's screams in the night, especially when it was windy, and I would pull the covers over my head tightly when we were staying there. At the top of the terrace was a pub called the 'Halfway House' and I always wondered where it was halfway to. We would climb on top of each other to reach the pub window and see me dad and his dad inside and on the way back, when we passed the blackened house, we would make a run for it. The doors in that long row of houses were never closed and the women used to sit on the doorsteps talking.

My uncle told us a story of a man who on his way to the pit had turned around again to go home. He met some more men on his way that were going into work and they said to him;

Wheeze tha going? Thar going wrong roo'ad ant tha.

The man replied without stopping and said;

Belts brok.

So the men turned and went home themselves and as they passed people on the way to work they repeated the same thing, 'belts brok'. It turned out that the belt the man was talking about was his trouser belt and he was nipping home to get another. Everyone had thought he meant the drive belt at the pit head and they all missed a day's work.

No-one liked to miss work in those days. Money was tight enough and there weren't the benefits that there are today. As alarm clocks often got switched off 'for a few more minutes longer in bed', many slept in and 'overlaid' as they called it. Most of the men in the neighbourhood including me dad had a old man that came around the houses early in the morning. This man was called the 'knocker upperer', he was a retired miner who made a bit of money from knocking the men up for work and unless you came to the window to acknowledge him, he would carry on tapping his long stick at the bedroom window. If you were to ignore the tapping that he first made, he would scrape something on the window that was fastened on a long stick. It was such an awful sound, just like a screeching noise, but it always worked. Me dad used to yell at him;

Would yeah stop de bloody scratching, fer God's sake? Jaysus, I heard yeah the first time.

The old man would yell back;

Well get thi bloody sen up then, I ent bloody gorr all day tha knows.

Dad would yell, 'bugger off' and the man would shout back, 'thee bugger off annal.' When the man came every weekend for his money, they would stand talking to each other in such a friendly way. Monday would come around and it would start all over again.

As we were growing up and becoming aware of our looks, we would walk everywhere to be sure we didn't miss anything or, should I say, anyone. We also liked to be noticed, much to me mam's disapproval.

We used to plug the record player through the window into a socket, so it would sit on a chair in the garden, and then we bopped away to the Mersey sounds until we heard the sound of the ice cream van coming up the road. Me and Nora would look at each other and run in to see if our hair was all right. No, it wasn't the ice cream we were interested in, but the driver and his mate. They were only young and all the girls in the entire street had a crush on them. Once they asked us if we would like to go to the speedway races in Sheffield. I wasn't sure what that was, but it had something to do with motorbikes and racing. We climbed into the ice cream van and laid low on the van floor, still eating a cornet while it drove passed the houses where we lived. We were so thrilled to be asked. It never went through our minds that we could be in danger, in that way we were so naive, but when we arrived at the stadium, we were too late and the gates were shut, so we couldn't go in. They drove us back home and no more than that. It was just as well that we couldn't get into the stadium because we would have been a while. It was summertime and when they dropped us off at the top of the road the whole street was out. My mother's face was like thunder.

God Nora, me mam's down at bottom of street looking for us.

How did she know? She can't ev seen us gerrin in the van, we gorrin at bottom o street.

Dunt know Nora, but I'm not looking forward to this.

Nora had a big hairstyle because of all the back combing she did and apparently her hair was bobbing up and down in the ice cream van as we drove up the street. A girl opposite to our house had recognised the hair as belonging to Nora and went running to my mother telling her we had been kidnapped. I'm surprised me mam hadn't already rung the police, but we hadn't been all that long, although if we had been able to get into the speedway, we would have been hours and she would surely have called the police. I won't tell you what me Mam said when I got home, it can't be printed, but somehow she managed to stop the ice cream van coming down our road again and we missed them and the free ice cream.

Can you imagine Nora? Headlines in the Evening Star; "Girls kidnapped by ice cream man". Then we turn up, just eating ice cream.

Nora laughed and said;

Am glad we dint gerrin to stadium, who wants to watch cars racing or whatever it was.

My only memories of the early sixties were getting ready to go out. It could take hours, there were no hair dryers then and washing long hair was a nightmare. Sometimes we would lay our hair on the ironing board, put a towel over it and iron it. Otherwise it was a case of drying it in front of the fire, to the sound of me mam's;

You'll get neuralgia, drying it like that. Dunt come rooaring to me.

She always used to say that. "Dunt come rooaring to me when you do".

She was once telling me off for washing my hair before going to bed, obviously leaving me with wet hair, and she yelled;

Yer'll end up deeing frum pneumonia. Dunt come rooaring to me.

I'll not mam, al go to heaven instead.

You'll gerra bloody crack in a minute.

She was harmless enough; she had her work cut out with all the kids because Dad never yelled at us at all. I can't ever remember a time when Dad raised his voice to anyone at home, me mam was certainly the boss, apart from when trying to stop him going for a drink straight from work. There was one time she was giving him some stick because he was late home and Dad sat there drinking his tea on the sofa. Me mam got angry and hit him on his knee with a stiletto heel. It must have hurt him bad because he threw the cup straight through the lounge window, but he still didn't yell at her. Me mam was laughing at how red Dad's face was with the pain. That was so funny and just as well no one was outside in the front or the cup of tea would have hit them.

I can't really remember much more than the things that I did, selfish as it may seem. I had no interest in the news or what was happening in the world. One night while I was getting ready to meet Nora, my mother was watching the news and crying over someone called President Kennedy;

What yeah crying for Mam?

President Kennedy's been shot.

Who's he?

Mam didn't even answer, and then yelled;

Dunt you be late in like last neet, en purra coit on, it's bloody freezing art theear.

The sixties were a good time and I am happy to have been growing up then. There were so many people at our house all the time, friends, relations and neighbours. We had really good neighbours on our street. One of my other friends, Irene, lived next door and we were always in each other's houses and she sometimes slept at ours even though she only lived next door. There was still a lot of the tomboy in us and we would climb trees and stuff like that. We never stayed indoors; whatever the weather and we had really bad winters then. The milk bottles on the door step would be three inches taller as it froze, icicles would hang from the roof, and the windows in our bedroom would have ice on the inside. It was freezing in that particular room because it had three outside walls and no carpet, only cold lino. When it was windy, you could hear the wind blowing down the drainpipes at the side of the house and we would pile coats over us to keep warm.

We played out in the deepest snow and we would build snowmen with socks on our hands to keep them from getting cold. Sometimes we wore

Dad's socks because they were bigger. Gloves often got lost and we never had any at the right time. The socks always ended up with holes in and we would be in trouble. We would roll snow for hours trying to make the biggest snowman in the street and after building the snowmen, we all went round throwing snowballs at other snowmen to make them fall down. This caused fights and when Michael had come over from Ireland and was here living with us one time, he put stones in his snowballs. This caused a huge fight between him and a lad on the street, but Michael always won. He was always fighting with someone, including myself, although our fights were more verbal; he told me a while ago that I was a cow when we were kids because I would bite him.

On one particular day, donned in wellies and coats, Irene and I went over the field to where the new school was being built and there were lots of puddles covered in ice. We liked to jump onto the ice and break it, taking turns on the way. Irene said it was her turn, but it wasn't her turn, it was mine. We argued a bit and I let her have my turn, but it so happened that the ice wasn't covering a puddle, it was covering a hole filled with water and she fell through it up to her waist. Apart from her being saturated, we were lucky it wasn't any deeper. They were still working on the school and there were big holes everywhere where they had dug down for the foundations. We went home then to face the music, I was as wet as Irene from falling down laughing.

Music would blare out from Radio Caroline and we would all sing along to Tom Jones and all the other songs of that time. This included my mother who was more like a sister in some ways. She would join in with our friends and she had such a quick and witty sense of humour that she was liked by everyone. Just as the pirate radio stations started up, lots of other things were beginning to change and when in 1965/66 Mary Quant came on the scene there was a dramatic change in fashion and hairstyles. The mini skirt was launched and the psychedelic colours that came with it, knee length white boots, and hairstyles that were long and straight with a long sharp fringe or hair was cut into a shoulder length bouffant that required backcombing at the top to 'lift' the hair. Oh, for those days again. Due to miniskirts being so short, out went stockings and suspenders and in came tights, which were much more expensive then than they are now many years later. They cost one pound a pair and my first wage at fifteen, years of age, was just two pound ten shillings, but they were tougher and with careful washing lasted quite a while. We hated nylon stockings. Many a time we would have to use a sixpence because the buttons had come off the suspender belt, leaving the stockings wrinkled as they hung there. My legs were like matchsticks anyway, I was so underweight and very tall. We found that sixpence worked the best, although at other times we'd had to take buttons off our cardigans in emergencies. This was a time when a bra made everyone look like they had pointed boobs, then the 'cross your heart bra' was introduced and boobs were reduced in size dramatically.

The material of clothes also changed. Polyester, acrylic and courtelle were introduced making clothes nice and easy to wear. New makeup came onto the market and, of course false eyelashes became very fashionable. I remember me and my friend Sandra putting make-up on in the kitchen. We had to lean over the table that had the toaster on it, in order to get closer to the mirror. The toaster was still warm from being used and we were careful not to burn ourselves, when the simplest thing would have been to move it. I leaned right over the toaster to put on my eyelashes and dropped the tube of glue into the toaster. Because the toaster was still hot I couldn't get it out again and the glue started to melt, so I left it and we finished getting ready and went out. A few days later me mam was complaining about the bread being 'off', and I didn't really take much notice at first. Then all the family was going on about the bread tasting different when it had been toasted. I kept quiet and hoped it would burn itself out;

Its only a little tube, Sandra, how long could it take to get rid of that?

I'm surprised it dint glue their mouths together.

Well at least then, she wouldn't be yelling at me. I'll not be eating toast for a couple of months, just to be on the safe side.

We walked down the street linking arms, laughing.

It was hard being the eldest, it was all new to my parents having a teenage daughter and I was always in trouble for something and my mother and I were arguing all the time.

You're not going art like that. That frock is too short.

It was a mini dress with flowers on and it was very short I admit.

It int me frock mam, it's cos me legs are too long.

Which was true, Sandra and I were the same size in clothes but mine were always miles shorter than hers.

In this house for half past ten lady.

Aw, can't ha cum in at eleven? Am fifteen, all others have to be in for eleven.

Half past ten and purra coit on, befooar ya catch yer death o cold. Dunt come running te me if yea do.

Me mam could toast bread with her tongue at times.

We used to go dancing on Friday at a place called the "Georges" in town, because it was St Georges Hall. There were fantastic groups that went there and we'd bop and sing along to the sixties sounds, but me and Nora had to leave at ten to walk down to the bus station and catch a bus and then walk home from the bus stop, which was a ten minute walk, just to be in by ten thirty. When we got off at the bus stop, we had to walk through a very dark recreation ground, either that, or walk the long way round. Then we would walk a little before reaching a long narrow snicket that divided Nora's street from mine, the snicket was very dark and we both hated it as it seemed such a long way. Whether coming from my side of the snicket or Nora's side, we would both walk to the centre. We would say together, one, two, three, 'God save me' and then run our separate ways like hell, shouting out to each other.

I would always put a coat on in front of me mam, then once outside, I would take it off and hide it in the washhouse after closing the door behind me, then I would pick it up again on the way back inside the house when I got home.

Mam was always worried about me and my sister bringing 'trouble home,' as she called it, when we were in our teens. Funny really, my mother never said that to any of my three brothers in their teenage years.

It was in the early seventies and I was married when we first had a car and I learnt to drive. Now we could go anywhere and it opened up a whole new way of life for me. We had never had a car in our family. In fact, I can only remember one car owner that lived on our street during the time I was a child.

It's strange how things work out. When my two boys were very young, we all went off for the day with my parents to this beautiful place called Haworth, the home of the famous Bronte sisters. This was an idea of my mother's; she was really intelligent and did a lot of reading. My mother knew everything about this place and chatted on, almost as though she had lived there. I had never realised that this place was connected to the film 'Wuthering Heights', a favourite of mine, but Mam had read a lot of books written by the three famous Bronte sisters.

I was so envious of the locals who lived and worked in such a beautiful village as Haworth, and I imagined myself living there, chatting to friends on the famous cobbled high street which was full of curiosity shops and quaint cafes. The hills around this village were just teaming with the history of the moorlands and I wished I could close my eyes and step back in time for a while and see this street in times gone by. Living conditions in those days were probably not very good though, so I would only want to spend a few minutes, no more than that.

The strangest things happen in life, as if they were meant to be. At the bottom of the street stood some old terrace houses and in one of those houses lived a little girl; this little girl was to be my daughter in law and the mother of two of my grandchildren, twenty years later. In fact, the famous Bronte church that we had walked around and viewed, along with the other visitors to Haworth, was to be the church my first grandson Nicholas would be christened in. Further down the cobbled street above one of the quaint shops that we had browsed in, my son Christopher would share a bedsit at the age of twenty five with his girlfriend, also a native of Haworth.

I never came to visit Haworth again until the day we viewed the pub we were offered in Oxenhope, the next village to Haworth, but I will always remember my very first day out there and my vision of living there and standing on the High street having a conversation with my neighbours.

Shortly before leaving the Woodmoor, we had taken four days off to visit Scotland, while Mam and Dad looked after the pub. Even though it rained for the whole time there, it was still a welcoming change. It was the second time I had been to see the famous mountain, Ben Nevis and not seen it due to the heavy mist that surrounded it. We travelled up through Scotland and stayed in different places, including Loch Ness. One particular place that we went to visit had a lovely hotel that overlooked the loch. We asked for a room there, but the receptionist said it was full, much to my disappointment. However, she made a phone call to someone and we were offered a room that was attached to the hotel. We were told it was a house that had rooms available when the hotel was fully booked.

We were shown to our room and walking up the wide sweeping staircase, it was almost like stepping back into the nineteenth century. Although the room was not 'en suite', the bathroom was right outside the door. We left our baggage and went down to the hotel for something to eat. Neither Chris nor I were people who could drink alcohol after a heavy meal, so we decided to have an early night and get more from the next day. The room was very nicely decorated with pink velvet curtains and matching bedding. It had little floral displays in pink on the dresser and two large windows overlooking the loch. The bathroom also had pink curtains, but they were in a much softer fabric, and matching towels and little ornamental decorative bits and bats to finish it off. There was also a gentle perfumed smell to the room that came from the soap. Pink has always been a favourite colour of mine and I was thinking that if I had a bedroom like this, with big windows, I would choose pink.

I stood at the window, looking out over the loch and pictured myself living in this house in days gone by, I imagined myself in a long dress with petticoats and a large hat, getting ready to go down to the shops.

It was still quite light and I stood and watched the sun go down before going to bed. It didn't take much time to drift into a peaceful sleep, the bed was so comfortable and everything had a fresh smell to it. I suddenly woke up with a feeling of someone being in the room. I looked up and a very beautiful lady was smiling at me. At first I thought it was the owner of the house. She was so near to me that we looked straight into each other's eyes and I couldn't speak. I stuck my elbow into Chris which to my surprise woke him. He must have sensed or felt something because he didn't get mad at me, but the lady floated back into the corner of the room where a sink was situated and then went through the wall.

Did you see her Chris? She was stood smiling at me.

See who?

That lady.

What lady?

A lady stood at the side of the bed and she was smiling at me.

You were probable dreaming, get back to sleep, we've travelled a lot today and you're just over tired.

I'm telling you she was real, she was only inches from my face.

No answer, he was fast asleep but I kept awake a while in case she came back, until eventually falling asleep.

The next morning when I woke, the lady was the first thing that entered my head; I jumped out of bed and started knocking at the wall around the sink.

For God's sake, what are you playing at, it's seven in the morning, get back to bed.

I'm looking to see where that woman went.

She probably went to bed and is still there now.

But I carried on tapping the wall and suddenly it sounded hollow. I went out into the corridor and then into the bathroom and tapped on the wall there which was also hollow. The bedroom obviously had once joined onto another tiny room, but the hollow part was only the size of a door.

We had to go to the hotel next door for breakfast and as we were leaving the house, I noticed a photograph on a table of a woman dressed in finery. The woman in the photograph was the one that I had seen. I mentioned the woman I had seen to the waitress and asked if the house next door had ghosts.

Oh, you're talking about the original owner. There have been a few people who claim to have seen her.

She asked if we had stayed in the front room overlooking the loch. We told we had and she said;

That was her bedroom; she had a dressing room in there which was eventually made into a bathroom. Very beautiful she was, or so I'm told, I've worked here for years and never seen her.

I looked across at Chris and said;

Told you it wasn't a dream, why would I say she had drifted into the corner of the room where there used to be a door, when I didn't know there was one there.

Chapter Seven

We moved into the Shoulder of Mutton on a Thursday. I drove the van with some of the furniture along with my brother Kev. Some of our friends from the Woody also came to help with the moving and the previous landlady had kindly allowed us to take some of our stuff there earlier in the week which had been really helpful. Because we were high up in the van, we had a splendid view of Oxenhope and the surroundings areas. We drove up past Denholme Gate, turned the tight hairpin bed, then we drove through a tree lined lane, past the farmlands and moors. When we reached the very top, the whole of 'Bronte Country' came to life in front of me, with sheep scattered across the fields. We could see a reservoir just in front of us and the sun glistened over a second reservoir in the distance. The hillsides were dotted with barns and an assortment of residential cottages, some dating back probably six hundred years. As we drove on the view grew larger still and an old mill stood in front of us with a tall chimney. The day we came to view the pub I hadn't taken much notice of the view, we were following directions to find the pub, and the other times we had come were late afternoon when it was dark.

Mam and Dad and the boys followed later, as Chris had to stay for the changeover at the Woody. We must have looked like the Beverly Hillbillies on arriving. It was only a small van we had borrowed from my father-in-law and it was full to the top. We climbed out of the van, along with the two dogs and Sherry the goat.

Before going inside, I had to put the goat on a dog chain and take her for a walk to find somewhere for her to graze, and another lead on each dog, to find a place for them to relieve themselves. I must have looked a right comical sight. The dogs had a pee and were eager to go off exploring and they were annoyed at having to be tied to a tree until we got sorted out. I tethered the goat securely and started unloading some of the cases and lighter items and my brother and I started to take them upstairs.

Walking into the upstairs front room and seeing the view of the reservoir with swans gliding on it was breath taking. A reservoir surrounded by moorland with winding streams running through the hills, like silver ribbons, and mist rolling down the hillsides. The main bedroom had two large windows and was very bright and airy with lots of room. The kitchen, like the other rooms, was clean and modern and looked over a farm that was almost joined to the pub. They had hens and ducks and there was the sound of 'cock a doodle do' amid the quietness.

There were three bedrooms altogether. The main bedroom had front views and side views, and was very large and bright. The other two bedrooms had good views, but the bathroom was weird. There was a fire escape at the back of the toilet with a half glass door that was used for access to the upstairs without going through the bar. The back of the pub had a car park and a huge wall that divided us up from the moorland and the houses high up in the hills.

Mam and Dad arrived with Chris and the boys and straight away they got stuck in with helping us unpack. I really don't know how we would have managed without their help. Dad helped Chris lift the heavy items while me and me mam sorted the clothes out. We were ready for a sit down, after all the lifting we had done, but the first job now was to find a suitable place for the goat to graze. We had come from a town pub to a country pub and, unbelievably, there was nothing for the goat to eat apart from the nettles, in the hedges. This pub unlike the Woodmoor, only had a car park and a few hedges, she seemed quite happy enough eating the nettles so I left her tied up and went into the kitchen. We unpacked the food and made some lunch but realised we had no milk;

"Well then, while you do some unpacking me and yer dad will nip out and find a shop down in the village", Mam suggested.

I was so busy that I hadn't realised they had been gone two hours. I was just about to go looking for them when they came through the door, absolutely shattered. In fact, I had never seen my mother with rosy cheeks before. The walk to the shop was so pleasant with its wonderful views and it was downhill all the way, so they had not realised the amount of walking they had done. Of course, being a village, the customers in the shop were used to chatting and they were very laid back and unrushed, so quite a long time was taken up there and, coming out of the shop and looking at the hill they were about to walk up they were both shocked. They asked someone what time the next bus was to the top of the hill and they replied 'tomorrow'. There was just one bus a day. There were no mobile phones then and our phone had not been connected, so they no choice but to walk. My mother never did like walking and I creased myself laughing. I can tell you now; they both slept well that night.

The next day I drove into town to find the supermarkets and on my way back I somehow got lost. I drove round country lanes as we still had not been connected to the phone. I never saw a person to ask the way to our place and ended up in country lanes that went on and on and were too narrow to turn around in. It was so quiet and it was ages before I got home, but I enjoyed the journey and I wasn't even missed.

Due to the lack of grazing for the goat we had to give her away to a farmer, which was sad, but we had to think of her. There was plenty of space for her there and it was on a hill with plenty of grass, which had to be a better diet than nettles.

The boys were off exploring while we prepared to meet the customers for the lunch time session. The first ones we spoke to ran the local taxi firm, a couple called Mick and Joan. Mick had longish hair and a moustache and Joan was pretty and dark almost Spanish looking. Both were very friendly and made us feel very welcome, Joan was to become a very good friend of mine. The other guy with them was a well built young man who didn't seem the smiley sort but did speak, although it was hard to understand him at first. When I asked him if he worked in the village, his reply was 'yeah, I work for wa'er bored'. It took several attempts to find that he worked for the Water Board. A lot of locals there, I found out later, did not put Ts into their words such as la'er instead of later, or wan'ed instead of wanted. I found in time that I was forever being teased about my broad Yorkshire accent. The young man's name was Gary and we were to see a lot more of him as he came in almost every night and he also became a good friend.

Before Mum and Dad went home we thought we would have a drive around and get familiar with our new surroundings. We drove towards Bronte waterfalls but because of the weather, we decided to just drive around for a while until we stopped to admire the view on the Pennine Way. There was a howling wind outside as we parked up and against all advice, Dad insisted on going out for some 'fresh air'. His clothes billowed as the wind caught hold of him and started to take him off. Once the wind had caught hold of him, he couldn't stop running, and on returning, his head was bent forward and his hands were straight down by his side and his feet were way behind him as he fought his way back in the car. My mother yelled;

You silly bugger, you could have carried on running ore top o that hill theear.

The wind still had an eerie howling sound when we got back to the pub. We all stepped out of the car and Mam started to mimic Cathy, of Wuthering Heights. Running towards Chris she called out;

Hinchcliff, Hinchcliff, it's me, Catheee.

Dad piped up;

It's not Hinchcliff, its Keighley.

You're both wrong it's Heathcliffe.

Me mam said; "Aw yeah, it is"

Me dad laughed and said; "Oh, I thought yis were talking about the town".

These 'Wuthering Heights' winds were something we had to get used to. Our car park was surrounding by high walls and the wind got trapped there giving out the most sinister, eerie sounds. Inside it would come down the chimney, howling in different tones, loud and then soft again. Mam said it sounded like lost souls travelling around the building. I visualised little faces blowing air out through their mouths, and sometimes it would become very loud and last a while. It always seemed to have been raining since we arrived there, a fine, drizzly sort of rain, the sort you get in a mist. Looking back, I realise that it could easily have been the mist, rolling down the hills, a lot of the time.

My parents were sad to go home, especially with their being so far away now. I waved them off, as Chris drove away with them, saying he would be home again in about three hours. The place was so quiet upstairs without them and I knew the boys would miss them terribly as I would.

Adrian and Christopher had settled in at school but it must have been a hard time for them the first day, especially being at separate schools. Funny really that the primary school which Christopher went to, was the school overlooking the whole village and the hills, that I had looked at twenty years ago, when I commented on how lucky the children were, that were taught here. Adrian met three really good friends on his first day, a friendship that up to today has lasted twenty six years. Christopher seemed to have many friends although not quite like Adrian's somehow. He was usually drawn to the more mischievous ones that were very much like him. They were both much happier at their schools there and both of them still say it was the best place they have ever lived in.

It took quite a time and a lot of effort to be accepted in this small village and really, from the start, I knew Chris would never settle here. He was definitely not a man for the country and its way of life. Even though the idea of a country pub at the time was appealing to him, lovely views meant nothing to Chris and he found the people a lot different to the Woody bunch. The previous landlady had run this pub by herself and was very popular and well liked so I hoped that I would eventually be as well liked as her. She was a nice lady and although she had only moved to the village, she left us alone and never interfered with how we ran the pub.

Although the living quarters were clean, I decided to put my own personal touches to them, starting with our bedroom and then the bathroom. The curtains in the bedroom were already there in pink velvet and very nice, so I had bought new bedding in pink and put pretty pictures up on the walls and scattered matching cushions. In the bathroom I changed it in a similar way with pink towels, pink soap and flannels, finishing off with little bows scattered here and there. I was looking through the bedroom window one afternoon and appreciating the lovely view, when I had a strange feeling that someone was stood near me. I looked around the room and there was no-one there, then I got whiff of a lovely familiar smell and my mind went immediately to the room we had stayed in for a while in Scotland. Although I wouldn't have wanted anyone around to hear me, I found myself saying;

Yes it is like your room now.

Saturday afternoon was the best time in the week for getting to know people. The first Saturday afternoon was the first time I had spoken to Gina. She was a tall, twenty two year old with lovely blond curly hair and a pretty face. She had been going out with her boyfriend, Dave since leaving school. He adored Gina and they were good together, he was also very funny without even telling jokes. Dave and Gina introduced me to Louise who was also a lovely girl and these friends made me feel at home there right from the start. Gina spoke of seeing me on the morning we moved in taking the goat out of the van;

You were struggling with the goat and trying to hold onto the dogs and looking everywhere for somewhere to tie them down.

Well, before you say it, yes Gina, we looked like hillbillies.

Gina giggled and agreed that we did.

We had a disco at the weekends and Dave was the D J. One evening he came in white trousers and a black shirt, looking really smart and started off with his usual records. I commented on how smart he looked to Gina and she said;

Yeah, he wore an outfit like that last summer. He called me over and asked me to look at his trousers. I asked him why and he said;

"Gina, I farted and I think I followed through. Have a look, Gina, and see if you can see anything. It feels a bit damp",

Gina had trouble telling me through her laughter. She continued;

Well, I set off laughing. He had a nasty brown stain all down the back and had to stand near the wall all night, without a drink, to make sure he didn't need the toilet.

There was always a good atmosphere in there as the old juke box was full of Irish music. The Black Velvet Band must have been the most played song, ever, on that juke box. There was a really friendly feel to that place and in no time at all I got to know the locals well.

Actually, it was quite easy to get to know everyone that came into the pub, as there were hardly any strangers that came in. It was in the middle of no-where and the tourists, who were going to Haworth, didn't need to come through Oxenhope, so we relied on people coming in to the Shoulder that knew where we were. We were very quiet during the week, but the weekends could get quite busy. The locals usually walked all the way up from the village or got a taxi, but very few ever drove there.

We held a fancy dress party for Halloween as we had done at the Woodmoor and, again everyone in the pub made an effort to dress up. We had skeletons, bats and all kinds of cobwebs, artificial blood and eerie sounds all around the place. A few of the locals had taken us to a fancy dress shop in Halifax, for our clothes and I dressed up as a female vampire. The customers made a great effort to dress up. One came in a bin liner with food plastered all over it and dirt, and she had a plaque at the back which read 'I'm a dirty bag'. Some were frightening to look at and there were some that you had no idea at all who they were.

A few weeks later our friends from the Woodmoor hired a coach to bring them to the Shoulder of Mutton. They had told us they would pay us a visit when we were leaving and we were so pleased to see them all again. We had booked a band for the night and had a great evening before we finished in the early hours and said goodbye to our friends. It was late when they left us and, apparently, they had driven up the lane for a few miles and had just left

Oxenhope when their bus broke down. As it happened they broke down outside a pub, which was serving after hours. The driver went in and asked to use the phone. He was quickly followed by a few that needed the toilet, and the next thing, the whole bus load got out and ended up drinking in that pub until early morning, while the bus was fixed. I laughed when I was told of this and pictured Ez saying to the landlord;

Gis a quick gold will tha.

Everyone had left in high spirits, so I have no doubt as to how they must have livened up the place.

Winter was soon on its way and it was so much colder than Barnsley, in fact, two coats colder than anywhere else, as the locals used to say. We even bought thermal underwear, though vanity stopped me wearing mine in the end. The country lanes seemed so dark when we went out at night and after coming from well lit streets, it took some getting used to. However, I loved this place, but already I knew Chris didn't.

One really cold night, I pulled the curtains back to look at the weather as it was so cold and for a bit of fun said;

It's snowing.

I was only joking, so as to see their reactions and, as I thought, they rushed to the front door to look, then came in again looking at me, and laughing I said;

In Russia.

It's surprising how folk are fascinated by snow. We welcome the first fall of snow flakes and admire the pretty scenes they give us, the snowmen, sledging and snow ball fighting, but then we moan about it after a while. It did snow though later, really snow. Some customers who had made their way here when there were just a few flakes had to stay the night. The road was completely blocked by closing time and no-one had noticed how heavy the snow was out there, with the curtains being drawn and the entrance behind the bar being an inner door.

I noticed a small group of people passing a cigarette to each other and took pity on them, thinking they had no money.

Chris, why don't you buy them some cigs, their having to share one, they have a puff and then pass it on----what're you laughing at!

Their smoking pot, yer silly bugger, didn't you know.

No, I thought they were smoking a roll up, is that what that smell is.

Later in the evening, people gathered around the bar, still smoking weed or whatever it was and it was passed to me.

No thanks, I get high enough on drink without ought else.

But Chris had to have a go of course; after a while he staggered upstairs to the toilet instead of using the downstairs loo and was gone ages so I went upstairs to find him sat on the loo, his trousers down and with the door wide open, asleep!

Chris, Chris. Wake up. I thought that stuff was supposed to make you feel 'high' not put you to sleep.

He looked awful and then said he felt sick.

They all slept on the floor of the pub, there were bodies everywhere and some said it was a dream come true to be locked in a pub for a night. We had a great time.

We had just cleared up after closing a few nights later when I looked out of the window. There was a full moon, the snow was falling lightly and the scenery was beautiful with almost a blue hue to it:

Chris, Chris, quick come and take a look at this.

What? I'm hungry.

This view, come and have a look.

He slowly and reluctantly looked out of the window.

Yeah, nice. What have we got to eat?

Lets go for a walk.

It's after 12.o'clock. Are you mad?

It'll be lovely, feeling the snow falling on your face, feeling the crunch of the icy snow beneath your feet.

What did you say we had to eat?

Oh, piss off; I'll go on my own.

I put my coat and wellies on, but decided it was too scary to walk past the graveyards at midnight. Strange when you think about it, they are the same corpses during the day and its fine to stroll around the graves, but at night people are frightened to be near one. The dead won't know the time of day. I stood in front of the pub holding my head up towards the snowflakes with my arms outstretched, catching the snowflakes on my tongue, before reluctantly going back inside. What a waste. The scenery was so fairy tale like and the snow was so pure and white. I had been used to living in a mining town where the snow was quickly blackened by smoke from chimneys and mines. I walked up the fire escape to the bathroom and Chris was just about to go to the loo, so I banged really hard on the glass and made him jump. I went to the bedroom and stared out at the snow, I would have loved to have gone for a proper walk in it.

The previous landlady had told me how trustworthy this village was;

Leave your purse on the bar and go away, it'll be still there when you get back. Leave your cigarettes and people will help themselves to a cigarette.

I found this to be so true. When it was quiet, we often left a few customers during the day to get their own drinks and put the money in the till, especially if I was out shopping and Chris had cellar work to do.

These winter nights were certainly the best for getting to know the locals well. Although obviously not as good as far as making a profit was concerned. It was the same crowd that always stood at the bar and we would talk long into the night and this is how I came to get to know Alison. She was the daughter of the shop owner in the village, and had two brothers who were also locals in here and seeing as we were usually the only women after hours, having a drink, we became very close friends. In fact, she hated the late nights, it was her boyfriend who liked to stay behind, Alison drank very little alcohol then and when we later moved, Alison came with us.

Even though this pub of ours was out of the way, we had lots of youngsters from the village who walked up to the pub on most nights of the week. By now I was reading palms as well as talking about star signs. The young ones would stand and listen, while I told them about our 'ghostly visitors' in the last pub. Or should I say that we were the 'visitors' in their pub. The locals also had tales to tell. They told me of a man who loved game sports and was showing off his new hunting knife, to just a few regulars round the bar. This happened before we took over the licence. The bar was held up by strong beam like structures and he threw the knife at the extremely strong beam, to show how good a knife it was. On its journey, the knife simply disappeared. It was after hours and the few people that were in the bar looked everywhere for the knife, all the furniture was turned upside down, but they all insisted it disappeared before hitting the beam; it had disappeared into thin air. I once read in a book that spirits do not like knives or swords.

There were no ghostly happenings here as yet, apart from a few unexplained things. Every night at the same time the door into the lounge bar opened and closed as if someone had just walked in. It was always at the same time I believed it to be a spirit coming in for his 'usual'. There are lots of pubs that have hauntings in Haworth, Oxenhope, Stanbury and the surrounding area, but then it's so bloody cold they probably come in for a warm.

After hours, I had my usual crowd of people who stood at the bar with me and Chris would stand with his crowd. I used to read their palms and tell them stories of ghosts; I would scare them to death at times telling them about the spiritual things that have happened over the years. At the end of the night, some of them were terrified of the thought of walking home and often went by taxi, because apart from the darkness, you had to pass the old graveyard as well. However, they kept coming back for more and as I was pulling their pints one night I told them;

There are always spirits around us. Sometimes you might catch a smell of a pipe or cigarettes if they liked to smoke. Other spirits leave an aroma of the flowers or perfumes they liked. When they are near to us, normally the room will go slightly chilled, but if they want to talk to you they will gently blow in your ear.

I left them to wonder a while on that note and collected a few glasses and put a record on the juke box, I quietly tiptoed across to one of them that was singing along to the song and blew gently in his ear;

Aaargh, Aaargh.

He screamed and ran round in circles and I laughed so much my face hurt.

I told them of the Banshee one night, when it was very windy and cold outside. I told the same tale that had been passed to me, in a very low voice, just as Molly had told my mother, looking around as if the Banshee could hear. They all leaned in closer to hear me as I whispered quietly as Molly had done, when all of a sudden the juke box started to play and made us all jump including myself. If there was no money going in the juke box, it was set to play one record, to sort of remind you it was there. The song was Donavan's 'Catch the Wind', which starts off; 'In the chilly hours and minutes of uncertainty'. We laughed and I continued as the wind in Oxenhope screamed outside, an ideal setting really for the talk of the Banshee.

I told them of Irish wakes and how it was a special occasion for the women and how people would look through newspapers to find out who had died.

They leaned across the bar resting on their elbows. Most of the people that came in during the week never sat down, they would stand at the bar for hours.

Have you any more tales, Maggie?

Loads, have you heard of the little people in Ireland, you know, the leprechauns?

I have, but they're not real though are they, just myths?

Oh, but they are real, they have been seen for hundreds of years, all over different parts of Ireland. Even today there have been reports of them being seen. One person, only recently, saw a small figure with a tiny sack and another saw one little man standing next to a tree until he scurried away with such speed; apparently all these sightings were from well respected people and there are others that have seen a light that could not be scientifically explained.

Well how big are they then?

Two to three feet tall. They are men that wear a green or red woollen waistcoat and knee length trousers, long green stockings and silver buckled shoes. They have an apron with lots of pockets and always carry a hammer and they wear a cap. They also have a little pouch that they carry money in.

Why do they carry hammers?

Because they mend shoes for fairies.

Mend shoes for fairies? I never know when to believe you Maggie. Warra load o cobblers.

Ah ah very funny. I'm telling you it's true; there have been reports of leprechauns being seen all over Ireland for hundreds of years. They are little creatures who can move so quickly that they are very difficult to catch. People have tried, but as far as I know no one has succeeded in catching one. They are solitary creatures that mend shoes and are very well known for their practical jokes on humans which are not funny to us. Some say they are evil spirits, but I don't think so.

Evil spirits?

That's what some say. It's been said they don't like humans who they consider to be money mad and untrustworthy. One story that was told to me as a child was that a wealthy landowner in County Tipperary had knocked down walls that were considered sacred and cut down a tree believed to be the home of local fairies. Bad luck fell on him immediately. He lost a herd of cattle which suddenly died and other calamities happened to him and his family.

Are they over here or just there?

I don't know. There have been hundreds of sightings but not one has ever been caught. They are very hard to catch. I heard that they talk away to themselves and sing while mending shoes for the fairies. There are lots of fairy rings that have been found in parts of Ireland and loads of people claim they have seen fast moving creatures when walking through these areas.

Do you believe all this then Maggie?

Of course I do, as much as I believe in the Banshee. They can't all be wrong you know. Even the Irish Poet, Yeats, has written about the leprechauns, so I'm told. I've seen pictures of some that wear a jacket with seven rows of buttons and a cocked hat. Dad told me years ago that it's the trooping fairies, that wear green and that leprechauns wear red. When a leprechauns feels mischievous, they say that he will leap and spin on the point of his hat with his heels in the air.

I left them all to ponder and poured another drink and I could hear Chris talking about the universe and the big bang etc. They were discussing cave drawings, astronauts, aliens and the pyramids, so I joined in;

It's obvious really when you think about it. The pyramids were built by giants, when I say giants, I mean men about twelve feet tall, but well proportioned and with amazing powers. It would take thousands of men to build those structures and hundreds of years, so where did they get food and water from, in a place like that. Food doesn't grow in sand and where did they get water from? I bet it was built by giants and they built the pyramids in a week.

They fell about laughing as usual.

Where did the giants come from then Maggie?

Well, I worked that one out; they came from outer space as astronauts from another planet. That's where the cavemen got their drawings from. Everyone has seen drawings of spacemen on television that were found in caves and cannot be explained. The Bible itself describes something that came down from the sky, with people wearing what looked like helmets and there was fire coming from the bottom of the machine as it landed. Honestly, to me that sounds like an astronaut in a space shuttle or a rocket.

"The Bible You read that in the Bible?" Chris asked in astonishment, as if I had never read a Bible. I hadn't really, even though I went to a Catholic school, but I had read this somewhere and had looked it up in the Bible and found it.

No, I read it in a book and then checked it out in the Bible, Ezekiel or something like that. I still have a little Bible upstairs. Hang on a minute, I'll show you.

Even though I hadn't read a Bible since leaving school, I still had a little white one upstairs in the bedroom cabinet for 'protection', along with my rosary beads. I ran upstairs quickly to prove my point.

Right then you lot, are you ready.

We're ready.

Right then, I'll begin;

From the book of the prophet, Ezekiel, chapter one, verse four:-

"I looked and I saw a windstorm coming out of the North, an immense cloud with flashing lightening and surrounded by a brilliant light. The centre of the fire looked like glowing metal".

Chapter one verse five:-

"And in the fire was what looked like four living creatures. In appearance their form was that of a man".

Verse twenty seven, are you ready?

"I saw that from what appeared to be his waist up he looked like a glowing metal, as if full of fire, and that from there down he looked like fire; and brilliant light surrounded him".

Now you tell me, doesn't that sound like a space ship or a rocket landing? And what about the drawings of people in caves with helmets on?

I'm speechless Maggie; it certainly sounds like someone in a rocket or spaceship. I'm going to buy myself a Bible and have a good read of that. Write that name down on a bit of paper for me.

I was really getting into this discussion and could have said a lot more, but when I returned from taking the Bible back upstairs, they were discussing how life began. I listened as they talked of Darwin's theory of coming from the sea and I said;

Anyway, I'll tell you how I think we came to be here.

They were all ears now, after showing them evidence of my last revelation.

I think this has been a planet before and it was destroyed. At the time it was destroyed there were astronauts who had gone up into space; they could do nothing to help as they watched the people on the planet die.

"Well what happened to them if there was nothing left of the Earth?" A voice piped up

The astronauts travelled around until they found an appropriate planet and settled there, because they couldn't come back, as the planet might have been destroyed by floods, fire, or something. The astronauts by now had grown into giants because of the different foods and different atmosphere. Thousands of years passed and there were new generations growing all the time, as they lived longer, obviously.

I stopped for a minute to serve one of them while they chatted away and were debating whether or not there was truth here somewhere, and I carried on;

From the information passed down to them from their forefathers, they were able to build space ships and eventually they made their way back to Earth. Everyone knows of Darwin's evolution theory, there must have been some organisms still living on Earth to provide food and plants. Anyway, they found their way to Earth and taught the cavemen new things and then they built the pyramids because they were giants, but I don't know why they built them yet, I haven't really thought that far yet, but I'm working on it. But I do think it could even happen again when this planet goes caput. I remember having the same dream all the time when I was young, about sitting in a star or a planet, not on one, but inside one, with a very special person who I did not want to leave behind. We were looking down at the blue Earth and the 'person', I was with, was telling me I was going to live there and it was millions of miles away. I remember having that recurring dream as clearly today as I did when I was young, just as I remember all my other recurring dreams. The first time it happened I was very young. How would I know what colour this planet was? I certainly wouldn't know anything about reincarnation at that age, but I know I have been here before, in one way or another. I also think that if there was a Big Bang, then where did all the other pieces end up. They must have gone somewhere into space and perhaps there is life similar to ours.

That's true enough. If it had split in two there could be another planet like ours but if it shattered into pieces then there could be loads of them.

Pull us another pint Chris, I need one after that. All these years I have wondered if this planet was once visited by aliens.

You might be right there, after all there's a lot of unexplained things in this world and if we did come from fish, as Darwin suggests, and gradually evolved into humans, then there may be mermaids after all. What do you think Maggie?

Yeah, but some might have gone the other way, a fish head and a human body.

Ugh, what an awful thought. Int it time you lot was heading home?

Anyway, if birds come from the sea as well as every other living thing, then that's where the fairies must come from, miniature flying humans.

Night, Chris, night, Maggie.

Be careful of those birds on your way home, they might be fairies and if you frighten them, you may have the leprechauns after you, or worse still it could be the Banshee.

Frighten *them,* I'm shit scared.

Well, maybe there are fairy rings down by the beck with little men mending their shoes, sitting under a large toadstool. You never know.

Chapter Eight

God, I wished he would hurry up and answer the phone.

Hello, Shoulder of Mutton.

Chris, it's me.

What's up? Why are you crying? Where are you?

In a car park in town and someone's pinched me jeep and I'm not crying, me nose is running from the cold. It's freezing.

I had been so excited at finally owning a Suzuki jeep. It was my pride and joy and they were very popular at the time. I had gone into town to do some Christmas shopping. My arms were full of Christmas shopping bags and huge boxes and it was getting late and already dark. I struggled down the hill, to where the car was parked, and to my horror my jeep had gone. The car park was almost empty apart from some three cars and one articulated lorry. I had to walk back up the hill, still loaded down with shopping, to find a phone box, by which time I was shivering with cold.

I'll be there as soon as I can; I'll have to get a lift.

It was so cold standing in the car park waiting for him, tears started to run down my face at the thought of losing my car. My nose was running and I couldn't get to my tissues. I was also afraid of being mugged, the shops were closing and suddenly I felt really vulnerable. I was so relieved to see Chris arriving. He walked over to me and took some of the shopping just when the articulated lorry was pulling away. There it was, my little red jeep, it had been hidden behind the truck. When we arrived back to the pub in silence, Chris went to the bar and I went to unload the shopping and hide the Christmas presents. I walked into the kitchen to pop the kettle on and I saw Christopher stood looking at me. I was shocked and screamed out;

Oh my God Christopher, what have you done?

His face and clothes were covered in blood. Before looking to see if he was all right, I ran down to the bar;

Chris, Chris, our Christopher's bleeding. There's blood everywhere;

He ran up stairs, close behind me, and there stood in front of us was Christopher, wiping his face with a towel. He had picked up the tomato sauce bottle and shaken it really hard and the top wasn't on properly. Chris said nothing, but then he didn't need to. What a day!

Oxenhope and Haworth are spectacular in the snow and quite a few times over the years helicopters have had to drop food parcels over Black Moor, which is located just behind the Shoulder of Mutton, high up on the moor. This was when other local areas had no snow at all. I had to phone the school, in Keighley, just before Christmas, to say my son would not be in today, due to the road being blocked by snow. "What snow?" was the reply; the school was only fifteen to twenty minutes away.

Christmas in Haworth is amazing, with its Olde Worlde little shops and cafes. In fact, it looks like a scene from a Christmas film, with carol singers walking down the cobbled streets past the brightly coloured window displays.

It was just a few days before Christmas when I went into Haworth for a look around. I was on my own, for the first time. It was a lovely drive there, the shops on the Main Street were all trimmed up for Christmas and it was so cold that day. I walked around the grounds of the Bronte house, the Old Parsonage, looking at some of the graves while the winter sun shone down on my head. There were so many members of families that had died with such a short space of time between each other. There was one particular grave, of a man who had five wives, all buried with him, down there. Even more oddly, he didn't even bother to put their names on the gravestone. The grave simply read 'Here lye the bodies of the five wives of William Sunderland' along with a few more members of the family. Looking at the graves which held babies and young children was so sad. Some of those poor Mothers had one burial after another for their children, and one of the graves had a stone carving of a little baby resting on a bed with his head on a pillow. I could have stayed for hours walking around here but I had to make my way back now. On my way back to the graveyard entrance, I took a different route and came across a grave with sixteen children. Twelve of them were infants. My God, how that poor woman must have felt, knowing that every pregnancy she had, might end in death. I had already looked at a grave that held seven children who had died before the age of two. But to lose sixteen babies with only one surviving child, that managed to reach the age of nineteen years, did not bare thinking about.

I thought to myself, after Christmas I would do a little research into Haworth and the way of life in the Bronte years.

Although I had looked around the Bronte house many years ago, I promised myself that after Christmas I would come back and have a proper look inside the house, now that I was living here. Before leaving the Bronte grounds I stood a while and imagined myself in a long dress, wrapped up in a shawl, holding a basket in my hand. I imagined riding a horse across the moors in a black cloak and bonnet and I imagined myself walking down Main Street, talking to the locals. Walking back to the car, I heard my name being called. It was one of our locals. I stood there talking to her on the cobbled street and I had a feeling of having done this before. It was the time I came here for the day in the seventies and had pictured myself talking to someone and living here and that really felt so weird. This was something else that had come to fruition.

I bought some fresh bread and a few more groceries from the little shops and people were shouting 'Merry Christmas' to me on my way out of the door. It felt like a scene from the film 'Wonderful Life'. In one shop, they had those old fashioned white aprons for sale that people wore in the old days to keep their clothes clean and long, white, heavy cotton night dresses.

The cold air was hitting my face as I made my way back to the car park and I was glad my nose wasn't running, as with my hands full, it might have frozen on its way down my chin and turned to icicles, just like you see on mountain climbers. I decided that I must buy more appropriate clothes now. In fact I might treat myself to one of those Victorian nightgowns and perhaps a white night cap.

I went back to Haworth on Christmas Eve morning, with one of my friends, and called into the shops to say Merry Christmas to some that I had got to know. We were handed glasses of sherry by quite a few traders and by the time I got home I felt drunk. It was only ten thirty in the morning. I will always remember that day and wish that Christmas was always like those in Haworth.

Christmas Day arrived and everyone went home early for their Christmas lunch. I cooked the dinner while Chris finished off downstairs. We had the usual traditional dinner and I had bought a Christmas pudding that you could put in the microwave. I never really got the hang of microwaves and I had put the pudding in for too long. All of a sudden there was an almighty bang. The pudding had exploded and there were only crumbs left. The pudding had been nuked.

Being an out of the way little pub, we weren't expected to open in the evening of Christmas Day, so after lunch we thought we would have a family Christmas with the boys and Adrian suggested Trivial Pursuit. Both Adrian and Chris were clever at this game, so this was going to be a challenge. It started off with laughter, as Christopher and I simply guessed if we didn't know the answer and said some pretty stupid stuff. Adrian asked a question about Lenin:-

What part of Lenin was considered to be small when they did his post mortem?

"His foot" I shouted out in a guess. Both Chris and Adrian laughed and Adrian said;

Don't you think that it would have been known that he had a short foot when he was alive?

Christopher was only young and obviously didn't understand the question. His answer was;

His trouser legs.

Adrian coughed up a drink he was just about to swallow, almost choking;

Why do you think it's his trousers legs?

Because I heard me mum say that linen shrinks.

Christopher stormed off crying because of being laughed at, Adrian was almost crying with laugher, Chris was laughing and I was shouting at them to stop laughing. When Christopher came back, we started again and I answered a question correctly that neither of the other two knew and because they didn't know the answer they accused me of cheating. This happened twice and I got angry so we fell out. We decided to watch the television. By the way, it was Lenin's brain that was small.

It was unbelievably quiet on this road. Hours could pass or even a whole day without seeing a vehicle. I remember a time when we arrived back from somewhere and a truck was parked up. The driver jumped out of his cab and said he thought it was a ghost town; he had been waiting for directions for ages and hadn't seen one person at all.

Another time, when we had been out, there was an old customer of ours from the Woodmoor waiting on the doorstep. It was freezing cold and he had ridden all the way up here from Barnsley on a push bike;

My God, Barry, what are you doing here? You must be frozen.

A little.

Come in and I'll make you something warm to eat.

Oh no, thank you all the same. I brought some sandwiches and have just eaten them, but I will have a cup of tea please, if you don't mind.

I ushered him inside and put the kettle on. Barry was a well spoken and very educated man, but unfortunately he liked his drink and this eventually stopped him doing anything intellectual. There was one time when he came into the Woody and asked for drink;

–I've just been done for drinking and driving.

But you don't drive.

No, I was coming down Harbour Hills, a very busy road, on my push bike a bit drunk and the bike was swaying from one side to another and the police stopped me.

Don't you mean that you were swaying? The bike was only doing as it was told.

We had a cup of tea and a chat and it wasn't very long before he was setting off back to Barnsley. I made a flask up for him and told him to ring us when he got home. It was so cold that his nose looked like a red beacon. This was not to be the last time he biked all the way to see us.

I loved the snow in Oxenhope; the scene from our windows was like a postcard, hills covered in snow, looking like cakes covered in icing, the beautiful winter white swans working their way through the ice and the fact that you were snug and warm indoors watching this scene. One Sunday afternoon Gina and I hid behind a wall with a pile of snowballs, throwing them as people walked out of the pub and hiding before they saw us. Unknown to us they worked their way behind us and bombarded us with snow. Chris was mad at me and said I should grow up. I don't think so.

"Chris, I think I'll do some baking, mince pies I think, with brandy in them."

I could see it now, passing my mince pies round the pub, the customers biting into them and tasting the brandy, mmmm.

Chris's eyes rolled to the ceiling as I took a brandy bottle upstairs with me. I would just have one glass as I made the pies, but made the mistake of topping the glass up, every now and then; seemingly I had the one glass, only it was never empty. 'Disaster'! It is not a good idea to drink brandy when you are baking. The pies were awful. The pastry was awful and I had been overgenerous with the brandy which bubbled over and burned. They smelt nice though.

Christmas was out of the way and I did my usual shop down town. I was late back and decided to serve a large meat and potato, shop bought pie. The pie just needed heating and that would save time cooking. Never one to follow instructions, I placed the pie straight onto the shelf to make it crispy and closed the door. I put the plates out and had done the vegetables. It smelt delicious and everyone was starving. When it came to taking it out, the crust was very crispy indeed but the insides had fallen through the shelf and the meat and potato was splattered all over the bottom of the oven. This was not to be the end of my disasters in the kitchen. Chris had often complained of lumps in the gravy and I had recently bought a large pointed sieve, I thought I would sieve the gravy to get the lumps out. I poured the gravy into the sieve, holding it very carefully over the sink to make sure I didn't spill any on the table. To my horror, I had let the gravy go down the plug hole and was left with the lumps. I had been used to draining vegetables and I think I got a little side tracked.

However, I still decided to do pub lunches and bought a few cook books. I thought that I would start with just the basic kind of food, such as trout, seafood platter, hot beef baguettes and chicken and chips in a basket, plus sandwiches and salads. Living in the country meant that there were so many chickens; that eggs were about one penny each, so I made mayonnaise and salad sandwiches as a change and egg mayonnaise sandwiches for pool nights, along with meat sandwiches.

The nearest bakery was a car ride away at a place called Crossroads, I had only just ordered my bread and tea cakes when I heard the fire engines. I looked out and saw they were heading to where I lived, then it hit me, I had left twenty eggs boiling on the hob and Chris was downstairs behind the bar.

I paid the lady and drove like the clappers to get back home. The smell hit me as soon as I got out of the car. Even though I was outside of the pub the smell was awful, but strange as it seemed the fire engine was nowhere to be seen, it had been going somewhere else. However, my pan of eggs had exploded, after the bottom of the pan had completely burnt away, in fact disintegrated, and they were stuck on the ceiling. The smell was, well you know how a rotten egg smells, this was twenty rotten eggs and a burnt out pan that had melted. That's why all the doors and windows were open and people were drinking outside. I then had to go back to the bakery because I had left my bread behind. After a while, I decided there wasn't much call for pub lunches, this was not a lunch time pub, especially in the winter months and a lot of food was being wasted. Not to mention the kitchen disasters.

There was a lot of talk of ghosts on our cosy evenings, but I never felt anything spooky or unnatural here, except the one time when I was suddenly woken up in the night by a sound and I was aware of someone in the room. I turned my head to the left where Chris slept and saw a woman was looking down at him. Now this woman had no body that I could see, just her head, but at the same time this didn't look out of place. It was as if her body was hidden by a mist. She had a 1930s hairstyle, a long beak like nose and a really wide smiling mouth. She was looking down on Chris and smiling. She looked at me briefly and simply faded away. I shook Chris violently and woke him up and he told me to go back to sleep. The next evening I told a few at the bar of my vision and Alison looked quite startled and said;

You have just described the old landlady that used to live in this pub years ago.

'How long has she been dead? I asked.

She's not dead.

Not dead, it can't be her then.

I think it could, she's really old now and lives in the nursing home where my mother works. When she's awake she often talks about The Shoulder and sometimes thinks she is still the landlady here. When she sleeps she shouts out things like, 'Harry they're skinning rabbits in the taproom again'.

Weird, to say the least, an undead ghost! Astral travelling perhaps?

We never really saw much of Adrian or Christopher. Adrian was practising playing the guitar and stayed in his room a lot, when he wasn't with his friends, or went on his long walks. He also liked to read a lot and often ate his meals in his room. Christopher, on the other hand, seemed to be out all the time, with his friends. They would build tree houses and he would be gone for the whole day, apart from mealtimes. The difference in these two was so great. We had bought Adrian a bow, as he was interested in archery and he was having a look at it in his room when the arrow shot off through the window. He told us exactly what happened and took full responsibility. It was just as well the garage next door was closed because it could have certainly killed someone.

Christopher, however, in contrast, would try to lie his way out of anything. For instance, he was downstairs in the tap room playing pool with his friend, as he often did after school in the winter. We were out this particular time and when we came back he told us someone had thrown a brick through the window and true enough there was a large brick lying there on the floor. It didn't take Sherlock Holmes to work out that there was glass on the outside but none on the inside; it was obviously a pool ball that went through the window.

Against my wishes Chris bought Christopher a pellet gun. One afternoon a man came knocking at the upstairs fire escape door, which was behind the toilet that Chris was sitting on at the time, making him jump. He shouted angrily to the man to go downstairs to the back door and he would be down to see him. How anyone could put a fire escape up to the bathroom with a doorway behind the toilet. I'll never know. He went down to see the man and he was not very happy at being disturbed whilst on the toilet. He opened the back door and I went down to see what it was all about. An elderly man stood there complaining of Christopher firing the gun at his greenhouse. Chris said;

Christopher wouldn't do anything like that, it must be someone else.

At that point a very sheepish looking Christopher turned up. He told Chris that it was his friend that had done it, not him and Chris was happy to believe him. However, I did not believe he was telling the truth and said so. I apologised to the man and said we would pay for the damage. The gun was taken off Christopher, his pocket money was stopped and he had to 'bottle up the shelves' for a few weeks to cover the costs.

Speaking of guns, we were told of the night when the farmer next door was fed up of a fox killing his chickens, so he wrapped up warm for the night and sat on a chair with his gun in his hands to wait for the fox to come. He stayed there all night, but had fallen asleep. Alas, the fox had a field day while he slept uncomfortably on a chair all night. Apparently, not long after this, his son, who was fed up of being woken up very early in the morning, by the birds singing, was so annoyed that one morning he thought he would fire the gun to frighten them away. He certainly did, along with hitting the power line and cutting everyone's electricity off.

We had this lovely chap who came into our pub regularly. He was the strangest and most likeable person I have ever met. His name was Clem and he looked a little like Sonny Bono of Sonny and Cher with his long hair and long moustache and he sometimes wore a deerstalker hat.

Clem lived in a caravan with his dog and was either a farmer or a farm hand, I never really knew what he did, but I knew it was something to do with farming.

I was told that his caravan had no heating or hot water and believe me, Oxenhope in the winter was cold, but nothing bothered this guy. He was a heavy drinker and loved his alcohol. I asked him if it was cold in his caravan and he told me;

It gets so cold sometimes in the night that I have to knock the ice off my beer that I keep at the side of the bed.

Clem was a man you would never get bored with and apart from being one of the most content people I have met, he was a very intelligent person, and he spent a lot of time reading books. Whatever the subject was that was being spoken of; Clem would always know something about it. He was also good at telling stories. This is a tale he told me many times;

Many years ago there was an old couple who had no home to live in; they travelled around sleeping rough and getting whatever they could. One day while looking for somewhere to sleep, they found a large old drum and moved in there. They found boxes and bits and pieces to make a home and one day when her husband came home he found his wife crying. He knelt beside her and asked what the matter was;

We don't have any curtains in here.

But, my love, we don't have any windows.

Still she cried for these pretty curtains she had envisaged in her mind and one day her husband came home with some paints and painted some windows for her to put up curtains around them. Clem would always smile broadly when telling me this and I really don't know if it was a true story or just a fairy tale, he was so convincing.

It was in the spring when a customer came in laughing to himself. After ordering his drink he said;

Clem and Barry are having a shoot out down in the village; it's like a scene from a cowboy film.

With real guns you mean?

Yeah, they had an argument over a dog being shot for worrying the sheep. I don't know which of them owned the dog, I wasn't going to hang around, and everyone was getting out of the way. I don't know who started firing first, but they were shooting at each other and ducking behind the hillocks.

Farmers often shot dogs for worrying sheep, in some areas. I was told this when our dog went into a farmer's field and came back with blood all round her mouth, she had been chasing chickens and obviously, from the evidence around her mouth, she had caught one.

Many years after leaving the pub trade, I was with my daughter-in-law driving to Haworth and there was a big traffic hold up on the road. Everyone was just creeping along very slowly, when usually on this particular country lane the cars were able to overtake. I realised it was Clem driving his tractor and I swear he was asleep, because I made him jump out of his skin when I shouted hello to him. He hadn't a care in the world.

Chris, I think this place looks a bit dowdy.

I was looking around the pub one lunch time and decided that the place needed a face lift so, after convincing Chris that it would bring in more customers, he finally agreed. We arranged to have new curtains fitted and someone to re-upholster the seating.

After all the work was finished, I thought a few finishing touches would be good and I had read that fish tanks were very fashionable now and also therapeutic. I mentioned this to Chris

Fish are supposed to be lucky; I read it in a magazine.

We could do with a bit of luck and I like the idea of a fish tank. There are lots of accessories to put inside and they look nice lit up.

We went into town after closing in the afternoon and bought a big fish tank with all the colourful plants and accessories. We bought lots of little brightly coloured fish including two much bigger ones that Chris had liked, even though they were very expensive. We eagerly set the tank up and put it where it could be seen by everyone and with the lights inside the tank, it looked really well. The pub was looking nice now, I thought to myself, looking around the room as I was about to leave. Perhaps some tall, grassy plants would finish it all off. Because I didn't know one plant from another, I decided I could do the same as my friend, who had a pub nearby. She had flowers delivered and then changed every few weeks. The firm that did this also looked after the flowers and replaced the ones that had withered. Thinking they must have firms that did the same thing with plants, I brought the phone books downstairs and Gina and I started to look in the books to find these people. We looked for plants, but, of course, they were advertising plants to buy or they were advertising garden centres, so we looked under the plant hire page, but they were all machines and trucks and things, we were on this page just as Chris came across and looked to see what I was up to;

Why are you two looking on the plant hire page?

Without me answering, he guessed straight away and he burst out laughing. He told them at the bar and everyone was in uproar. I decided to buy silk plants instead.

As for the fish, someone put cigarette ends in the tank and poisoned the two expensive fish. The fish must have thought that they were fish pellets. Later in the week, a stupid idiot swallowed a couple of fish just for a dare. I thought I would look for a nice picture with fish on, instead of real ones, as it certainly wasn't lucky for the fish.

I was telling some of the girls at the bar of my embarrassment, caused by the plants and about another time in my life when I had made a stupid assumption;

Years ago, when I was in my early twenties, I phoned a turf accountant to ask how much it would cost to turf our lawn. He was very angry with me and told me to piss off and I was left there on the line wondering what I had done to upset him.

We all had a laugh about this and one of them told me she wouldn't have known that a turf accountant was something to do with horse racing, either.

As the subject of horse racing had come up, we all agreed that it was cruel for a horse to run in the Grand National, as many were hurt.

Oh I think it's so sad for the horses when people bet on them each way;

In what way?

Those poor horses have to run back again when they have reached the finishing line and that's really cruel for the poor horses.

We were creased with laughter, because she thought that was the reason they called it each way. We talked about the embarrassing moments in our lives and I said;

I was always a gullible and naive person when I was young and often the butt of jokes. When I first married in the 1970s, no-one had telephones in their houses that I knew, apart from business people and of course mobile phones had not been invented. Because my husband worked far away from home and I was pregnant, we decided to have a phone connected. I didn't have anyone to call and sat looking at the phone wishing someone would ring me. One week later, the phone did ring. I rushed over to answer it and in those days, you always answered by saying your phone number, such as hello, Barnsley 6317 etc. After the bleeps a voice at the other end introduced himself as a BT engineer and said he was checking the line for a fault. His voice sounded a bit muffled and far away, but I managed to make out what he was saying, and indeed thought the phone had a fault. He asked if I could please hold the phone at arm's length and whistle, to test the sound. I eagerly obliged because I hadn't used it at all yet and wanted to make sure it was all right. He thanked me, but asked if, before he went to make his report, could I stand away from the phone and say something. I asked "such as"? He said "just say something, like Baa Baa Black Sheep", I did as I was told to the sound of laughter. My brother Tony, who was almost hysterical at the other end of the phone, had put a handkerchief over the pay phone and stood slightly away to disguise his voice. Why I would expect a BT engineer to put four pennies in a phone box to speak to me just about says it all.

There was so much laughter about embarrassing moments at the bar that evening, that I was still laughing to myself the next day.

My sister often came and stayed at the pub for a couple of nights and this was always something that I looked forward to. We would stay up late when everyone had gone home and chat. All around the bar on the top shelf were bottles of whisky, really old whisky in different shapes and sizes of bottles; in fact it was quite a collection. We were looking at the dates of some of them and decided to taste a few. It wasn't very long before we were halfway round the shelf with the intention of tasting them all. When I fell off the stool I was sitting on, we laughed so much and couldn't stop laughing, putting our fingers to our lips and making a shushing sound. Walking past the window were a few of our customers. They were arriving home from a nightclub and I went outside and asked them to come in, but very quietly. They came in through the taproom window, so as to not wake up Chris. We stood around the bar talking and laughing, as quietly as possible. We were having a great time until I heard Chris stirring.

God, it's half past three, he'll kill me,

Everyone by this time was very drunk and trying to sneak them quietly out of the pub, was very difficult, everyone was in high spirit and making a 'shushing' sound. After finally closing the door and turning out the light, we went upstairs. I tripped and Teresa being behind me fell on top of me. Chris appeared at the top of the stairs, looked at me and didn't say a word. Not a good sign.

A few nights after that, Teresa and I thought it would be good to go up to the next pub just for an hour. Chris was playing pool and he didn't mind, he was speaking to me again now. The pub was within walking distance, but as it was on a very dark country road and due to the fact that it was uphill all the way to the top, we decided to drive there. I wouldn't have been able to drink, but we were only staying a short time anyway. As we got nearer to the old graveyard I was talking away to Teresa, when something caught my eye on the road as the headlights lit up the darkness. We carried on and my sister said 'that was a briefcase'. I stopped the car when my sister added 'it might have money in it'.

"Oh my God, yeah, or it could be a doctor's briefcase". I was already manoeuvring my gearstick into reverse, thinking rewards. Teresa spoke up in excitement;

"Or...... it could be drugs". Her head now was almost back to front.

"What if it's a bomb?" I had only just got the words out when I realised that I had gone too far and reversed over it. We faced each other and said at the same time;

"It wasn't a bomb".

I moved forward very slowly and we climbed out of the car. It was very cold and dark and we were at the side of the graveyard, so we quickly picked up the briefcase and jumped sharply back into the car with the 'find'.

It was badly bent and locked which made it even more intriguing. Try as we might to open the case we couldn't, (purely to find the owner!). We carried on back to our pub, had a few drinks and sneaked it upstairs to prise it open with a crowbar. What did it contain? You may wonder. It was the papers of a bloody train spotter and not the film 'Train Spotter', but a real train spotter. Realising there would not be any great rewards, the next day we phoned him up from a letter that was in his briefcase and arranged to meet in a pub nearby, only to find he actually looked like a typical train spotter; sorry you train spotters, no offence.

I was telling one of my customers about the briefcase and how we thought at the last minute that it could have been a bomb. The subject then turned to bombs and eventually the war and I listened into their conversation;

I used to live near a man that flew a German bomber in World War Two; he was a really nice bloke.

Well, like all the rest of the men fighting in the war, it was a job they had to do. My great uncle lost his leg in the war but used to rub the missing limb with his hand and say it was cold or it was aching.

I've heard about that before, about people being able to feel missing limbs.

The conversation went on and somehow got around to Ireland as one of them had come to live here recently from Dublin. He spoke about the North Strand bombings in Dublin in 1941 and the other man was a bit confused at this.

But the Irish weren't in the war, they were neutral weren't they? How come they were bombed?

The Irish customer told him how a German Luftwaffe plane had dropped four bombs on a Whitsuntide holiday weekend.

Usually there were searchlights and flares to warn the German planes that they were flying over neutral territory and air raid sirens were used to warn people, but that night the sirens did not go off. Of the four bombs that were dropped, the last one and the biggest landed on the North Strand, killing twenty eight people and injuring ninety or more. The Germans quickly apologised and gave compensation for the people who had lost their homes. There were over two thousand people made homeless.

I agreed with him, as over the years I had heard Dad talk of that terrible night and said;

I remember me dad telling me about that, he was about fourteen at the time. He told me how they all hid under the bed until someone shouted that they should go into the cellar. All the tenants moved down into the basement, terrified as the noise was deafening and even shattered some of the windows on the street. They lay with mattresses on top of them, most of them not even dressed. Dad told me;

We were all huddled together believing dat we were going to die and someone shouted "We have to get out, dis building will collapse and bury us", so we ran out onto the road with our hands covering our heads.

I couldn't stop laughing at this;

You went and stood outside on the road when they were dropping bombs around you.

But later when I thought about it, getting away from the basement was probably the thing I would have done. There had been a few of those tenements buildings that collapsed over the past few years, through being structurally unsound, killing families that were in there. Dad said they all rushed around to the North Strand bombsite the next day to look at the big hole in the ground and that there were still people looking for bodies in the rubble. He said there was glass everywhere and people were crying.

Chapter Nine

In the early hours of the 26th of April 1986 a nuclear reactor exploded near Chernobyl, on the border between Ukraine and Belarus, throwing tons of radioactive materials into the air. The media estimated that the disaster released one hundred times more radiation than the atomic bombs dropped on Nagasaki and Hiroshima. The world panicked.

Talk about panic, the word quickly got around, even before we heard it on the news, that the cloud was heading our way. People were saying you had more chance of getting cancer if it rained over you and all kinds of speculation was rife, such as could it be in the water or in vegetables, animals would eat the poisoned grass and everyone would eventually get cancer.

We watched the television all the time for reports of the disaster and looked up at the clouds moving nearer our way and they certainly did move our way and it rained quite heavily. I had been to the supermarket and when driving through the village, I noticed that it was very quiet and the supermarket was not as busy as it usually was either.

On my way back home I saw a young boy running down the road, followed by a bull and a farmer who was chasing the bull. The boy jumped over a wall that went into a field and I thought to myself "Oh bless him, out here in all this rain". It wasn't considered a good thing to ask a child if he wanted a lift, but I still felt guilty for driving past. At least he had escaped the bull and he had his hood up over his head to protect himself from the rain.

I was home a good hour before Christopher walked in, soaking wet in a jacket just the same as the boy I had passed, had worn. My mind sort of whirled round, then he told me he had missed the school bus that dropped him outside our pub and his friend had lent him his jacket;

I was walking home when a bull had got loose from a field and ran into the road, so I jumped over a wall to escape it. I saw you drive past and shouted, but you didn't hear me.

Oh my God, that boy that I was feeling sorry for was my son and to make things worse he had walked miles uphill, all the way home, completely wet through, while I had driven past him. Christopher was often in trouble for not coming straight home, but this day I hadn't realised the time, if I had I would have gone to look for him.

Why didn't you ring me?

I did and no-one answered.

No-one answered because I was out shopping and Chris must have been in the cellar. Adrian had gone straight to his friend's house.

But I've been home an hour, why didn't you ring from the village and I would have picked you up?

I didn't have any money left; I bought some crisps and a coke.

You could have reversed the charges and anyway, where's your own coat?

I don't know, I think someone took it by mistake.

Go and get a shower quick and wash that rain off your skin and I'll make you some tea and wash your wet clothes.

I didn't know what to believe with Christopher sometimes. He was always in trouble and would tell lies constantly to stop me finding things out.

As usual life goes on and the conversations soon started to turn to other topics.

The weather started to warm up and Mam and Dad was staying with us again. I was so excited now because I had found new places to take them. I took them to Stanbury, a few miles away passing open moorlands and reservoirs. Adrian walked to Stanbury lots of times. It only had one street but still had three pubs, two in the village and one further on called the 'Old Silent'. Many famous celebrities have stayed at The Old Silent, including Bing Crosby. It is also reputed to have ghosts and many of the guests have reported seeing them in their rooms. It is easy to see why when you go there, it has a really old feel to it even though it has been modernised. When I first ever went in there, there were two old fashioned leather armchairs with high backs and a big old dog that lay in front of a large log fire. The old clock ticked away as the pendulum swung from side to side and I would have loved to stay there for a few nights. Further up the road were the famous Bronte waterfalls and this was the place where a few years later, I would have liked my first grandson to have been christened, with natural water placed over his head and the family all around, just like being christened by Mother Nature herself.

As you travel along the road through Stanbury, you will eventually come to Wycoller Country Park which is classed as one of the prettiest parks in Lancashire. The area is famous for its association with the Bronte sisters who mention many of the landmarks in their books, 'Wuthering Heights' and 'Jane Eyre'. Wycoller village itself can't be seen from the road and cars are excluded, making the place even quieter and more tranquil, just nicely tucked away amid the hills and fields. Although it's quite a walk from parking the car, it is a very nice walk beside a stream that flows gently into the village. I found it hard to believe that this fairy tale village was brought slowly back to life after almost being abandoned. From the 15th Century Wycoller was a sheep farming area and a weaving community lived there until power looms were invented, leading to the village's decline. In 1820 the population of Wycoller was 350, but weavers began to move away to nearby towns and closer to the developing mills. Apparently thirty five dwellings have been lost since then and maybe some of the weavers made their way to Haworth, following the work.

I do like an old ghost story of the places I visit and this was no exception; Wycoller and Wycoller Hall have had a few sightings of ghosts. During the reign of King Charles II according to legend, Simon Cunliffe, the local squire, was out fox hunting when the fox ran across the bridge and into the Hall, up to the top of the stairs and into his wife's bed chamber. The hounds pursued the fox and attacked it. Cunliffe rode his horse up the staircase and was angry to see his wife terrified at the scene. On hearing her screams, he raised his hunting crop as if to hit her with it and she died of fright. Her screams, the noise of his horse clattering across the bridge and up the stairs, the crack of his whip and the hounds chasing the fox into the Hall have been heard by many over the years.

I was fascinated with this place, although my mother found the walk a little longer than she would have liked. I was particularly interested in the seven bridges that cross Wycoller Beck including the pack horse bridge that was said to be eight hundred years old, although over the centuries it has been reconstructed. Clapper Bridge is close to the ruins of Wycoller Hall and probably dates from the late 18th or early 19th Century. Clam Bridge is more than one thousand years old and is listed as an Ancient Monument and it is just a slab of stone that lies across Wycoller Beck. The bridge, which has been swept away by floods twice, cracked again in two places and was repaired in 1991. We laid on the grass awhile and listened to the birds singing. In fact that was all you could hear and as I lay back with my eyes shut, I pictured the scene in my mind's eye of life here in the earlier centuries. A voice broke into my dream;

Cum on, wake up, we've a long walk back to the car. It'll take ages.

Mam, we haven't been here an hour.

I know, but I keep thinking of that walk back and I can't rest.

It isn't that far a walk, but we'll go back if you want.

So it was time to go and I made a promise to Wycoller that I would be back.

On the way home I told her that one of the bridges in Wycoller had been used in the film 'The Railway Children'. My mother had watched 'The Railway Children' many times and said with a little sadness in her voice;

It reminds me of when me dad died and we went to Yorkshire from Lancashire on a horse and cart across the moors with all our baggage. I was nearly five years old and I remember the journey. At first it was exciting, our Tom was making us laugh and Rene was telling us a story from a book someone had given her for the journey. Me Mam was crying nearly all the way home and eventually we all cried, then me hat blew off and we had to stop. We all jumped off the cart and chased it over the moor; it was a very windy day. I never did get my hat back and now I was crying for two reasons. We were never told where we were going and I was scared and I'm sure Tom and Rene were as well. I was too young to fully understand why everyone at home was so upset at seeing us off. I thought we were going on a day trip like we did once. I fell asleep and woke up crying for me dad.

My mother looked so sad and was obviously remembering very painful memories as she suddenly stopped talking. I wanted to put my arms around her and give her a cuddle and take away the painful memory, but I was driving trying to hold my own tears back and then I had an idea;

Tell you what; we'll have a day going to some of the places where The Railway Children was filmed.

The next day we were up early and we set off in my red jeep and I took Mam to see the house where the children went to stay after their journey in a horse and cart, as it was only down the road from us. The film was set in Haworth, Oxenhope and nearby areas and I took her to all the places that I knew of from the locals. We started at the Bronte Parsonage where

Dr Forrest's surgery was filmed and had a look around the museum and then set off to Mytholmroyd Tunnel between Haworth and Oakworth. We continued on to Oakworth Station and the cottage that stands next to the station, where the station master and his wife, Albert and Nell Perks, lived with their children. We had a great day out and she cheered up.

The part of Oxenhope that we lived in is called Leeming and it is very quiet. There is no reason to come through Leeming unless you live there or are visiting someone and, apart from the locals who come into the pub, we rarely saw our neighbours. However, there was one day in particular that brought the whole of Oxenhope to life and that was Straw Race Day. Straw Race was an event that started in the seventies and is held every July. People came from all over come to take part, most of them dressing up in fancy dress costumes. The teams that take part pay to enter the race and all the proceeds go to charity.

Since moving in to the Shoulder of Mutton, just about every customer had, at some point, talked about the Straw Race and this was obviously a very special day.

People taking part would run through the village from one end to another, carrying a bale of straw and drinking a pint at each pub on the way. They have raised quite a lot of money over the years for charity.

We were warned to have plenty of staff and expect thousands of people in the village. We were also told that the village pubs had entertainment inside and outside, plus they all served food.

We organised a large marquee and hired a musical monkey grinder organ, which was very authentic, and we started to book bar staff as soon as possible.

Mam and Dad were coming and my brother, Patrick, and my sister in law, Marilyn, along with their four boys. This meant that we would have twelve people staying and only three bedrooms. We thought the best solution would be to buy a caravan that would double up as a place to sell hot dogs, burgers and cold sandwiches. Chris's parents were coming too but they wouldn't be staying the night.

Mam and Dad, Patrick and Marilyn could cook and serve the food. Chris's Mam, Dad and sister could work in the marquee serving drinks with the other staff there. Adrian, Christopher, my four nephews and a friend of Christopher could run stalls that sold sweets and soft drinks and Chris and I and the bar staff would serve in the pub bar. We needed to have two people to serve the runners, through the window that looked onto the road.

They had priority and had to be served without waiting, because they were running a race and could not be held up. We also had people to collect glasses, although we were informed that we should use plastic glasses due to the amount of drinking outside, but they still needed clearing away. I found it so hard to believe that we needed that entire staff for just one day; I wondered where all these customers would be coming from and hoped they would all turn up.

We went to look at caravans; we only needed a cheap one that was clean and hopefully we could sell it afterwards. Mam and Dad had come though earlier in the week and were going to stay for a while until after Straw Race Day and my brother and family were coming up the day before the event.

I was always pleased to see my relations. We had lived very near to each other all our lives and although I loved my new life, I did miss them all.

We were up at the crack of dawn, preparing for the big day, and the Monkey Organ Grinder man was first on the scene setting his equipment up. It sounded just like an old fashioned fairground outside. I could not believe the size of the marquee which was huge and luckily the weather was good so the whole front was open. My sister in law and me mam were slicing the tea cakes and setting the caravan up for cooking, with Dad and Patrick carrying food from one place to another. The caravan did have an oven in it, but we also used the cooker that was inside the pub. Onions were peeled and chopped, cold sandwiches were made, wrapped and put in cool places, sauce bottles were taken outside to the caravan. The outside toilets arrived and were put in place. The boys put the tables together and laid out the crisps, sweets and soft drinks and I worked out that we had twenty six staff altogether. I started wondering if that would be too many, although some were family.

People started to arrive, followed by the runners in their fancy dress. The organ player was playing now, so were the juke box, and the music we had set up in the car park. The quiet deserted little place that we lived in suddenly came alive, just as Chris's family arrived. I think they were as shocked as we were with the number of people there so early in the day.

The runners were arriving in their dozens, and as the crowds moved on to the next pub, more were arriving at our pub, Chris was forever changing barrels, I was running in and out taking change for the tills and fetching bottles from the cellar. We had twenty six staff and we could have done with more. By now the caravan had queues of people waiting to be served; even the boys were rushed off their feet.

We had one man, Eddie, who was a regular customer of ours, who took charge of the bar inside and he was brilliant, thank God, I don't know how we would have managed without him. He was never still and sweat poured from him. He later went on to get his own pub in Silsden and made a very good landlord. Eddie had a very dry sense of humour, such as when he came into the Shoulder one evening with his usual smile;

I've had a right day today. I went to feed the cows later than I normally would and the ground was so boggy that I had trouble carrying the food to the troughs. The cows came rushing towards me and at the time my feet had sunk down into the bog and I couldn't move. I lost my balance, fell backwards spread eagled in the mud, while my wellingtons were still standing in the mud. The cows grabbed the food while I struggled to fight my way to a standing position again.

The afternoon went on without any hitches, apart from thinking we had run out of bread rolls. I was discussing this with me mam and I said;

We can't have, I bought much more than I thought we would need.

Well they have all gone, we're using tea cakes for hot dogs now, and I can't understand it.

Before too long it was closing time. In those days there was no all day opening, and we really needed time to clean up in readiness for opening up for the evening, which we had been told would also be very busy.

We finally had the chance to sit down for five minutes. Everything was cleared away and the caravan was cleaned and ready for the night. I went into the bedroom to get changed and there, on the bed, were five dozen rolls and five dozen teacakes, along with Chris eagerly counting the pile of money we had taken.

The customers starting pouring in early doors and we had entertainment on. The locals really enjoyed Irish folk music and the band we had booked for that night was extremely good, giving a wonderful atmosphere.

Usually when people are drinking for that amount of time, there's trouble at some point. We were behind the bar when a couple of young lads starting fighting and we threw them out. A short time later someone came in and said there was a dead body outside with blood pouring down his face. We dashed outside not knowing what to expect, feeling guilty for turning them out to finish fighting. I was the first out and knelt down beside him, not really knowing what to do other than call for an ambulance. At that time I knew nothing of taking pulses or any kind of first aid. I was suddenly aware of me dad standing behind me;

Is he dead?

He seems to be breathing, I think.

Dad bent down low and shouted to the young lad;

Are yis dere son?

To my amazement the boy said yes and sat up. He had been asleep and it was only a small cut where he had scratched himself on a stone.

Chris noticed that someone had stolen the back door key when we walked back in. This wouldn't normally have bothered me; I would have just put it down as a prank, but there were hundreds of people that day who knew we must have taken a lot of money. This caused concern so we phoned the police and a locksmith to change the lock. Excitement over, everyone went back to their drinks. The band had finished for the night and we were cleaning up once more. Patrick and Marilyn went to bed and the six boys were sleeping in the front room in sleeping bags. Mam and Dad said goodnight and went to sleep in the caravan which was in the car park.

We always liked to relax after a hectic night and Alison, Gina and Louise stayed for a drink with their partners while we discussed the day;

I can't believe there were so many people here today.

It's always busy, but there seem to be more taking part every year and luckily the sun always seems to shine on Straw Race Day.

I don't know how they do it, running up those hills and carrying a bale of straw, especially after drinking a pint of beer at each pub.

I thought it would be best to lock the doors because we were drinking after hours and the police were in the area. I locked both doors and we carried on with our conversation. Alison said it was time she went home a little after that and I unlocked the door for her and locked it again. Suddenly, there was this hammering at the door. I opened it and it was Alison;

I've seen a ghost.

A ghost?

Yes, in the car park, just two white legs and no body

White legs and no body?

Isn't it funny how you sometimes repeat what people say when they are trying to tell you something?

Of course, we all ran outside and because of the lights inside, the car park was blacker than ever. When my eyes adapted to the dark, I saw me Dad stood there with a bunch of weeds in his hands looking very sheepish in white pyjamas. The pyjamas looked luminous in the darkness and stood out, putting the rest of him in the shade.

Dad, what are you doing? It's two in the morning.

um, just picking dese up.

What?.....weeds? You were picking up weeds?

Because the caravan had no toilet, we had given them a back door key to the pub and because it was very late, Dad had assumed everyone must have gone home, so he tried getting the key in the door, which of course I had locked and left the key in the lock. After trying the door, he was forced to take a pee outside in the hedges, but as he had walked over towards the hedge, Alison had come outside and Dad had to bend down quickly, pretending to pick weeds, because he was embarrassed. It was so dark and because he only had pyjama bottoms on and had bent down, his top half was invisible.

The next morning Chris was in the bedroom again counting all the money we had taken the previous day, getting it ready for banking. We were having breakfast in the kitchen, talking of the night before, and laughing at the same time. When Mam said;

Yer Dad had tried to open the caravan door, but could only open the top half.

Dad butted in;

Yeah, I was desperate to go for a pee and yer mam was shouting, "Paddy, for God's sake what're you doing". And then again "Paddy"

Dad exaggerated the word by saying Paddeeee

Me mam laughed and said;

He was making a racket and I was worried that he would wake everyone up.

Only because you were harping on and didn't give me time. Yis kept yelling at me.

Mam was such a bully with him at times but always in a funny way. She laughed as Dad told us how it all started;

"I can't go to sleep, I need a pee", I said to yer Mam, but when I found the bottom half of the caravan door locked, I went to Joyce and told her.

Well, climb over the bloody thing and keep yer voice darn.

He hadn't realised when putting his leg over the bottom half of the door, that the steps were much lower down at the other side and he went crashing to the floor to the sound of me mam, shouting, "Paddy, for God's sake, what yer bloody playing at?"

Mam was laughing her head off now and said;

It was all quiet again when he finally got out of the caravan, then I heard someone scream. I jumped out of bed and saw yer Dad with weeds in his hand.

Because I knew my parents well, I could easily picture the scene and laughed for days after. They were so funny together, those two.

The day after the Straw Race, it was very still, not a sound from anywhere, and the only evidence of the day before was straw scattered all over the road. Leeming had gone back to sleep for another year.

This village and Straw Race Day reminded me of an old black and white film that I watched years ago, Brigadoon, it starred Gene Kelly; it was a musical about two Americans that visited the Scottish Highlands on a game hunting holiday, only to get lost on the first night. While looking at their map, they began to hear soft music; then a village appeared out of a mist, even though there was no village shown on the map. The village was under a magic spell and was invisible to the outside world apart from one day every one hundred years when it was full of life, music and dancing, as well as fighting. Brigadoon came alive once every one hundred years and Leeming came alive once every year.

I was cleaning the shelves behind the bar when one of our locals had come in and made me jump

Seen any fairies recently Maggie?

Yeah, there's one stood in front of me.

Hah, hah, hah, very funny. Have you ever heard of the Cottingley Fairies?

Is this a joke?

No seriously, there's supposed to be fairies that have been seen in a beck and it isn't far from here, it's in Cottingley which is only fifteen to twenty minutes away by car. They were seen by two cousins, in 1916 or around that time. As far as I know they are still living and swear it is true to this day.

He told me as much as he remembered about the story of the little girls and I was very intrigued. I used to pretend we had fairies in our garden, when I was young, and made stories up about them.

The next time I was in town, I bought a book about the Cottingley Fairies and was surprised to find how much had been written and decided there must have been some truth somewhere.

Apparently, Frances Griffiths and Elsie Wright are famous for their story and are still talked about today. It all started off with a photograph taken showing Frances with the fairies in 1917. Elsie had borrowed her father's camera and he had given her instructions on how to use it. They went down to the beck among the trees and after an hour returned in excitement.

Elsie and her father, who was one of the earliest qualified electrical engineers, went into the darkroom to develop the film and there were fairies on the picture. Her father remarked on the fairies, believing they were made from paper and the girls told him they were real. The second picture showed a gnome and her father stopped Elsie from using the camera and assumed they were a hoax.

In 1918, Frances wrote to a friend in South Africa and sent her some photographs, on the back she had written about how friendly she and Elsie had become with the fairies. Frances even mentioned that it was funny she had never seen them in Africa, when she had lived there, saying that it must have been too hot for them.

Frances spoke of the war for a while in her letter and mentioned that one photograph was of her in the back yard, taken by her Uncle Arthur, and the other was the one of her with the fairies, that Elsie had taken. Francis spoke of the fairies as if they were an everyday occurrence and of little importance. She wrote to her friend saying that a fairy named Rosebud was fat and that she had made her new clothes.

Although her father didn't believe the photographs were genuine, Elsie's Mother, Polly Wright did and three years later in 1920, she went to Bradford, with a friend, to attend a folklore lecture. The lecture included references to fairies and following the lecture she mentioned the fairy pictures to her friend. They were overheard by a friend of Edward Gardner, a leading theosophist, and the friend passed on the information to Edward. Edward Gardner asked to see the photographs and on seeing them, suggested that he take them to someone who would authenticate them.

In December, he wrote to Mrs Wright thanking her for the three photographs and announced that they were the most interesting and wonderful photographs he had ever seen.

Gardner had come into contact with Harold Snelling who was a genius at being able to tell whether a photograph was fake or genuine. In his letter to Gardner, Harold Snelling believed the two negatives to be completely genuine, even going on to say that they showed movement in the fairies.

These photographs eventually came to the notice of Sir Arthur Conan Doyle and after hearing the opinion of Mr Snelling, it was agreed that a second and expert opinion was needed and an appointment was made with Kodak's manager. Two other experts were brought in to examine the photographs at great length and it was agreed by all, that the plates showed no sign of them being faked. Unfortunately this couldn't be taken as conclusive genuineness and Kodak wouldn't give them a certificate.

It was decided that Edward Gardner would travel to Yorkshire and interview the family in their own home. In the school holidays, during August, Polly Wright had written and asked her niece Frances to come by train to Cottingley from Scarborough where she had gone to live with her mother and father after the war. Polly told Frances that Edward Gardner would be travelling up from London with new cameras so they might have the opportunity to take more photographs of the fairies.

Edward Gardner travelled from London to Bradford by train and took the tram out to Cottingley Bar, three miles away. He had brought with him two cameras and two dozen secretly marked photographic plates. He gave the girls the cameras and instructions on how to use them, telling them that it would be best to photograph the fairies on fine days.

The girls did manage to photograph more fairies, but one fairy in particular stood out. It was actually the last photograph taken of the fairies and the most striking of all. The photograph showed a fairy of a more mature age, who had recently arisen from sleep and could be seen very clearly, with flowing hair and beautiful wings.

As our customer had said, Cottingley wasn't too far from here and one summer's day, in the afternoon, I drove out there. I had instructions as to where the beck was and I also had my camera with me just in case. The beck where the fairies were seen was hard to get to now because new houses had been built and everything had changed. I felt a little disappointed and walked across the road to where the beck flowed. I was looking over a bridge at a stream that had a little water fall and ran into the River Aire. Something suddenly caught my eye. Dozens of dragonflies came swarming down to the stream, moving very quickly and flying over the rocks and water. They were beautiful, really brightly coloured and graceful, almost as if they were giving me a display. I tried to photograph them, but they were flying so fast that it was impossible to take pictures.

I don't know what to think of the Cottingley Fairies. There have been many differences of opinion over the years; especially as one of the girls' father's had a darkroom for developing photographs. But then even at times when the girls were fed up of all the publicity, they always maintained that they were telling the truth. My own opinion is that very few children could keep a secret as spectacular as the Cottingley Fairies for so long without 'confessing' to their best friends that they were a fake. The girls must have been forever questioned about it being as famous as they were. Beside which, Elsie and Frances were not the only ones to admit that they had seen fairies in that area.

In the 1980s a forester, while working in Cottingly Woods, admitted to seeing fairies. The forester, a former wrestler, claims that he saw the fairies in the woods and that there were three of them. He states that were about ten inches in height and believes the girls were telling the truth and that it was not a hoax. Sightings of fairies have been reported all over the world, for years. Who knows, 'Tom Thumb' might have originated from fairies.

Could it be that the girls really did see fairies or is it possible that they saw the same dragonflies as I had seen on my visit to Cottingley? Photographed them and changed them into fairies, by cutting clothes out of fairy books and sticking them onto the photographs during the developing process. I have seen dragonflies in the past, but I had never seen them in a group as they were on that day. The romantic in me wants to believe the young girls, after all, why build up a hoax such as this, knowing that they would be constantly questioned by experts? They didn't want to become famous; they had fame thrust upon them. I drove home and got caught in the busy traffic, while driving I was thinking how much quieter it must have been without cars, just the sound of the clip clop of horses pulling carts.

Chapter Ten

Often, whilst writing about my time spent in what is known as 'Bronte Country', I have remarked on the beauty and serenity of the area and the pleasant feelings that occur when travelling through and walking in this area. It would be easy to fall into the trap of believing that the Bronte sisters, whilst writing their books, must have lived in idyllic surroundings with little to cloud their view of life, as they looked out over the rolling moorland that lay on all sides of them. There was, however, a bleak and much blacker side to where I am now living, back in the time of the Brontës, during the early and mid nineteenth century.

The area covers large expanses of moorland which are made up of areas of peat bog and undulating hills covered with heather and bracken, which makes the soil so damp and acidic that nothing else can to grow. Add to this the fact that at this time there were very few trees to break the wind which relentlessly blew across the moors, both from the mountains of the Pennines in the west and down through the Yorkshire Dales and the Lake District, far to the north. Farming was almost impossible, apart from the sheep that roamed in every direction. Food and produce for the town of Haworth and the village of Oxenhope had to be brought in by horse drawn carts and stored in what was becoming a rapidly expanding industrial centre for wool combing, spinning and weaving. Indeed, Haworth had originally evolved as an assortment of weavers' cottages, built on either side of a very steep cobbled street which led up to a level area at the top of the hill, on which the church and the village centre had been laid out.

The cottages housed the looms for weaving the cloth and were designed so that machinery was above the living quarters in rooms with windows that looked out over the surrounding moorland, letting in the light that enabled the weavers to use all of the available daylight. The area became famous for its wool combing and weaving and wool was brought from the sheep farms, high up in the Yorkshire Dales, and production grew at an immense rate during the first twenty years of the nineteenth century. By 1820 production of cloth and wool from the Haworth area represented a large proportion of Yorkshire's output. The number of weavers' cottages had grown rapidly to cope with the demands of the woollen industry, but unfortunately, the facilities for sewage, drainage and even drinking water did not keep pace with the needs of the local community.

Around 1820 Haworth would have been a vile place to live. The only drainage was an open stone lined channel, which ran all the way down the main street, into which all the refuse from the houses, privies and waste from the animals that were kept by the residents was allowed to run. Life must have been extremely squalid, as there were no water closets, not even one, only stone built middens that housed heaps of rubbish, animals and the privy which had to be regularly dug out, causing huge dung heaps between the cottages and down the main thoroughfare. What constituted a fresh water supply ran among the housing and was used for washing and drinking alike, but the families who lived there were brought up with these conditions and accepted them as being normal. They did not associate disease and death with the way they lived; to them it was a way of life.

As mills were built to cope with the huge demand for textiles, the town expanded on all sides of the hollow that Haworth was built in. Whichever way you entered the town, you would have to travel downhill. The roads were steep and the new mills and factories, along with the rows and rows of very basic housing, were stacked precariously on any piece of land that would accept a foundation. The population grew rapidly, but living conditions were no better than before. In the mid nineteenth century living in the main town were about two thousand souls. A government report stated that these living conditions were as bad as the worst slums in London and that life expectancy was less than twenty years with forty per cent of children dying before they reached their sixth birthday. From a population of approximately two thousand people, over the ten years that the government survey was carried out, there were thirteen hundred burials in Haworth's cemeteries.

Strangely enough, the way in which the bodies were interred only fuelled the problems of ill health. This was because the local area was rich in stone, from the millstone grit quarries that were all around this part of Yorkshire, which made headstones and grave coverings reasonably cheap. It became a local tradition that the graves were covered with huge slabs of stone, many of them engraved with the names of the families buried underneath them. All were packed tightly together, as space was at a high premium.

My first thought was that this must have been a shrewd move; to have the graves virtually sealed up, must have reduced the risk of passing on any diseases that the occupants might have died of. The locals must have had the same thought, but we were both wrong as what they had done made matters infinitely worse. The graveyard had become a sea of stone, which covered everywhere, apart from the well worn pathways between the graves. Nothing was able to grow and there were no plants, trees or grass that would allow the bodies to decompose. The natural processes of decomposition were not allowed to take place and the remains only rotted causing toxic gases to rise through the soil and leak out from between the stone slabs. People did not even notice the pungent odours; they were used to them and paid them little heed. Worse was to follow. Rain, and it does rain quite profusely along the edges of the Pennines, ran off the impervious surface of the gravestones and soaked into the soil beneath and as there was nothing which could absorb the liquid, the ground became sodden. The graveyard was build at the top of the hill, above most of the town which was expanding in the lower regions of the hollow. Gravity was now to take over and as water always finds its own level, it sank through the hillside, taking with it the diseases that the people had been trying to contain.

It is no wonder that the Bronte family would not venture far from the parsonage, which was just above the graveyard. Patrick Bronte, however, had to fulfil his duties as the local vicar. He must have witnessed some harrowing sights, as he consoled bereaved relatives or administered comfort to the dying, especially when young children were involved. Being a father he must have always been aware that it could be his own family next, as he had already suffered grief when he lost two of his daughters and his wife. Patrick Bronte's remaining daughters, however, would have been loath to pick their way through the filthy and smelly streets and I feel sure that they must have felt very vulnerable, virtual prisoners in their own home, and perhaps this affected their imagination and their writing.

Almost opposite the Shoulder of Mutton, there is a mill which, along with the mills further down in Oxenhope, must have been very similar to the mills of Haworth.

I try to imagine those times and hope that that these mills and the surrounding houses were not as bleak as those in Haworth had been. Oxenhope was not as tightly packed with buildings and was mostly built as the industrial revolution progressed. They were new mills and housing, which took advantage of the running spring water which ran in abundance down the valley. Leeming, where the pub was built, was situated even higher up on the edge of the moorland with only a few populated dwellings on higher ground. There was much more fresh air and the winds that blew frequently would have blown the pollution away allowing the people to live cleaner, healthier and happier lives.

I really hoped so; such a beautiful place should not be ruined or remembered by what was, after all, a fight for survival and greed for money and wealth.

Many of the neighbouring towns were to grow rapidly, as the textile industry changed from being a cottage industry to a conglomeration of factories where mass production took place. Only seven or eight miles away from Haworth lay Bradford, a town which in the first part of the nineteenth century boomed into an intensely populated and polluted industrial area. At the beginning of the nineteenth century, its population was approximately thirteen thousand but by the middle of the century, only fifty years later, the population had grown to over one hundred thousand. All these people had moved there to work in one of the two hundred factories and mills that had sprung up to fuel the boom in textile production. This increase in production was gained at a terrible cost to the workers who lived in appalling conditions. Bradford became the most polluted town in England and was often likened to Purgatory. Cholera and typhoid were rife, killing up to a third of the children and many of the adults. This coupled with the harsh working conditions in the mills meant that the life expectancy of the inhabitants was only eighteen years. These conditions not only affected the mill workers but also the middle classes and the mill owners themselves, but profit appeared to be paramount and little was done to improve conditions for many years to come.

One man who stood out from the rest was a mill owner who had become one of the largest employers in Bradford. His name was Titus Salt. He became more and more concerned about the pollution and conditions facing his employees and as Mayor he tried, in vain, to persuade the local council to pass laws which would force the factory and mill owners to clean up the industrial pollution. When he failed in his attempts, he decided to build a new mill only a few miles away from Haworth. He chose a site on the banks of the River Aire, close to the railway and the canal which ran between Leeds and Liverpool, and he was to call this new industrial community Saltaire

Building work started in 1851 and the mill was opened, only two years later, on his fiftieth birthday, the 20th of September 1853. His three thousand five hundred workers, more than the whole population of Haworth, travelled the three miles from Bradford until Titus Salt had built over eight hundred and fifty houses to house the men, women and children who worked in his mill. Each street, many named after his children, was designed to hold one shift or team that worked in the mill and at the end of the row of houses was a larger house for the charge hand or foreman of the shift, so that control and team spirit were built into the lives of his workers.

He had designed the village around his mill and he had made sure that all the houses had an outside toilet each, along with fresh running water that was piped from his own reservoir and gas was also made available to provide light and heating for everyone. How different it must have seemed to the squalid conditions his workers had left behind in Bradford and indeed to the conditions most of the workers in Haworth must have been suffering.

Titus Salt was indeed a foreword thinking man, who tried his best to make the working conditions in his mill much more pleasant and safe for his employees. The mill was much quieter than others because the shafts and belting that drove the machinery, were run under the floors of the mill sheds and extractors removed the dust and fibres keeping the conditions as bearable as possible. He built Saltaire to completely new standards, providing public baths and washhouses, so that his workers would be clean in body, and he built a Congregational Church, which his workers were expected to attend, so that they would be clean of spirit. He looked down on them each Sunday, from a balcony at the back of the Church where he and his family were seated.

As the village expanded an institute was built to help with people's education and a hospital was opened to cater for their health in times of illness. A park was built and Titus Salt paid for land which he donated for a Wesleyan Chapel which was built by public subscription, a public library was opened and shops were built to cater for the workers' needs. Titus Salt was possibly 'teetotal' as he refused to allow, 'Beer Shops' or public houses in Saltaire. Instead he built almshouses where workers who had reached retirement age could live out their lives in Saltaire, freeing up the houses for new workers, without forcing people to become destitute.

In many ways he appears to have been a very modern thinker, but in other directions he refused to move forward. He was one of the first employers to introduce the ten hour working day whilst still insisting that young children, under the age of nine should work in the mills, many of them crawling under the working machinery to keep the floors clean. His workers were not allowed to become members of the newly formed trade unions and, yet, he was heavily involved in establishing the United Reform Society which endeavoured to bring together both middle and working class reformers.

Some people might think that he had an ulterior motive, when he designed his 'model village' and that really he only wanted to increase production and profit for his own financial benefit. It may come as a complete surprise to us to know, as it did to his family, that when he died he did not leave behind a fortune because during his lifetime he had given it all away. Perhaps, not surprisingly, on the day of his funeral, when he was buried in the grounds of his beloved Congregational Church in Saltaire, an estimated one hundred thousand people lined the route taken by the funeral procession. Apart from a few trendy wine bars, the village is still pretty much as it was which is absolutely amazing. He was certainly a great man.

I don't know if this particular evening was the result of planetary influences or if there was something in the air of this usually peaceful pub. We tried our best to make everyone welcome at The Shoulder of Mutton, including bikers; they had been in many times and, apart from being a bit loud at times, they were all right. Once again my parents were up here for a while and the place was packed out, this particular Friday night. Dad was stood at the bar with my mother and it got a bit rowdy, with a lot of swearing, which was bad enough, but when one bloke swore very loudly at the bar, Dad asked him if wouldn't swear like that in front of his wife and daughter. Well, from then on the place turned into a battlefield. The man hit Dad; I went round to the other side of the bar and punched him in the face. Dad was already fighting another biker; Chris was on the floor with three of the bikers punching him. I was smacked right under the chin, glasses were being smashed everywhere, and in fact the whole pub was fighting. Christopher was only eleven and he came downstairs like Rambo with a carving knife and my mother tried to drag him back upstairs. The police were called, but wouldn't come into the pub straight away, I went outside to see what they were playing at and asked them to come and sort it out, but they wouldn't venture into the pub because there were bikers on their bikes wielding sticks with which they were hitting each other, looking like horse riders with lances on a battle field. They were fighting each other now.

What the place looked like in the morning is hard to describe, but the floor was covered in glass and we had to go and buy new beer glasses, as there were very few left on the shelves. We were a bit concerned about any follow up from the bikers and Chris had all sorts of things handy to 'sort them out'. It was a Saturday night and the place was filling up with some of the rugby lads from Haworth, Oxenhope and Keighley. Now whether it was just a coincidence or whether they wanted to protect us I really don't know, but I had a sneaky suspicion they were looking for action. Anyway, it was like nothing had ever happened. A few of the bikers started to come back in, but we never had any more trouble and it never did happen again. Years later I met one of the bikers that I had hit in the face that night. He was standing at the bar in the Five Flags pub, looking very tall and menacing. I stood next to him and I ordered both myself and Tracy a glass of lager, hoping he didn't recognise me, but;

I know you; you used to be the landlady from the Shoulder.

Yes I was. How are you?

I was shocked that he remembered me and how tall he was. I found myself looking up to him and had forgotten that he was probably six foot four inches tall.

Remember that fight at the Shoulder?

That didn't take long to come out. It was about ten years earlier and I was dreading what was to come next. I replied;

How could I forget? It cost us a fortune in new glasses, not to mention three hours of cleaning up. What I thought strange was that people were fighting with their own friends. Had you all been on magic mushrooms or what?

He laughed at this; even so I still think there was something very sinister about that particular night.

Would you like a drink, Maggie?

No, I'm all right thanks; I'm just dropping my daughter-in-law home and I'm driving anyway.

They were good nights at the Shoulder, Maggie. You're still talked about today. You were quite a character.

I've calmed down a bit now, but I have very good memories of my time there.

You were like a f...ing wild cat.

So you're still swearing then I see?

We laughed as he put his hands up in defence. We said goodbye and as I looked up, I thought to myself. Did I really punch that guy?

Things returned to normal at the Shoulder of Mutton. We didn't have any more problems with the bikers, although they weren't all bad and most of them now were gradually coming back in.

It was early evening, which was normally a quiet time, but this particular evening there was no one in at all. Chris had asked me to watch the bar while he nipped out for something, I was there a while when finally a customer walked through the door;

Hiya. Is it the usual?

Yes please Maggie.

It's quiet tonight, where is everyone?

They're on their way up the road. I just heard that Jack's been barred from the Idiot Hut. He's been going in there for years, they have held a meeting and it was agreed.

Oxenhope village had a club that was called the Idiot Hut. It was a very popular place which some of the customers usually called into before coming to the Shoulder. I have no idea why it was named so, but apparently it had nothing to do with the customers being idiots.

Sorry to hear that, but there must be a reason for barring him. What did he do?

He crapped on the snooker table.

He did what? He crapped on the snooker table? He would have been more than barred from here, the dirty bastard.

He couldn't help it, it was an accident.

An accident? Why didn't he use the bloody toilet like everybody else?

I think we've got our wires crossed here. I'm talking about a cat.

A cat?

Here I was again, repeating words.

Aye, he's been going in there years as I said. Folk love him and he keeps the mice down.

Who does the cat actually belong to?

I don't know, but it's always in there.

All that fuss over a poor little cat. He probably didn't know he had done it, he might have thought that he wanted to pass wind. I bet that in his past life the cat was a man that played snooker and for a brief time remembered.

We both laughed at this and the customer said to me;

Do you believe in reincarnation then Mag, joking apart?

I certainly do. Do you believe we were here before?

Not really, because we can't remember anything and I think we would be able to.

Do you know what that could do to a person's mind to remember things from another time? It would drive us insane, especially if we were tortured or even if we were the torturer. No, I believe we have been cleansed of all memory with little snips of knowledge to survive. Do you believe that a new born baby dreams?

Well yeah, that's what experts say. Something to do with rapid eye movement, that happens when a person dreams.

You tell me then, what a new baby could possibly be dreaming about. They haven't had any experiences apart from being born, have they? If a baby dreams then they are either psychic and can see into the future or they are looking into the past and remembering something from that time.

You're right I suppose, they must have images about something, to be able to dream. It's funny when you think about it, how a baby instinctively knows to go straight to the breast for milk without being shown.

Survival instincts. They also know to cry when they are hungry. For some time a baby only has the power to cry and not much else.

That's true enough Mag. All babies do for the first few weeks is sleep and cry, feed and shit and then repeat it all. So, do you think that if people are frightened of water, it could be that they drowned in a past life?

Not necessarily, there were awful times on ships in the past for sailors and passengers alike. It could take months to travel across the seas. There were outbreaks of cholera and other diseases on the ships and a lot of sickness. Hundreds died at sea. You know those Jewish people that have ringlets down each side of their face and wear big tall hats, they might have a name, I don't know, but I freeze with fear when I see one of them and I don't know why.

Well there are dozens of books of people claiming to live other lives, so I suppose there must be something in it.

Anyway, changing the subject and going back to cats keeping mice down, a mouse jumped out of the bread bin when my brother Kev opened it to make some toast. Kev went running out of the room with his hands over his head, as if a bomb had gone off. It was so funny, his face was white and distorted, and it was only a tiny field mouse.

My brother was now living with us and, as tough as he appeared to be, he didn't like spiders or mice.

I started to tell the man about my son;

The other day I heard a commotion down in the pub. It was late afternoon after closing time, Christopher and his friend James had opened a box up and there was a mouse inside, so they put the cat in with it. I went mad with them, luckily neither was hurt. The cat and the mouse I mean, Christopher was hurt when I told him he had to bottle up the shelves. Can you imagine how terrified that poor mouse must have felt, not having anywhere to run.

He's good at pool your lad. I was watching him play the other day.

Yes he is. He's also good at going down to the village with his mates late at night. We were just about to go to bed, when the police knocked on the back door. I wondered what they wanted, as we weren't serving late. I let them in and Christopher was stood behind them. They told me they had found him camping out down by the beck and I thought he was in bed. He had sneaked down the fire escape, hadn't he? This was the third time the police had brought him home.

Kids, eh? We don't see much of your eldest lad; I've only seen him once.

Adrian was different in many ways to Christopher. He had always been much more mature for his age since being a child and I knew that he would go to university one day. He spent a lot of time reading books, even before starting school, and was forever asking what a certain word meant. With the use of pictures at the side of the words, he soon began to work things out for himself and he seemed to have a sort of photographic memory for the things he had read and learned, as he never seemed to forget anything.

Although Adrian liked to read a lot, he also had other interests. He taught himself how to play the guitar, and eventually played in a band, with friends that he had made on the first day he went to school in Keighley. The band was very good and in no time at all they were getting local bookings. Adrian also loved walking and archery, astronomy and physics and he had been abseiling. He also had a friend whose father was a vicar and did a spot of bell ringing at the Church. He did in fact go to university, but much later when he was married with two sons. He went on to achieve a 2:1 in law at Durham University. Christopher, on the other hand, was a very outdoor person, adventurous, mischievous and clever at building tree houses and into sporty games including darts. He wanted a dart board in his bedroom. Again against my wishes, Chris bought him one. He placed it behind the door in his room and as I opened the door, he threw a dart that just missed me. I also found that the door was full of holes where he had missed the board. The dart board went in the bin along with darts.

I also found the biggest catapult I have ever seen in my life and I said;

That's going in the bin as well!

It's not mine. I'm saving it for someone, it's for killing rats.

Killing rats? But we haven't got any rats?

My friend keeps it just in case he sees a rat.

I give up. Anyway give it back to him. I don't want to see that in this place again.

Out of the blue my cousin John and his partner Tracy came to visit us. It was such a surprise to see them turning up, all that way from Barnsley. John had taken my advice and left the pit to become self employed and run his own pub. They had been for an interview and were told that they would be sent on a training course in Bradford.

We're going to have to travel every day to Bradford. We can't afford to stay in a hotel, but we're really pleased to get the offer of our own pub from it.

Where is the pub course being held in Bradford?

He told me the name of the pub where the course was being held and it was on the main road to Bradford and not that far from our pub over the country lanes. Chris said;

Stay with us here if you want to. We'll manage and you can get a bit of practice behind the bar.

They were thrilled to stay with us and we introduced them to Haworth and other places of interest. It was fun having them to stay. One day I said;

Why don't we hire horses and go for a ride over the moors? I have always wanted to do that. I could visualise it now, the four of us galloping across the moors, the wind blowing through my hair, stopping at streams to allow the horses to have a rest and a drink. Alas, I was brought back to reality.

Chris said "You can't hire a horse just like that",

Why not? You can hire a car.

You can hire a car, if you can drive a car. You can't ride a horse.

You don't need a licence to ride a horse.

Do you think they would just let you take a horse out for the day, without knowing how to ride it? It's not a case of giddy up you know.

That was true, how do you get them to turn left or right. I had another idea;

Chris, we could hire a small plane. A man up on Black Moor has small planes and a landing site and you do have a pilot's licence.

Chris did indeed have a pilot's licence, but even if we had the opportunity of hiring a plane, I wouldn't have gone up with him. He got the licence when he lived in Australia and once took his friend for a ride. He made the plane drop and jerk and with panic on his face turned to his friend and told him the engine was packing in and that they would have to try and land in the ocean. I would have killed him on the spot the moment we landed, but his friend did manage to see the funny side, I suppose, after he had changed his trousers.

Margaret, we can't afford a donkey ride at Blackpool at the moment. Do you realise how much a plane costs to hire?

Well, a person can dream can't they? We'll go to the village chippy instead.

The pub they were offered turned out to be in the next village, called Cullingworth, higher up from where we lived and we were all thrilled. The locals teased;

Oh no, we're being invaded by Barnslians.

As I predicted he was good at the job and was very well thought of by the locals. John had such a natural personality; he was so pleasant and forever making his customers laugh 'til they cried.

It was good to have some of my family up here, we had many a good time at each other's pub and of course his mother, my aunty, came to visit him regularly along with my cousin Billy.

Chapter Eleven

Up to now I had managed quite well with the catering side of things. When putting on events such as birthday buffets, treasure hunts and things like that. By sticking to simple food and buying certain items from the supermarkets that were ready to eat, everything had gone down well. Plus I believed that fresh bread baked on the day was very important. I was also extremely good at making food look well presented. I had a natural flair for this and I could make a cheap meal look very expensive through laying it out well.

This time, however, I was asked to do an engagement buffet for a really posh couple. They had been recommended by a friend of mine, which was fine. Fine, that was, until they gave me the list of the type of food they wanted. When the pair had left, I was stood looking at the list with Gina and Louise.

What am I going to do? Have you seen this list? I haven't heard of half of the stuff on here and besides, I gave them a price based on the number of people eating as I have always done.

Because they were usually for the locals, my buffets were a set price per head and everyone had been happy with the food I had laid on. I didn't make that much profit, but that was made up by the amount of drink we sold.

We'll help you.

Gina looked at Louise and burst out laughing;

Louise, we can't cook. How can we help?

We can wash up, set the tables and carry things down.

Yeah, of course we can and we can butter the bread and things like that.

That's nice of you, thanks, but what are we going to put on the tables to eat? Half of the dishes that they are asking for are vegetarian dishes, I think.

Get some recipe books.

There isn't time and what if I make a hash of it.

We were silent. We were trying to think of what to do and the three of us lifted our glasses to have a drink, in unison. After a few minutes Gina spoke up;

Marks and Spencer's do a good range of vegetarian dishes and Morrison's might help.

Gina was good at thinking; she had often come up with ideas before.

That's a brilliant idea Gina.

The day after I went into town and had a look at what was available for the buffet, without it looking shop bought and it was just great. Marks had excellent vegetarian dishes of all kinds. If I put them on proper serving dishes, no-one would know. Morrison's were also very helpful on their fresh food selection and offered to have fresh food boxed up on the morning, along with freshly baked bread and a selection of Indian food.

That was sorted. I phoned Louise and Gina and told them what I had arranged. I was all set as far as crockery and cutlery were concerned because I had bought the previous landlady's catering equipment.

The day arrived and as promised both my treasured friends were there to help. We prepared the food that I had made myself. I had put on joints of beef and ham for the meat eaters and I had also bought a meat slicer which was worth its weight in gold. Louise chopped up the salad and Gina made some open sandwiches.

I nipped into town and picked the food up and it cost an absolute fortune. I had paid almost double the amount I had charged the couple and made no profit from all the work I had put in. I didn't care however, anything was better than telling the couple that I was unable to do it. Gina thought otherwise;

Yeah Maggie, that's all right, but what if someone else wants the same buffet for that price. You can't keep working for nothing.

I had definitely not thought of that and had no intentions of being in this predicament again. I thought for a minute and said;

What I need to do is write some set menus with a price and if they want different to what's on the menu, I'll tell them I'll get back to them later to give me time to think. Good thinking, don't you think?

We had a drink to unwind and a good laugh about it all and then someone arrived with the cake;

This cake is very fragile, be very careful with it, it cost a fortune. See you later, bye and be careful with that cake.

Well, she didn't hang around, did she?

What a cake, it was like a wedding cake; it had pillars holding the middle and top layers up with little doves going all around it as if they had just flown in and settled there. It really was a nice cake.

It was literally only minutes after the lady had gone when a dove fell off.

Oh shit, oh shit, I never touched it.

I stood there with my hands held high like a little schoolgirl trying to prove her innocence. We tried to stick it back but to no avail and with the pressure of touching it, another two fell off. These cute little doves played an important part of the cake decoration and would be missed if they weren't there. Time was running out and I didn't know the name of the person who had made the cake either. We tried all sorts of ways to put the doves back on the cake, even holding them to the icing for a full five minutes and then another fell off. I was panicking a lot by now; the couple would be devastated to find a doveless cake when they arrived.

What about icing?

No, because I won't be able to get it looking as smooth and anyway I haven't got any. I even thought of sticking pins through the doves but someone might eat one.

Gina burst out laughing and she had the most infectious laugh I had ever heard.

Or the doves might think they've been voodood.

I'll Voo doo that bloody cake maker, if any more doves fall off.

We all laughed at the situation while panicking at the same time. Hysteria I think they call it.

That women must have known what was going to happen, she wasn't here two minutes and stressed that we should be careful.

I think Louise was probably right, she certainly stressed to us to be careful with the cake because it was very fragile.

I know, but it'll be me they blame because it was all right when she left. Oh shit, what am I going to do?

It was thinking time again, and time for another glass of lager. I had a brainwave;

I've thought of something, chewing gum. At least it's not poisonous and no one will notice if it's only a tiny bit and anyway they always take the ornaments off before they cut the cake.

And so it was chewing gum, but only the slightest amount.

We tiptoed around the cake, gently placing the food on the table. In fact none of us dared even look at it, it only happened when we looked at it. I daren't put the juke box on in case the cake collapsed from the vibration. The doves could fly away or do whatever they liked when the party had started, at least we couldn't be accused of man handling the bloody stupid thing.

The buffet was perfect with a good combination of food to suit all. We stood back with pride looking at the table and I was glad it was all over, although I did feel a touch of guilt when I was praised for the food I had made. Apart from roasting the joints of meat, I hadn't made anything, including the sweet selection.

The evening went well and nothing more happened to the cake and as far as I know no one choked to death on the chewing gum, it was only the tiniest amount and looked like icing. I just hoped they had a place booked somewhere else for the wedding.

I was driving back home from Hebden Bridge and thought I would give me mam a call when I got home. Hebden Bridge wasn't that far away and a nice drive out. In fact who should I see on my journey home, but Christopher and his friend James. They were on their way back from Hebden Bridge on their bikes and they looked hot and shattered. It's all up and down huge hills, over moorlands and quite a way on a push bike. James had a flat tyre, and they were trying to pump it up. They were so relieved to see me, as it was a very warm day and they didn't even have a drink of water with them. I had to squash two bikes and two lads into my little jeep; it was amazing how we managed to do it. The boys dashed in for a drink and I went to ring me mam.

The phone was answered quickly as usual;

Hiya, it's me. Were you sat on the phone again? Fancy a week up here? It's a while since you came. We could go to Hebden Bridge; I've just got back from there and thought of you. It's your sort of place and not much walking.

Yeah, that'll be nice.

I travelled down to Barnsley to pick them up. They really looked forward to coming to stay with us. It was a nice break for them and I loved it when they were here. The day after they arrived we set off for Hebden Bridge, which was only twenty minutes away. We parked up and browsed around the shops and the old book shops in the village, had a little walk round the market before thinking about something to eat. The pubs were quite busy, so we headed for the car and drove towards Todmorden, where they had a good market.

As we travelled further towards Todmorden me mam shouted out;

There's a sign there for Littleborough, that's where I was born.

My mother knew very little of her father, he was never talked about throughout her life and it was only after my grandmother died that she was given a photo of him. On the photograph he was aged about twenty years old. This upset my Mother on first seeing it because she had not known what he looked like and now she did.

We'll have a drive there then, it isn't that far.

We drove to the centre of Littleborough, but because she didn't know the name of the street she was born in, it was a bit pointless.

Doesn't it say the address on your birth certificate?

No, it doesn't.

It must be a smaller copy then. We'll drive through to Rochdale and find the town hall.

We managed to get hold of her full birth certificate and it did indeed give us the address. We were so excited and drove quickly to the street asking people everywhere for directions. Eventually we found it, but unfortunately the houses had been knocked down years before, although the canal was still there. Mam often talked about a canal at the back, into which her brother Tom used to pee from the bedroom window. I felt sorry for her as she stood there quietly staring into the canal, probably remembering her brother, Tom, and her sister, Rene. We all climbed into the car and waited, giving Mam time on her own to grieve.

Tell you what, we'll call at the post office and see if any Hardys still live here. Everybody uses a post office, and after all he did come with his brothers to work in the mills. There must be families here.

It would have been so nice to have given her the joy of knowing something or somebody from her young life here, but unfortunately the post office where people went to collect their pensions, had not heard of anyone with the name of Hardy and it was only a small village. We looked around an old graveyard in the village, but could not find anyone with the name of Hardy, although they were mostly really old graves. There was probably a big cemetery somewhere around.

We drove home looking at the scenery and old houses; it wasn't long before Mam was back to her usual self, chatting away about the times that she could remember;

Me mam used to take us to a grave that was near a tree and made us promise not to say anything to anyone about where we had been. She said "Yer dad's buried down there", but I didn't understand at that time, I was only young. Sometimes we used to go on a long bus ride with her, to see people. I often wonder now if they were related to me dad. I always used to wish I had somewhere to go sometimes when I wanted to leave home. I used to wonder if I had another granny or granddad from me dad's side and if they were dead or not.

How come you weren't allowed to talk about your real dad then?

I don't know, it was like he never existed. We didn't have any photos of him when we were growing up. I can remember one photograph of me mam and dad though, it used to hang on the wall. When me mam and me new dad were arguing one day, he smashed the photograph. I was too young to understand what they were arguing about, but me mam and Rene were crying. When me mam died, we found out from someone that me dad died from a brain haemorrhage. It bothers me now every time I get a bad headache that I might have a brain haemorrhage like him.

Was it a brain haemorrhage? I thought he was kicked in the head by a horse.

I'm not really sure what he died from, but that's what I was told a few years ago. It might have been the kick in the head that caused the brain haemorrhage. That's something we'll never know. Me mam never mentioned him again after that picture incident.

Ah well, let's go back and have a whisky, shall we? This conversation is getting a bit morbid.

Good idea.

I felt awful at her disappointment at not finding anything out about her dad and wished there was a way of finding something, but everything seemed to come to a dead end.

After my lovely mother sadly died, at the age of sixty eight, I had this urgency to find out about her father. I had promised my mother, one day while I stood at her grave side, that I would find out something about him. Time and time again we set off to Littleborough until going there became a regular event. We searched everywhere looking, for I don't know what, but something had made me keep going until, on one more disappointing day, I decided I was never going to find anything about my mother's past and told myself that this would be the last time I would ever come to Littleborough.

On my way back to the car, I called at a newsagent for some sweets for the journey home. I was flicking through some books and found a glossy booklet that had some old photographs of Littleborough, taken by a local photographer. It had the street inside that my mother had been born on and pictures of some houses. I thought if nothing else, I had this.

When I got home I was very upset of not finding anything out about my grandfather and felt that I had let my mother down. I made a cup of coffee and settled down to look at the book. Inside there were pictures of a royal visit with children waving flags. The girls were dressed in long white dresses and pinafores, with big bonnets. The boys had hats on and trousers with braces and there were flags lining the streets. It looked a very happy time. I thought to myself, "my aunty and uncle could be in that crowd", it was the right timing, and me mam would have only have been a baby. I found a magnifying glass, but even so it was difficult to identify someone that young who was now over twenty five years older than me.

I flicked through the book again and was about to close it when something else caught my eye. On the back page was a photograph of a men's trip. This photo was taken at the end of the street where my mother was born, and I quickly picked up the magnifying glass and looked at the faces of the men smiling at the camera. One of the men who were stood at the back looked like my Uncle Tom. This was not my imagination, he had my uncle's eyes, and this man had to be my grandfather.

The following Sunday was a cold, dark, dismal day as we set off again to Littleborough and it might have been my imagination, but I think not. I could feel Mam and Uncle Tom in the back seat smiling and I felt sure today would be the day.

However, the same thing happened. Nothing at all happened. As we were driving and thinking of going home, we spotted a Heritage Centre and called in. We looked at some books and brochures of the area and bought a few souvenirs of Littleborough. The volunteers that were looking after the centre were an elderly couple and so I asked them if they knew of any Hardy's that lived in the area. I expected them to say no, which they did, but after saying thank you and goodbye, the lady said;

I don't know anyone called Hardy, but I know someone that used to be called Hardy before she married.

My ears pricked up and my heart missed a beat.

Really? How old is she roughly?

She'll be in her late seventies. She lives next door to her son, and she has a wheelchair now. She's disabled.

This was a wild guess but after all this time I was willing to take a chance. We asked her for the name of the street, which she kindly gave us, but she didn't know the number. She did know the woman's married name, however, and that her son was called Steve and that he lived next door to her.

It was such an awful night, cold, damp and foggy. A young man was walking past and we pulled up and asked if he knew of these people, which he did. Because we didn't want to frighten the poor woman to death, we knocked at the son's house and explained what it was all about. He was very friendly and helpful;

My mother lived in Barnsley. She used to talk about Barnsley when we were kids. She lived in a place called Cudworth.

He went inside his house for a key to his mother's, telling us she would be in bed, even though it was only early evening. Steve was just so nice. He invited us to sit down, asking us if we would like a cup of tea to which I readily said yes. Before going upstairs to tell his mother, he went to put the kettle on to boil and we waited patiently. All of a sudden there was a noise, the ceiling opened up and his mother descended down in a lift from the ceiling which we hadn't noticed. I will never forget that day as long as I live, we could hear her voice as she descended down into the front room where we waited with bated breath.

Barnsley? Barnsley? Who's from Barnsley? I'm from Barnsley.

She was holding on to a walking frame, the excitement and wonder clearly showing in her face. She finally sat down and I explained to her that I was trying to find information about my grandfather and that my mother never knew him and she had passed away herself now, at the age of sixty eight without ever knowing what had happened to her dad's family. I explained that she had always missed him and how I had made a promise to her, to find out something about him.

I could hear Steve in the kitchen making tea while she reeled off all the Hardy's names that she had known which was quite a number, but she never mentioned my grandfathers' name, Henry.

I felt very downhearted and said;

I was hoping you knew someone called Henry.

Henry, no there wasn't anyone called Henry.

Even though I was very disappointed, my first thought was "do we still have a cup of tea?" Her son was just about to bring it in and I suddenly felt embarrassed, because we had the wrong Hardy. I was about to apologise when she said;

I knew someone called Harry, but he died years ago, he was only thirty.

My jaw froze for a second, I couldn't speak. Finally;

Harry was my granddad. Harry is sometimes used instead of Henry and he died when he was that age.

She told us her name was Elizabeth and her father, Thomas, was my grandfather's brother. There were eight brothers and four sisters altogether in the family and some of them had come to Littleborough to work in the mills, during the depression.

So, you are me mam's cousin then?

Yes, I suppose I am.

She certainly had the same smiling eyes that my mother, aunt and uncle had.

I showed her the photograph in the book that had eventually brought me to her and she told me it was either my grandfather or one of his brothers as they all looked alike. She said it was certainly one of the Hardy brothers. I was in shock.

I remember your mother, Joyce, I was six years older than her and sometimes she stayed with us when Aunt Alice, your grandmother, went shopping.

Elizabeth phoned her other son, who she said was doing a family tree, and she went on to tell me the sad tale of how my grandfather died.

He worked at the mill just up the road from here. They were a very happy family and they lived round the corner at the bottom of this street. He was a lovely man, Uncle Harry, and everybody liked him.

I froze again as I thought back to that day with me mam and the very corner that we had walked towards near the canal. All that time her cousin lived just a few yards away from where she had stood, upset. A cousin that she never knew existed, someone that could tell her everything about the father she hardly knew. Elizabeth's lovely Lancashire accent came back to me;

Uncle Harry loved working at the mill. He sometimes came here for his dinner during working hours with his brothers and my mother would cook for them all. We were a big family then you know. We shared houses and ate at each other's houses. We made our own entertainment and your grandmother, Aunt Alice, fitted in well with the Hardy family, she was very happy here, good days they were. Would you like some more tea?

We told her we were all right and she carried on telling us of my grandparents' life here;

When Uncle Harry and Aunt Alice came to live here, she was pregnant with your mum. They stayed with relatives at a street named Howards Place, just around the corner from here. When your mother was born they found a place of their own just off Littleborough Road. They named your mother Joyce, but we all called her Joy because she was always laughing. Uncle Harry worked at Breda Vistada's mill as a silk spinner, not far from here.

Elizabeth told me that my grandfather had been kicked by a horse that he was working with. He didn't go to hospital though and it was forgotten about. She looked a bit sad as she told me;

He was never the same after that, his personality changed. He had always been a lovely man; he would pick me up and swing me about. I loved my Uncle Harry, but he started to turn nasty. He would shout at Aunt Alice and at times he could be violent, which was out of character for him. He also turned very religious, carrying a Bible around everywhere and reading passages out loud all the while. It was the kick on the head you know. It had done something to his brain, I was there the day the ambulance came and took him away and he was shouting for my dad, who he was very close to, screaming to him and begging him not to let them take him.

Did he go into a mental asylum?

No, he went to the hospital here, Birch Hill Hospital in Littleborough, but I don't know what happened to him then. I saw Aunt Alice crying and asked my mother what was up and she said Uncle Harry had gone away, I was never sure what she meant and didn't ask, but we all missed Uncle Harry. When he died Aunt Alice went away with the children and we never saw them again.

The door opened and I was glad. Although I was thrilled to find this lovely lady, it was such a sad thing for me to hear.

This is our Sid.

We introduced ourselves and told him briefly what we were doing there and he opened a folder with pictures inside and there, in front of my eyes, was a photograph of my grandparents sat together with a black dog at their feet, the first photograph I had ever seen of them together. Sid had other photographs of the Hardy family and even some of their parents, my great grandparents. He had clips from newspapers, birth certificates and all sorts of documents, all of which he laid out for us to see.

We had the information now to get a birth and death certificate and Sid kindly let us have a copy of the family tree he had spent all that work on doing. All this from a family we hadn't known two hours before. I loved them and felt that they were my family as well. They really were the nicest people to meet and, in-between all the talk and information, the telephone rang and Steve left the house returning with a tray of sandwiches that his wife had kindly made for us. I was amazed at their hospitality. No wonder I had felt the presence of both Mam and Uncle Tom on our way here. I was so pleased to have met them and was reluctant to leave, but I promised I would be back.

I went just a few times before I received a phone call from Sid to say Elizabeth had died. Apart from the sadness of her death, this meant that my Aunty Rene never got to meet her. Life was so unfair; I had met this lovely lady who had been so kind and helpful. She had become part of my family and now she had been taken away. We did, however, give my aunty a family tree and the birth and death certificates of all the Hardy family, plus some photographs that she was very pleased with.

We were invited to the funeral and of all the funerals that I have ever attended this was the best. The songs were nice, not morbid and the vicar gave a lovely sermon. Although I hadn't known Elizabeth long, I knew that she had had a lovely nature and would not have wanted people to be sad. Her four sons and their families respected this and the service became a celebration of her life. This continued after the service as everyone gathered and joined in a barbecue in the back garden and we had a great time.

Using all the information from Sid, I was able to do a family tree. My mother's family can be traced back to 1863 when her grandfather, a miner by trade, was born in Derbyshire. Thomas Graves Hardy later married Henrietta Robinson, both being nineteen at the time, in 1882 and set up home in Ilkeston where they had six boys and two girls. In 1898 the family left Derbyshire and moved to South Yorkshire. They moved into the old paper mill in Worsborough Dale and had another four children, one of which was my grandfather. I know that my grandmother came from Sheffield originally. My grandparents eventually married and had two children, Betsy Irene, who was known as Rene, and Tom, while living in Barnsley.

One of the things I found in the search was that, according to a newspaper cutting, my grandfather's Uncle George was arrested and found guilty of being drunk in charge of a horse and cart. This wouldn't have been so bad apart from the fact that the Hardy family were making a living by making blasting powder, for use when shot blasting was carried out down the coal mines. George was quite merrily trundling along on his horse and cart full of gun powder when the police apprehended him. My grandfather worked in the mine as a stone miner hewing out the stone to form the galleries that allowed the coalminers to cut into the coal seams. Later he became a colliery road repairer down in the depths of the pit, making good the miles of road surfaces that were used by the pit ponies and men who worked at the coal face or drew the coal back to the pit shaft, where it could be brought up to the surface.

I had just assumed that everyone who went down the pit must have dug for coal, but the truth is that most of them did other jobs which helped to extract the coal from the bowels of the earth.

Coal mining was in recession during the late 1920s and many families were finding it hard to find work, forcing men who had always worked down the mines to move away and seek work in other industries, often in unfamiliar parts of the country.

My grandfathers' older sister, Sarah Hardy, was the first of the family to go to Littleborough in Lancashire when she crossed the Pennines to work as a barmaid in a local hostelry. Sarah wrote and told her family of work in the cotton mills and Elizabeth's mother and her father, my grandfather's brother, joined her to work in the mills. As it became more and more difficult to find work in Barnsley, Henry (Harry) and Alice, my grandparents, uprooted their two children and crossed over to Lancashire where Henry secured employment at Breda Vistada's silk spinning mill where he worked as a spinning operative. My Mother was born shortly afterwards and I felt now that we had come full circle.

Sid had also given me a phone number for another of my mothers' cousins in Harrogate called Margaret. I rang her up a few months after meeting Elizabeth and, as soon as I said who I was, she started to cry uncontrollably. For all her life she had wondered what had happened to her cousins who she had spent most of her time playing with as a child. She fondly remembered them all and told me of the times they spent together.

Your mother was only four or five when they left and I remember her having a lisp. She was concerned about her shoes being dirty and said; "look at my thooses now". Aunt Alice was so upset the last time I saw her, but

I never knew they were going for good and I have wondered all my life if they were all right. Rene was crying because she didn't want to leave her school and friends, Tom was trying to make jokes, but it was an act to stop himself from crying and your mum had her thumb in her mouth and was clinging to a little rag doll as if her life depended on it. It was really sad.

We arranged to go and see Margaret at home in Harrogate the following Sunday, where she had a lovely meal all laid out ready for us. She was stood at the window in a pretty little apron with a tea towel in her hand. She came to the gate to meet us and it was very emotional.

Margaret had great nostalgia and passion for the life she had had as a child in Barnsley;

We all lived in one really big house with aunts, uncles and cousins and we were the only people in the area to have a flushing toilet. We used to play in the orchards and there were fields all around where we lived. Our grandmother who was six foot tall used to sit outside on a rocking chair preparing the vegetables while smoking a clay pipe.

Margaret talked of a happy childhood. Her eyes would fill with tears as she talked of the days down at the powder mill, about her cousins and the freedom she had felt for all those young years. I really liked Margaret very much, as I did Elizabeth, and thought how much my mother; aunt and uncle had missed through not knowing any of them.

Sadly, not long after this visit, Margaret died, but not before she had shared with me a legacy, a poem that she had written for herself and I know that she would not mind me sharing it with you;

Sometimes when I'm dreaming I go back to the Powder Mill,
Down to the bottom of Worsborough Dale and turn down Edmunds Hill,
Past the canal basin and over the railway track, I don't turn right up Dark Lane, I head for the old muck stack,
It towers on the skyline, getting closer every day; my heart just fills with sadness that will not go away.
For standing in the corner in a field of yellow corn, there is a house that's called the Powder Mill, the house where I was born,
I dream again of childhood days when life was free from care,
And as we wandered through the fields we had time to stand and stare.
At the trembling grass, the buttercup, the skylark up above.
Oh those happy childhood days, when life was full of love

Then I awake from dreaming, and I know I can't go back
My home is there no longer, it's covered by the old muck stack.

I sent for my grandfather's death certificate and its states that he died from 'Acute Dementia Praecox', but there was no post mortem. He died in St Helens, in the County Mental Hospital, which was then in Lancashire, but very close to Merseyside and Liverpool. He was only thirty one years old.

It wasn't until many years later when I was studying for a degree in Psychology that I saw those words again, Dementia Praecox. We were studying mental disorders at the time and I knew I had heard this somewhere. Suddenly it hit me as to where I had seen it before; it was on my grandfather's death certificate. I was totally shocked when I realised what this medical description of my grandfather's death really meant.

Without being too technical, the cause of death, as written on the death certificate, was;

Ia. Acute Dementia Praecox. The death certificate stated that there was no post mortem carried out, which presumably means that my grandfather was being treated for this disorder for some time and that the medical staff at the hospital were convinced that this is what he had died of. Ia. denotes a medical abbreviation for abnormal or diseased and as the psychological terminology for abnormal is; – a departure from the normal behavioural patterns of individuals, this is probably what they meant. Acute, when used in relation to diseases or to the symptoms of a disease means that it would have had a sudden onset and be relatively short lived. Dementia Praecox is the original term for severe Schizophrenia, especially affecting adolescents or young adults. The symptoms usually include sudden outbursts or embarrassing behaviour and these are the first obvious signs of dementia. The affected person may develop an unpleasant personality which becomes magnified and they may make accusations, unreasonable demands or even assault. Though, Ia. Acute Dementia Praecox is now obsolete, as a medical term, it was frequently used in 1934. Indeed it was still used until the mid 1970s when psychiatric understanding was overtaken by research and monitoring and Schizophrenia became the name for this condition.

For all those years my mother, unbeknown to her, had a grandmother who still lived within walking distance, plus twelve aunties and uncles living in different places. I also remember my Uncle Tom crying once, when he was drunk, saying that he missed his dad. I suppose he remembered him more being older, but on the other hand I asked my Aunt Rene about these sad times and she didn't remember any of them. I realise now that because she was the eldest at eight years old, it must have been a very traumatic time for her. Being the eldest meant she probably had the most responsibility and perhaps she had blocked it from her mind. However, she remembers her life clearly before his illness, and spoke of her dad carrying her on his shoulders across the fields to school and picking her up to take her home again. The fondness for him showed clearly in her eyes.

In those days mental illnesses were frowned upon. People didn't understand them as they do now. It wouldn't matter what had caused the illness, if you were mentally ill then you were classed as crazy, or, as we used to say, a nutter. In fact during the middle ages, it was thought that a person suffering from any form of mental illness was possessed by the devil or witchcraft and some people were very frightened of having a spell cast upon them. People were locked away and hidden from the outside world as if they had never existed, sometimes tied to a bed with chains. Books tell of crazy people being locked in attics or cellars in the past. In fact, in Charlotte Bronte's book, 'Jane Eyre' Bertha Mason, who was Edward Rochester's mad wife, is locked away in a room and was hidden and kept prisoner and depicted as being evil. I once watched it on television when I was a child and had nightmares for weeks, thinking of that mad woman.

I suppose on entering a mental institution even with the mildest of mental illness, such as depression, it would only be accelerated by being with others who were very mentally disturbed. It is so easy to pick up mannerisms from others, good or bad. How awful to think, as well, of the perfectly sane people that were sent there to be locked away by a spouse. This terrible deed did happen, sometimes for money reasons, or sometimes if one partner had met someone else they wanted to marry and so claimed that the other partner was mad. Money and power went a long way in those days.

Mental illness still has a stigma with it. People shy away and avoid speaking to a mentally ill person. I was guilty of this myself, until I worked for the Social Services and drove buses for the mentally handicapped. It didn't take long for me to realise that they were human beings who thrived on affection just like the rest of us. To some people it's almost as if the illness could be infectious, or it may be just the fact that they are frightened of something they don't themselves understand. As the saying goes, 'out of sight, out of mind'.

My grandfather may or may not have been kicked by a horse; the fact still remains that he died from a very fast degenerative mental illness, known today as severe Schizophrenia.

This was probably the reason why he was never talked about; the sadness of all this really is the suffering that my grandmother went through. They had been very happy together, I know that from what I have been told and losing him this way must have been very hard for her. How could she tell her children why their father wouldn't be coming out of hospital and that a once gentle man turned violent and shouted abuse when she went to visit him? I know that she had taken the children to see him in the mental hospital because my mother had told me a long time ago how she remembered her dad shouting at her mother and accusing her of going with other men and being really nasty towards her. This is a classic symptom of the disease and seeing their once mild mannered father turn so violent must have been a terrible time for them all. Although my mother said she only saw him on one occasion at that one time in the hospital, my grandmother carried on visiting him, along with other family members and she stayed loyal to the end.

I'm not sure what my aunty remembered of that time. I can only think that sometimes our self conscious keeps things down in the depths of the mind, which in some way must be better than living with traumatic memories. I have been a practising hypnotherapist for years now and believe that people can be helped to overcome past problems without reliving the trauma, which can be hard to let go of. That is the reason I will not do past life regression, real or not. This could open something up, causing even more problems. My Aunty Rene seemed to have lived a happy life. She was very active up to being over eighty years old and I can't ever remember her being depressed, until my Uncle Bill died after sixty happy years of marriage. My mother, on the other hand, seemed to go into depression a lot, as she got older, and she would often talk of her past.

For some time in her later life, my mother was convinced that she would have a brain haemorrhage because that is what she was led to believe her father had died of. Whenever she had a bad headache it would worry her and was probably made worse by the anxiety caused by thinking this way. At times, when we were looking for something of her dad's life, I would pray that something would eventually come to light and that she would find what she had been looking for all those years. However, my mother was a worrier and knowing that a mental illness was the cause of her father's death, would have always been at the back of her mind. Also research shows that it can be hereditary but whether or not it will develop depends on environmental circumstances. Up to now, thank God, no-one in our family has shown any symptoms.

It must have been terrible for my grandmother to leave a place where she was happy, only to go back to Barnsley and start a new life as a widow. Not only did she lose her husband, but she had to care for three children with very little money to live on. In addition she would still have been in shock; she was after all still only a young women. I will never know why she chose to come back to Barnsley, although in times of sorrow it's nice to be near loved ones and she did have a family.

I could now close a chapter in my life and hope that me mam would be pleased with my investigations, or was it through her that I found out as much as I did? I like to think so.

Chapter Twelve

Time went on and our pub was suffering. We were starting our second winter there and knew that this would have a knock on-effect on our finances. We had to cut back on heating to save money and I begrudged staying up late for those who came in at the last minute, particularly when the pub had been empty until nearly closing time. We had to think of leaving and getting another pub that would bring in customers during the winter as well as the summer. This broke my heart because I loved not only the place, but the people in this quaint little village.

Chris had never felt at home here, in fact he hated it. He was beginning to go into a depression more and more each day and it was made harder still because he had to sort the finances out and make ends meet. Things were starting to get difficult. We had spent so much money on refurbishment, which had been proved to be a waste of money really and had only made our finances worse.

I was reluctant to leave Oxenhope. I had made some lovely friends there, friends like Gina, Louise, Joan, Leslie and Alison and along with these close friends, I would miss the usual crowd, but at the same time I was fed up of struggling with money and falling out over it. I hated being behind the bar during the week waiting for customers to walk through the door. It was so boring and soul destroying, so yes, in a way I was also ready to move.

From the start there was something very weird about The Goat's Head. We were to play a pool match there one night, with the lads from the Shoulder of Mutton, and as soon as I entered the building I just knew that this would not be the last time I would come here. There was cosiness about the place that evening. It was run by a family who seemed to be well liked, the atmosphere was good and there were quite a few customers for an early week night. I looked around the pub as I settled down in the corner of the room. It was very old. I only saw the pub from the lounge and taproom but guessed it was built in the 1600s, or early 1700s. The wooden seating was Tudor style, with high backs. It looked good and fitted the style of the pub and I could picture the men, of days gone bye, sat on these seats smoking pipes, wearing big boots, big hats and a dog by the side of them. Yes, the seats certainly fitted the time of an old inn, but they were very uncomfortable to sit on. There was also wood panelling around the bottom of the walls to match the Tudor style, the walls were thick and very out of shape and the doorways were very low.

I was daydreaming again and found myself looking towards the bar. For a brief second I saw myself there, working behind the bar smiling and serving the customers. We made our way back to our place and I never gave it another thought until a few months later, when Chris had to go into the hospital to have his wisdom teeth taken out. The Hospital is just past The Goat's Head and I was travelling with my mother at the time and mentioned how I would love to run a pub like that and how nice it was inside. That was all that was said about The Goats Head for another three months or more.

There is a phone number a publican can ring to see if there are any pubs for lease, so we rang the number and the only one that was in our region, apart from town centre pubs, was The Goat's Head. I was so excited that I was unable to speak. Chris was also optimistic, but realistic;

It doesn't mean we'll get it just because it came up. Pubs between the country and the town are well sought after pubs, so don't get too excited.

Too late, I already was excited. Again, I saw myself there behind the bar, serving drinks.

We phoned the brewery first thing the next morning and they told us the Goat was already spoken for. A couple had already put in for it and there were even more people wanting this pub as it was a village pub, but with plenty of houses around it and on a main road to the north. I wasn't particularly interested in enquiring about another place now; I was sulking and decided to go shopping. Normally, I would go to the supermarket that I had gone to since moving into Oxenhope, but I went to another one that day instead. As I went for a trolley, the landlady of the Goats Head recognised me and stopped to speak. I was surprised that she did remember me really, when I had only been there the one time. It is customary to introduce yourself as fellow landlords and landladies when going into another pub, but that had been months ago.

I told her we had applied for the pub, but understood it had gone and I was really disappointed. As we went our separate way, she turned around and told me she would put in a good word for me as the final decision had not yet been made. I thanked her, but thought it would be too late for that. The interviews would have all been finished, but all the same it was very nice of her to say that.

Later in the week, we went to a licensee meeting about the launch of a new drink. These launches were always dead boring; apart from the meal we had afterwards. During the meal, a man sitting opposite made polite conversation and asked how we were doing at the Shoulder. I told him we were struggling and I went on to blame the brewery, as they had never put a proper pub sign up, that was visible from the road, and neither had they helped with the refurbishments. I went on moaning about this while the man listened to me sympathetically;

They don't bloody care about how much work we have put into the place. We've put money into it that we couldn't really afford, to make it look nicer and the Area Manager didn't even take the time to come and look. We have asked for a new sign time and time again. You have to be stood directly in front of the pub to see the stupid sign; the brewery couldn't care less so long as we sell their beer. Useless they are, bloody useless.

Chris gave me a kick under the table and scowled at me. I thought it was because I had sworn. When we were in the car and were on our way home, Chris told me that the man I had moaned to was actually the head of the Area Managers which was bad enough, but Chris was even more annoyed at me because he said that I had made matters worse during the promotion and embarrassed him.

Different people had stood up and talked about the launch and after the talks were finished, we were shown the new advertising campaign on a large screen. I was bored and needed to go to the toilet, so I stood up and to Chris's horror I said loudly;

Scuse me, I'm nipping to the loo while the adverts are on.

Later in the week we had a surprise phone call from the Brewery offering us The Goat's Head.

I couldn't believe it. I had pulled the Brewery down, complained about the Area managers and, worse still, joked about the advertising campaign. I was meant to get this place.

I started having second thoughts when I told the locals we were moving. I had made some good friends there, both male and female, and I particularly liked the fact that ladies came in on their own and sat at the bar. One young girl was called Julie. She was very pretty with long, blond hair and all the local men were attracted to her. Of course, when you meet someone looking like her for the first time, it's easy to feel threatened or jealous, especially when they sit at the bar laughing and talking to your partner. At first I did feel like that, but Julie was such a lovely person and I grew to like her. She was bubbly, very funny and never short of conversation. Once she was telling me about a time when she came out in really tight, drainpipe jeans;

It took me ages to zip them up. They were tight and uncomfortable, but when I looked in the mirror I liked what I saw and off I went to the Shoulder. After a few lagers, my stomach started to swell and I needed to pee. I couldn't move my legs to walk across to the toilet. I was so cramped, because the jeans were too tight and I wouldn't have been able to zip them back up anyway. I was bursting for a pee.

Julie had to wait while her boyfriend came in and when he arrived, he threw her over his shoulder and carried her off to the car and home before she passed out.

It was a Friday night and the place was packed as usual. The disco played and everyone was dancing, I really wanted to stay now. Adrian and Christopher always went along with whatever we decided to do. They never moaned and the chances are that it was very upsetting for them, as they loved it here, but unless a miracle happened we had no choice. This time though they were able to stay at the same school and Christopher was now in the same school as Adrian.

To make things even worse, we arranged to view the pub on a dreary, wet and foggy March day. The noise of the traffic made it even more unbearable after living in a virtually car free area. Everything looked different during the day inside the pub. The cosiness wasn't there, or perhaps it was the mood I was in at the time. We walked through what seemed to be a dark, dingy corridor. On the left was a tap room with three people in playing darts and two more stood at the bar in the main lounge. The landlady showed us around, including upstairs and it seemed huge to what we had now. The doorways were so thick and low. The walls bulged out, all different shapes and sizes, as if they ready to burst, through the building being as old as it was. There were three bedrooms, a large bathroom and a small kitchen. The upstairs living room was a decent size and there were a few doors which she never mentioned, so I took it that these were closets or cupboards.

I felt a little better after having a look around upstairs and from the kitchen window I could see a courtyard with buildings. The courtyard was sealed off from the road and the noise. Having a bit of privacy would be nice after living in two pubs without any private outside space for us to relax in. I still cried all the way home.

This was to be our last night at the Shoulder; Chris had been to pick Mam and Dad up in the afternoon. We had a bit of a farewell party and my friends were asking me to stay at the Shoulder and let Chris go to the Goat's Head. It was all very tearful and emotional. The friends I had made in the Shoulder were very good friends and I was going to miss them, especially Gina and Louise, as I had spent a lot of time with them. Alison and Lesley, another two really good friends I had made, were coming to work for us at The Goat's Head and I was thrilled about that. As well as their friendship, it was good to have their moral support.

We had the night off to be able to mingle with the locals for the last time and I hadn't seen Chris as happy as this since we were at the Woodmoor. The party went on very late and there was a lot of drink consumed. Adrian was brilliant behind the bar, he was great at socialising with the customers, especially Clem, who Adrian told me later, had given him some really good advice. What it was I don't know other than that Adrian really appreciated it. I hate secrets unless their mine.

We had taken the beds to pieces and put two mattresses on the lounge floor and there we all slept that night. All of a sudden Chris burst out laughing for no reason, very loudly, followed by me mam, and then everyone was laughing including Adrian and Christopher. Even today I don't know why, I can only guess that Chris was so happy to be leaving the Shoulder of Mutton, that he became hysterical and that his laughter became infectious.

The next morning the cleaner arrived;

If I hadn't known how to get to this place, I could have just followed the vomit. There's sick from the bottom of Oxenhope all the way up to here.

The previous afternoon, we had filled the delivery van and as we couldn't get everything in the van because of bad packing, the rest of our furniture and cases were left outside all night, piled up in the car park covered up, where they were left untouched. The furniture van arrived and we loaded the rest of our belongings. I said a tearful goodbye to the cleaner and walked outside to look once more across the hills and the reservoir.

I picked up the last of my bags and looked around at the Shoulder for the last time.

The day we moved into The Goats Head was the first time I had the chance to take a proper look around upstairs, as I had done in the two pubs before. Me mam loved it as soon as she saw it. The pub was built in a square shape with a courtyard in the centre and I was eager to explore everything around it, but first things first. The kitchen was the first port of call, so that we could make lunch and put the food away. It was quite a small kitchen that had little room to prepare food and as the landlady before us had been serving pub lunches I intended to carry on. I wondered how she had managed to cater for pub lunches in such a small space. In the corner of the room stood a pantry and really this was the first indication that there was something strange about to start. Me mam was putting food in the cupboard, while I passed everything to her, when at the same time we both jumped, but were unable to explain why. It wasn't that we had seen anything; it was just that something had startled both of us.

The bathroom was next to the kitchen along a small passageway. It was almost as big as the kitchen and because we had a large chest freezer, that we had no room for, we decided to put it in there for the time being, to keep what frozen food we had.

Margaret, a friend of mine who ran her own public house in Oxenhope, kindly offered to look after the bar to give us time to move in. This gave me the chance to explore this old building before the evening. It was a mysterious looking place with nooks and crannies everywhere. My mother was as excited as I was. Dad was helping Chris to unload the furniture van along with my sons, so Mam and I decided which room was to be whose. There were three corridors, one leading to the bathroom and kitchen, one to the lounge and two bedrooms and one that led to a bedroom at the top of the stairs. The one at the top of the stairs was set away from the rest of the rooms, so we decided that this would be Adrian's bedroom. It would mean he could play loud music without disturbing Christopher when he was watching television.

The lounge overlooked the front and side of the building, the side window overlooked the car park and beyond the car park was a recreation ground. The walls in the lounge bulged so much they made me laugh, the doorways were small and the thick walls weaved in and out. When we were in the bedroom that we had chosen for ourselves, we noticed another door there which I expected to be a walk in wardrobe or cupboard. I opened the door and was surprised to find it led into another large bedroom which was very spacious and had two windows at either side. It was sunny and warm in here and, unlike our room, this one overlooked the courtyard. The walls again were thick and bulging and because it had never been decorated, it was still possible to see the crumbling plaster. There seemed to be strange shapes in the wall, they looked like faces to me, but then this building was very old, how old I wasn't sure at first, but later I saw a plaque on the wall outside that had 1689 carved onto it.

To get to the courtyard we had to walk down the stairs and through the downstairs lounge and I found it a bit embarrassing at first. It seemed as if all the customers were eyeing us up. I said hello, but felt very self conscious even though they seemed friendly enough. I supposed I was in fact being judged and compared to the last landlady, just as in the previous pubs.

The courtyard was amazing. I felt so comfortable here. It was sealed off from the outside world altogether, the busy road outside ceased to exist, there were heavy wooden gates that reminded me of the gates they have on castles, and the gates were under an archway that reached up almost as high as the building. Huge stables stood to the right, where straight away in my mind's eye, I could picture the staff of the old inn, in days gone by, taking care of the travellers' horses. The barn had the original old beams and the windows were just narrow slits and I believe they could have been even earlier than the rest of the building. Although there was no straw or animals in the barn now, there was still that certain smell of olden times and I stood there picturing a scene of men lifting the straw with their pitchforks. The courtyard floor, which was originally cobbled stone, had been paved over, in recent times, with bricks and in a corner was a huge rock and I wondered how a rock as big as this could ever have got there and what it was used for. On the walls of the building were strong chains with rings. I guessed they must have been for tethering up the horses and I supposed that nothing much had changed over the years in the courtyard, it was like stepping back in time.

The back of the building was such a contrast to the front, as at the front of the building there was a very busy main road that led to the North. Streams of heavy wagons and cars stood revving up at the traffic lights making an awful noise. The hospital was just up the road and the ambulances often had to put their sirens on when approaching the lights, which were virtually outside our front door. In the back, the quietness was so welcoming. It was spring time when we moved in and a blackbird was perched on the roof, croaking and sounding angry. It was looking my way and I assumed it had a nest somewhere around here and wanted me to go out of the way while it took food for the young ones and so I went indoors.

Back inside the building, while still finding my way around, I found another small room the size of a closet, but the thing that intrigued me the most was that the closet was only about three foot high and three foot wide. It had been cut out of the wall for storage. I walked towards the kitchen to finish some unpacking and noticed that the wall dividing the kitchen from the bathroom was also very thick, in fact so thick that my mind was working overtime again and I began to wonder if there was an hidden room in there or perhaps a priest hole. I had read a really good book years ago about priest holes. A priest hole was the term given to a hiding place during the period when the Catholics were persecuted in England. By law, from the reign of Elizabeth I, in the middle and late sixteenth century, priests were not allowed to give Mass and if they did attempt to do so then it would mean imprisonment for High Treason and they could be tortured or even be killed. This meant that under these persecutory laws, the number of secret chambers and hiding places increased in the dwellings of Catholic families. Nicholas Owen, a Catholic martyr, built numerous priest holes. He was a carpenter and went under the name of 'Little John'. Owen built hiding places so well that even skilled carpenters could spend up to two weeks searching and still never find the priest holes. Owens had the ability to hide a room, in-between walls, disguising the entrance so no one would know it was there and he never told anyone else about these secret hiding places. He was not much bigger than a dwarf and always worked on his own, yet he managed to break through thick stonewalls, to make hiding places in the centre, and it is said that no one knows to this day how many he may have built. Some of the rooms that he built, from the inside, looked like proper churches with pews.

Not too far away, East Riddlesden Hall had secret hiding places. A priest hole was found in the fireplace and there was also a priest hole hidden in Ripley Castle in North Yorkshire. Priest holes could be anywhere, not just in mansions or castles and in 1691 a priest was hanged outside the door of a house where he had given mass, only a month earlier, in a secret room.

That evening I was very nervous, going down to the bar for the first time, knowing that all eyes were on us. It started to fill up very quickly as it always does when someone new takes over a pub, but at least I had my friend and barmaid, Lesley, who came from the Shoulder to work with me for a couple of nights and there was also another of my friend, Alison, who had more or less moved in with us, sleeping on the couch, and of course my son, Adrian, who helped out behind the bar.

There were quite a few men leaning on the bar and they that started to make conversation. It was early evening and a good time to relax and get to know a little about Steeton as a place.

One particular man had a beautiful collie dog. The man looked to be in his sixties and he had piercing blue eyes and smoked a pipe while resting his arm on the bar. My nervousness must have shown because he looked so sympathetic. He introduced himself as Tony and said to me;

There's no need to feel nervous lass, the folk are all right round here.

Well, it does seem a nice place. Are the regulars of a mixed age, or is it more for the younger generation?

Oh, we have all ages coming in here lass, but I'm just going to warn you now, although most folk are all right, as I said, be aware of these three men, they are nowt but bother.

He put his pint down and pointed to me with his pipe in his hand, his eyes looking right into mine;

Gera pen and write these names down. They'll try it on cos you're new and they will let you think they're all right, but they are nowt but trouble as I said. They want barring from't place, that lot, trouble they are, nowt but trouble.

I thought to myself; great, three thugs, what a good start. I reached for a pen and wrote the names down feeling a bit disheartened.

I asked a bloke, who was stood at the bar, one I had spoken to earlier, to let me know when these three came in without telling him why, although he did look at me with a puzzled look.

Each time a 'rough' looking customer came in I wondered if this could be one of them. Gradually it filled up with people, mostly men at first, but no thugs and I was beginning to relax a bit.

Two elderly men came in and joined another man, who had stood quietly on his own at the far end of the bar, he was also elderly. He also had a beautiful dog, a sheep dog, just as nice natured as the dog Tony had at the side of him. The two men ordered drinks and they were really nice polite gentlemen. One looked a bit like a sergeant major; he stood so upright with a handlebar moustache. The other gentleman looked as if he had just recovered from a stroke because he could only use his left arm. They both smiled at me as I went to take their order and they wished us all the best for the future and politely asked how we were getting on. I told them I was all right apart from being a bit nervous about the thugs I had been warned about, one of them looked very concerned and asked;

I can't think who you could mean; we have no thugs in Steeton,

I went to get the bit of paper I had written the names down on, it was on the shelf behind the bar now, as the bloke I had given it to had gone home.

I read the three names out;

He said they were called, Peter, Bernard and Jim.

One of the men almost choked on his beer and the other laughed so loudly;

Who told you that?

Pointing towards the one called Tony, I said;

The man stood over there with the pipe and the collie dog.

I looked over to Tony and it suddenly clicked, I looked at the three men and back over to him. He smiled, tipped his pipe and winked.

No! I don't believe it, who's who then?

These four elderly men were to become very good and funny friends of mine and I have wonderful memories of them.

The locals seemed really friendly as they came to the bar and wished us well and I was looking forward to getting to know them all. That was until a few women came in, the worse for wear from alcohol. One of them shouted out to some-one at the bar;

Which one is the landlord then?

One of the men stood at the bar said;

He's just gone upstairs to get some change, but this lovely lady here is the landlady.

The women looked at me, unsmiling and in a bitchy way;

We're not interested in the landlady; we're only interested in the landlord, we heard that he was dishy.

Although I felt annoyed, I quite calmly said;

Well, that's very unfortunate, ladies, my husband is particular, not peculiar. Now what would you like to order?

They looked a little stunned to know they hadn't upset me and politely ordered and paid for their drinks. I smiled at them sweetly, as they left the bar, and muttered under my breath, "Arse holes".

The evening went very well. The pub was packed full of people and we had four bar staff besides the two of us. It was a big change from what we had left behind, having more customers, and I felt really happy at the end of the evening.

When everyone had gone home we relaxed with Mam and Dad for a drink and I made us all some supper. We discussed the evening and then we all went to our rooms. My parents slept in Christopher's room, in twin beds, and Christopher slept on a camp bed on the floor in the same room. Adrian finally turned off his music, in his room and we all settled down.

I was surprised to find I couldn't sleep, especially with not having had much sleep for the last two or three days. My mind was racing with wonder. I was imagining priest holes with skeletons of people trapped from years ago. People unable to get out when the walls were knocked down around them, blocking them inside, waiting for some-one to come for them until they eventually starved to death. No-one would realise that they were behind the thick, heavy walls, trapped. The walls being as thick as they were could have meant that there was little air and coming out too early could result in torture and possibly death.

Not a good thought to be going to sleep on, but eventually I drifted off, dreaming of skeletons trapped inside walls, that lay there for centuries. Then, suddenly, I woke up to the sound of horses trotting. I was not dreaming, I was wide awake then. I sat up and still heard them. I lay awake and thought of the courtyard, perhaps ghostly spirits still came to rest here on their horses. Oh shit! My imagination was really beginning to worry me.

This went on for the first three nights, then I decided to tell me Mam, but I didn't get the chance, she told me first;

I didn't want to tell you this but for three nights I've heard horses trotting outside. The first night I thought that I was overtired and imagined it.

Oh my God, mam, so have I.

Unknown to us, Dad was stood in the doorway and overheard.

I heard it me self and I didn't say anything.

I told Chris what we had all heard and he said that he hadn't heard anything as usual, he was such a deep sleeper; I didn't want to ask the boys either, in case it worried them, but four days later Adrian came into the kitchen yawning;

I've hardly slept since we moved in here. I hear noises most of the night; the sounds are like horses trotting. I think it might be the pipes from the toilets downstairs.

Water pipes.

The trotting noises were from a leaking tap in the men's room downstairs and when that was fixed, the trotting stopped.

Truth be known I was a bit disappointed.

Our first Saturday afternoon was very busy. There were only the two of us working and we were rushed off our feet. This was the day I met Karen.

She made no effort to hide the fact that she was going to flirt with Chris. Karen had the shortest skirt on and the longest legs I had seen for years. She had a large smile which seemed to be permanent and was quite pretty, her hair was mid length and curly. I was a little unsure of Karen at first, but it wasn't long before I did find her to be a really nice, but weird person. Karen's husband, Mick, and his friend Des were also very friendly people and we all became firm friends during our time at the Goat's Head. We spent some very good and hilarious times with them. Mick was quite a good looking chap. He was very dark with piercing eyes like his father, Tony, had and he clearly liked his drink by the size of his belly. Des, on the other hand, was of much smaller build, even though he also drank large amounts of beer. He was always laughing and he didn't try to hide the fact that he had a 'thing' about Karen. Mick ordered another beer and asked;

What made you want to come to Steeton from Oxenhope then?

Chris explained to them that he preferred a pub that had a taproom because he had liked the first pub we were in and the pub games. I joined in the conversation and told them about coming here once to a pool match and about my vision;

I just knew that I would be behind the bar of this pub, I saw myself standing there.

I also told them about the day that we came to view the pub and how depressing it had looked at that time of the year and that I had started to wonder if we had made the right choice. I told them about my being a little upset on the way home, but how I loved it here now. Mick placed his drink on the bar and told me;

I remember that day you came to look at the pub. I was playing darts in the taproom and was just about to throw a dart. I heard the door open, you walked in through the door and I saw this beautiful woman, dressed in a long fitted black dress and wearing large black sun glasses, just glide pass me.

This was all said in front of Karen and she slapped him straight across the face. They then carried on as if nothing had happened and she continued to smile and flirt with Chris, in a harmless way, I would say. I really liked these people. They were good company and Chris also liked them. In fact he seemed much more at home here.

Karen said to me one day;

Have you heard of the smarty trail Maggie?

No, what's a smarty trail?

Oh, it's very good. You buy lots of smarties and put them on the floor starting a trail that leads to the bedroom.

Why?

Because young boys love smarties and they follow the trail into the bedroom.

Anytime a young lad walked into the pub, she would shout;

Maggie, do you have any smarties behind the bar?

The following Saturday Mick came in on his own and Karen came a little later with a box under her arm. Mick ordered a drink for her and asked what was in the box;

It's an inflatable castle for Stephen.

Stephen was their two year old son and Mick looked again at the box and then at Karen;

A castle? Oh yeah. And who's going to blow that up then. Me I expect.

Karen got very angry and replied;

You don't have to blow it up, clever dick, it's inflatable.

I have to say that I felt sorry for Karen not understanding why everyone had laughed at her statement.

To try and get to know the locals better we decided to have on a treasure hunt, finishing off with a disco and free buffet. We toured around the area to find clues that were fair to everyone. We went every day for a week with Des, Mick's friend. He knew the place really well through living there all his life. The clues were to be in country areas to stop cars from littering the main roads. As we were finishing clearing up after lunch time, ready to set off, I said to Chris;

I had a dream where I was on a narrow country lane with lots of bends. I was in the back seat and you were driving and Des was sat next to you. Then the car went round a bend so fast that it hit a mother pushing a baby in a pram. The lane was in the middle of nowhere and the sudden jolt, as we hit the mother and child, woke me up.

Des arrived and we climbed into the car with our writing pads and set off. Des was pointing places out to us when I immediately recognised this lane from my dream and knew Chris was driving too fast. I shouted to him to slow down, as there was a bad corner here and there might be someone pushing a pram. Surprisingly, he listened and slowed down. Just around the bend, in the middle of nowhere, with no houses anywhere that could be seen from the road, was a mother pushing a pram. We would certainly have hit her, if we had been going faster.

Stranger still, the women smiled straight at me and later in the evening something made me think of that incident. The pram was very old fashioned, it was an old type carriage pram, and although I could not say what clothes the woman was wearing, I remembered that she had a hat on. Had this accident happened in the past? A tragic accident on that narrow lane, I don't know but both Chris and Des saw her and asked how I could possibly have seen her from around the corner, especially as I was travelling in the back of the car. I thought this might be worth looking into later.

The atmosphere was very good after the treasure hunt that evening. The place was packed out, I had made a really good buffet and people were getting stuck in eating and chatting. As I was going around with my video camera, all I could hear was talk of the treasure hunt. Someone accused the winners of turning the signs round, and there were light hearted disputes, but it was a fantastic day and the conversations continued the next night.

After a few weeks, it was getting too much for the staff that travelled from Oxenhope to work for us and although I was sorry to see them go, I did understand. This meant interviewing new staff to work for us and so I asked some of the locals. This was how I met Rose. She was a character, she was very funny and she never failed to crack a few jokes every time I saw her. She was very small and frail looking and struggled to breath. She had to use an inhaler because she had something wrong with her chest, but oh she was so funny. I loved working with Rose and we became very good friends. Rose lived across the street and was a very independent woman who lived with her teenage daughter. She worked as a cleaner during the day for four different people and at night she now worked, as a barmaid, for us, at The Goat. This hard work was all because her dream was to have her own Triumph TR7, a two seater sports car. Rose was always having trouble with that car but wouldn't change it for anything.

There was never a dull moment with Rose and as she was very popular with the locals, we were lucky to have her with us. Although she was independent, she was forever looking for Mr Right. Rose joined dating agencies and told me of the dates she had been on and I was always concerned about her going to these 'out of the way' places to meet them. Sometimes they were as far as Ilkley Moor, in the middle of dark country lanes, but she was happy as she was and she told me funny things that had happened, on these meetings, and we would laugh.

Early one morning, around seven, we were still in bed when Rose shouted up to us;

Maggie, Maggie, can I borrow your Chris for a jump?

A what?

A jump. I need a jump Maggie. Get him up, and then he can jump me?

Rose, how did you get in? Have you been here all night or what?

No, silly bugger, cleaner let me in. Tell Chris I want him quick, I need a jump, or I'll be late for work.

Chris went down to see her and it turned out that her car wouldn't start, so she needed Chris to jumpstart it, as she was late for work.

Saturday afternoons were my favourite time with the locals. It was also a busy day, especially when we were asked to make pie and peas for the local football team. I was rushed off my feet with running up and down stairs from the kitchen. It was easier to carry the dishes in twos than carry a lot on a tray more slowly and carefully. Pie and peas were very popular on a Saturday and with help from Rose and the extra large oven and pans, it all ran very smoothly, until one day that is;

Rose I've lost that bracelet that Chris bought me last week, I can't find it anywhere. I've looked in the bedroom, bathroom and all over the place.

When did you last see it?

An hour ago or more, on my arm.

I knew Rose was thinking the same as me;

You must have it dropped in the peas. That pan is like a witch's cauldron.

Oh no, you don't think it's in someone's dish do you? It's only a small delicate thing.

Check the bloody pan first before thinking the worst and going around asking if anyone has eaten your bracelet.

I stirred the pan of peas and it wasn't in there.

Well, you know what that means Maggie; you'll have to go down and ask all the customers from the last batch that went out.

Oh God, Rose, I can't do that. You go and ask.

No way, you go. It's your bloody bracelet.

You go; you're braver than me Rose.

Bugger off.

Just wait 'til you want me to do somat for you.

I had no choice than to go downstairs and explain to the footballers what had happened. At the second table that I went to, a woman smiled at me and said;

Is it a white gold bracelet that has a twist to it?

Yes. Oh I am sorry, but it must have fallen off in the peas because it's a really big pan. I really am sorry, the safety catch must have broken and………

Oh, it wasn't in the peas love, it's on your arm.

I was puzzled at what she had said. I looked on my arm and it was there, it must have ridden up with my sleeve and hidden under the folds of the material.

I walked back upstairs with a glum face and told Rose that someone nearly choked on it, before telling her the truth. Her face was a picture.

I did so much running up and down those stairs it was no wonder that I was so slim, especially on Saturday afternoon. However, we also had a keep fit class at the pub, held before the evening opening, and I ran it myself as I had at the Shoulder. There were usually half a dozen regulars, including Karen who was the fittest of all. Sometimes we might have a few more that came and we did the Jane Fonda workout which was really energetic. Talk about no pain, no gain, it was a full hour of intensive training. It was great because I could eat and drink without ever gaining weight.

Because the locals had enjoyed the treasure hunt, we thought we would have a golden oldies night, where we could dress in 1950/1960s clothes. I loved to dress up and dressed in a teeny bopper outfit with a net underskirt and flared skirt, tight cardigan, a little neck scarf and white pumps and socks with my hair swept into a ponytail. Alison wore a similar outfit with polka dots and we thought we looked great. The old songs went down really well and it soon started to fill up with customers of all ages, including my friends that I had made on the first night, Tony, Bernard, Jim and Peter, (the thugs). One of our customers, Jack, would always sit in the corner singing along to the music. Jack was always in trouble, a bit of a villain really who made me think that he was the missing link between Arthur Daley and Del Boy. At first Chris took a liking to him, regardless of what people had told him perhaps because he reminded him of my cousin Billy from the Woodmoor. Jack was funny and made Chris laugh, but this quickly changed when he realised that Jack couldn't be trusted. He would sit in the corner with his pint and cigarettes and he usually wore a pin striped suit and tie. He looked a perfect gentleman in every sense, but was disliked by some people because of the bad deeds he had done in the past, including to his own family. He flitted about, living in different places and at one time moved into his mother's garden shed. That's how bad things were for him and eventually he was thrown out of there. I really liked Jack, he was so funny and in different circumstances he would have made a right character in television because he was naturally quick with the answers, often when being verbally attacked. Nothing fazed him. I have seen people really have a go at him, insult him and threaten him but he would always smile and speak to them later as if nothing had happened. It was very hard to dislike Jack. He was also a terrible flirt with the ladies, including myself;

Hey up Jack are you all right? I see you have your Al Capone suit on. Did you get mixed up about the era tonight? It's a 50s and 60s night, not a Bugsy Malone night.

Very funny Maggie and there's me coming in just to see you my darling.

Jack, are they Chris's cigs you're smoking? He'll go mad.

Only had a couple, he won't miss them.

Chris misses nothing Jack. Get that packet of cigs put back behind the counter before he gets back....is that his pint as well?

Oops, I thought it was mine.

You'll never change Jack.

Would you really want me to change, Maggie my love.

Chris walked behind the bar and opened his packet of cigarettes and I quickly went on to serve a customer that was waiting.

I turned around to see Jack smiling at Chris, and then I saw Chris offer him a cigarette. Jack looked over to me and winked.

Chapter Thirteen

The weather was starting to get warmer and I sat in the garden after closing one Sunday afternoon. I lay back on the chair looking up at the white fluffy clouds when something caught my eye; it was the window that had cobwebs on it. I had seen this window before, obviously, when I had been outside, but I was still baffled as to which room it was in as there weren't any cobwebs on any of the other windows. A cloud had reflected on the glass and it almost looked as if someone was moving inside. A big gust of wind startled me and I had a strange feeling of being watched. The courtyard felt alive with ghosts from the past and I loved being out there on my own. I would look at the barn and the stables and try to bring it alive by picturing the scene inside my head. What it would have been like in the 1800s? After being lost in time for a while, I picked my empty cup up from the floor and I made my way inside and went upstairs. The sun shone brightly as soon as I opened the door to the bedroom adjoining our bedroom. It was warm and pleasant, having windows on both sides, and I would have loved to have had a lounge like this. How strange to have to walk through one bedroom to get to another. It surely must have been a bedroom at one time, although it must have been a very long time ago because it looked as if it had never been decorated. My son, Christopher, and stepson, Russell, had made a makeshift swing from the rafters. The room was well lit during the day, but during the evening it was very eerie. The strange looking faces on walls looked as if they were following me and I swear I heard noises from that room during the night. I wouldn't like to sleep in there on a night, but that was probably because it was just a bare room without wall covering and a carpet on the floor. I wondered where the other window was that could be seen from outside. There certainly wasn't another door in the room, apart from the one I had come through.

Early evening I went back down to the courtyard to see just where the window should have been. Some of the locals were sat in the courtyard now that the sun was shining and I asked what the rock was for. One of men said;

Oh yeah, they used to hang witches here you know. You've heard of the Lancashire witches haven't you? There was a right old witch hunt around these parts.

He finished his pint and said "see you later", just as I had got over the shock and wanted to hear more. Later, it was a quiet night and I was asking some of the locals about the witches and, of course, they all had something to say on the matter;

Have you been down the other cellar yet?

There were two cellars with separate doors opposite each other. One was the cellar for the beer barrels, which I had been down, but I had not been down the one opposite and, of course, I had to have a look now. The steps were narrow and it was dark and dingy. It was only a very small cellar with uneven well worn steep steps that were a little tricky to walk down. Hanging from the walls were tools, tools that I had never seen before. Long handles with spikes, they were certainly strange looking things. A voice behind me suddenly made me jump;

These were the tools they used to torture witches with before they hung them in the courtyard.

Another customer nodded;

That's right, they used to prick them with these instruments and if they bled they were innocent but if they didn't bleed they were found guilty and then hung.

Chris shook his head in disbelief when I told him what they had said;

Take no notice of them; they're just making it all up. They were probably tools used for farming. I can't believe you fell for talk of witches being hung in the courtyard. The rock was used for people to climb on and off horses.

Well, I'm not convinced, Chris. Pendle isn't far from here and it is notorious for witches and anyway why do they call it The Goat's Head?

I don't know. Go on then, why do they call it The Goats Head?

I don't know why they call it The Goats Head, but I know it is associated with devil worship and witchcraft. You would have thought that if it had something to do with farming, then it would be its whole body and be called The Goat.

But it would still be a goat, whether it was a head or a whole body. I give up. I'm off down to the cellar to change a barrel and just hope I don't trip over a dead witch on my way.

I was determined to find more information about the Pendle Witches and the goat's head symbol and that evening I asked for directions to Pendle with the intention of persuading Chris to go this Sunday with Mam and Dad.

It'll be a nice day out and me mam would love it there. They'll be going home in a few days and they say it's really fantastic scenery and you can go to the top of Pendle Hill.

Not in a car, you can't.

Well part of the way I think you can, and there's a shop there that has bits and pieces that have been dug up from the time the witches lived there, all behind a glass case, and they sell books and have witches hanging from the ceiling and.....

For God's sake we'll go, just shurrup about it. You're giving me a headache.

That's good; I'll go and tell me mam then.

Because the weather wasn't too great, we decided to leave Pendle until the next time my parents came up to visit, so in the meantime I thought I would check up on the goat's head symbol. I went to the local library and took a few books home and I have to say that checking the books out at the desk was a little embarrassing and hoped the girl behind the desk didn't think I was a devil worshiper. I settled down to read them after lunch and wished that I hadn't. They scared me to death and I was eager to get them out of the place and back to the library.

I was shocked to see the goat was linked to witchcraft. The goat connection may be even more significant than the cat, or so it seems, and it goes back to antiquity. A powerful clan in ancient Greece, the Palentids, claimed they were originally descended from a sacred goat and the horned and hoofed Greek goat-god, Pan, is one of the most important entities of witchcraft. Earlier, Thor, the Norse god, was worshipped before the other gods of Valhalla. Some say he existed as early as the stone-age and they believed that Thor drove a great chariot, pulled by two giant powerful goats, symbolizing thunder and lightning. Medieval legends say that the Devil created the goat. Satan himself often appeared with goat's horns, and sometimes changed his shape completely into a goat. All of a sudden, there was a very loud bang, the sound of thunder and it really frightened me. I thought that I had brought something back from the dead, but it was the draymen delivering beer. I decided not to bother reading any more of the books and I wished that I hadn't read the few pages I had read.

I was too busy to think about the books and the witches at the time. I was now looking into priest holes and wondering why that room was closed off. God knows what I would find in there, skeletons huddled together holding a prayer book, a tabernacle or perhaps tools to torture witches or even old coins or jewellery. I really had to find out why the room with the window was shut off, but breaking through the wall was something I had to be concerned about; I was already in trouble for putting a hole through the small cupboard I had found earlier, the tiny cupboard that was only about three foot square. Christopher had helped me chisel through the thick plaster to see if there was a hiding place behind the wall, but it had obviously been put there to store crockery for catering. Chris was not too happy having to plaster it back up again. He knew nothing of what I was about to do now, but I was too excited to think about the consequences at this point.

After lunch and after I had cleared the tables, I left Chris downstairs with the few remaining customers. I went into the spare room with Christopher and started to tap the wall adjoining the room where the extra window must have been and all the time I was tapping, I was hoping there was nothing too sinister in there, but at the same time, if there wasn't then I would be disappointed. We soon found a hollow sound and immediately started to attack it with a hammer; luckily it was only plaster board and easily replaced which was just as well. When we had made a hole, I peeked through and saw it was a small room. I made the hole a little bigger and, while Christopher stood back watching, I stuck my leg through to the other room and yelled;

Christopher, help, someone's pulling my leg.

Then before I frightened Christopher too much, I said;

Just like I'm pulling yours.

He was not amused, but then he was used to having a dotty mother.

We had made the hole just big enough to be able to climb through it and we realised that the floor on the other side had some missing floor boards and that it was quite a drop to the courtyard down below. This would probably be the only reason they had sealed it off. It was a room that was over the gates and must have been considered dangerous. On further investigation, we found that it wasn't really that dangerous, it only needed repairing, and so we sorted the floor out and it became a den for Christopher and my stepson, Russell, where they put up a tent. However, after much argument, I drew the line at letting them sleep in there at night. Chris was neither mad nor surprised.

That evening I was surprised to see some of the locals had come to see us from The Shoulder of Mutton;

Hello, it's so nice to see you again, I was only thinking about you yesterday.

Hiya Maggie, are you settling in all right, here in Steeton?

Lovely, nice village and nice people, but I do miss you lot. I hear that the new people have left The Shoulder already.

Well, let's face it Maggie, you're a hard act to follow.

Really, that's nice of you to say so.

After a few drinks and hearing the latest news from Oxenhope, we reminisced of the nights in The Shoulder and the laughs that we had and, of course, the ghostly tales;

Remember when I blew in your ear and you thought it was a ghost. God that was so funny.

You scared the bloody daylights out of me. Go on then, tell us, have you seen any ghosts here yet?

Not as yet, but I can 'feel' things sometimes, especially as the pub is so old. There's a plaque in the courtyard that says 1689, so it's pretty old. Some locals say the outside buildings are older still. Anyway, did you hear that I found a dead body? Well, not really a body, but a skeleton. The police were involved and everything. It should be in the papers this week, I was told.

I pictured the headlines in my head "Landlady finds missing person in cupboard".

A skeleton. Maggie? You're joking.

No, honestly, I had been looking around the place, looking at all the little nooks and crannies, when I thought that I would have a look at the barn and the stables. You know what I'm like for exploring. In the stables, I found an old cupboard that was locked. After searching all over the place for a key, without any luck, I decided to force it open. The musty smell was horrible as I opened the door, because it had been locked for all those years. I almost fell backwards with shock when I saw a skeleton crouched in there.

A skeleton? I would have died.

You can say that again, I nearly did. In fact, I didn't scream because my mouth had completely gone dry and, at first, I thought it was a pretend one that someone had put there as a joke, but ugh, the smell. I don't know if you have ever seen a skeleton, a real one that is, but this one had long scraggy hair and holes where its eyes should have been and a big hole in the middle of its face where the nose was. Oh yeah, and its jaw was hanging and showing the teeth. I was amazed at the size of its teeth and isn't it funny that a skeleton always looks as if it's smiling at you.

How can you laugh at something like that?

I can now, but I wasn't laughing at the time.

Do they know who it was?

Yes, he was a local. Hang on a sec while I serve this gentleman.

I slowly walked back to the astonished looking group, who were waiting to hear more;

He actually had identification on him; it was on a medallion around his neck.

You mean the skeleton had his name on the medallion? My God how lucky was that.

Who was it, do you know yet? Was it someone that lived in Steeton?

Yes, the medallion read; Nick Ryan, hide and seek champion of Steeton 1950.

I'm surprised they didn't lynch me. It had taken some of them a few minutes to realise that it was a joke.

They fell about laughing, especially when I told them what I had done to Christopher with the leg pulling.

You're weird Maggie, we never know whether you're joking or not.

Another drink lads?

We do miss you though and we still talk about you all the time. We're always talking of the times we daren't walk home late at night past the graveyard, after you used to scare the living daylights out of us. One night James went home earlier than us and hid in the entrance to the graveyard and made a groaning sound. You had been telling us that strange things happen when there's a full moon and we were walking down looking up at the moon when we heard a noise coming from the graveyard, a groaning sound. You should have been there Maggie, it was so funny. We ran back towards The Shoulder ready to bang down your door before we heard this laughter and realised it was him making the sound.

We all burst out laughing again and I missed those nights at the Shoulder;

That was the night we were telling you of a crazy woman's ghost that used to run naked down Leeming screaming her lover's name. Do you remember? Her parents stopped her from going out with a soldier and she went crazy.

Yeah, you scared me a bit there because I thought I heard her one night, but I think it was the wind coming down the pipes. I was sure she was calling out "Alfred..."

How did you know his name? We didn't tell you. If you remember, we had forgotten it. Did you really hear his name?

I laughed and told them that Alison had told me.

I loved The Shoulder and although I liked the cosiness of those nights with the few that came in during the winter months, we were really struggling with money. We tried everything to bring in the customers. I would say I made the best friends that I ever had there, both male and female.

Remember the time when that male stripper didn't turn up for the hen night and the ladies were all disappointed?

My God, I certainly do.

We had a group of women in early doors that were on a hen night and we had booked a male stripper for an hour before the pub got too busy. The male stripper didn't turn up, leaving the girls disappointed, and as a joke Chris said that he would pay £30 to any man who would do a strip. We never expected to get an offer, but one of the young local farmers who was in with his mates, offered to strip, of course, he was encouraged quite a lot by his mates. The crowd was going mad clapping their hands and stamping their feet and they cheered loudly as he climbed on stage, although we did have every intention of stopping him before he took his boxer shorts off. It turned out to be such a laugh, because he was so clumsy. They shouted and screamed as he started taking off his big farming boots, after struggling with his laces, followed by two pairs of long woollen socks. He kept toppling over as he lost his balance. He slowly took off his shirt and he had a thermal vest on which looked to be buttoned to his shorts. This caused loads of laughter and shouting for more, as he unfastened one button after another. Then he slowly started to unfasten his trousers and pull them down. The place was in uproar when he revealed his thermal vest had been buttoned to thermal leggings, which also had buttons on both sides and a baggy backside that hung down. The laughter didn't end there; as he struggled to get his leg out of his trousers, he lost his balance and fell down again. At this point we stopped him, to jeering from the crowd, and we paid him £50 instead of the £30 for his courage and the laughs that he had given us all. After all it had been going to cost £100 for the stripper anyway, which couldn't possibly have been as funny as him. The girls were having a great time and the atmosphere was electric. He later told us that he had enjoyed it and thought of doing it for a living after that. I told him that it wasn't the stripping, but more of a comedy act with all the warm clothing that he had had on. I was still laughing to myself after my old friends had gone home and hoped they would keep in touch.

Across from the pub was a memorial garden where Steeton Beck flows in a stone lined channel across the land where the old corn mill and malt house used to stand. These had all been demolished leaving a beautiful area which contained many tall, mature trees and grassy areas which surrounded the village war memorial, a tribute to the men of the village who had died in the two world wars.

Whilst sitting in these beautiful surroundings, I made a decision to look into the history of the area as I had done at the other two pubs. I was interested to find that for hundreds of years Steeton had been a stopping off point on the route down the Aire Valley, being situated only a couple of miles from Glusburn where the hillsides become less steep and a pass forms through the Pennine mountains, leading to the West and Lancashire.

Taking this pass leads a traveller through Cowling and Laneshaw Bridge, a small village near to Wycoller, where we had been before and leads onto Colne and Barrowford which are dwarfed by the imposing Pendle Hill, an area I intended to visit later.

Ignoring this pass and carrying on up the valley, brings you to Skipton, a major junction for trade and people travelling from York and Harrogate on their way to Preston and Lancaster in the west and Kendal and the Lake District lying further up in the north west.

Roman legions must have travelled through and possibly stayed in this area, as for many years the original road from Keighley, further down the valley, followed the route of a Roman road known in modern times as Hollins Lane which becomes Hollins Bank Lane as it descends past Hawkcliffe Woods and into the village. What a sight it must have been to see the Roman soldiers marching along, in columns with their standards held high and their helmets, armour and swords glistening in the sunlight.

They must have always been alert for an ambush or attack from the Celtic people, who lived there before the Romans conquered them and it must have been at this time that some Roman and Iron Age coins were lost, only to be found in the twentieth century, along with a Bronze Age axe.

It is difficult to say when the actual village of Steeton was first formed, but it was certainly a thriving community in 1086 when the Doomsday Book was compiled. At that time, the village was called Stiverton, which literally meant Stephen's town, and had been under the control of a Saxon called Gamelbar, a supporter of King Harold who was killed by an arrow in his eye during the Battle of Hastings in 1066. This part of Yorkshire must have been very important as, after the battle of Hastings, when William the Conqueror became King of England; land was taken away from the Saxons and given to the Normans in payment for services rendered, during the new King's military campaign.

Gilbert Tyson carried William's standard during the Battle of Hastings and would, therefore, have been almost shoulder to shoulder with him at the height of the fighting. These lands in Airedale, which included Steeton, were payment for loyally serving the King and it seems strange that when William died and his son Rufus came to the throne, the Tyson family took the side of a failed rebellion against King Rufus and lost the land they had been given.

The land was granted to the Percy family, who were to own the land for the next four hundred years and I found it surprising that the 1379 poll tax records showed the population as being only fifty nine people, comprising twenty one married couples and seventeen single inhabitants, who were probably the children of the families. What a marked contrast to the size of the population in the 1980s when there were approximately three thousand five hundred people living in the area.

To the north of Steeton flows the River Aire which had to be crossed by a ford or a small footbridge, if you wanted to travel to Silsden and beyond. This could be a treacherous journey as the valley floor was a flood plain and could become extremely waterlogged and boggy. Indeed, in later years when the railway and canal were built, the watershed proved to be a large stumbling block causing many construction difficulties.

To the south of Steeton, lie the steep hillsides that divide Airedale from the moors of Keighley and lead through Whitley Head, Redcar and on to Laycock, Oakworth and Haworth. Steeton Beck tumbles down this steep hillside, travelling through Whitley Head into the village and it is alongside this beck that we find the remains of the original corn mill and later textile and bobbin mills, which used the power of the beck to drive their water wheels. Many of the houses built in the mid nineteenth century remain today and are very popular with residents who wish to convert them into modern dwellings.

In the nineteenth century the major influences that changed the shape of the village, were the building of a new stone bridge over the river, the new railway station that gave access to the steam trains which could take you to anywhere in the country and the building of the new road between Eastburn and Keighley, which moved the focal point of the village away from the original High Street and created the two now familiar pubs, The Goat's Head and The Old Star.

Coming back to the present, the sun was shining and I hoped that this would be a good summer, although this was a much busier pub and I didn't have as much time to explore as I had had at Oxenhope. I was doing pub lunches and the morning would be spent buying fresh bread and salads from the village and after lunch I had to clean the kitchen down and put everything away. After everything was clean and tidy, I sat in the courtyard drinking coffee and soaking in the silence when I caught sight of something moving on the ground, only ants I thought. June was my most favourite month of the year, not only because the days were longer, but I knew we still had July, August and September left to look forward to.

I noticed a couple of ants beneath my feet and then realised that there were quite a lot of them scurrying about in different directions. I couldn't help but watch them as they rushed about as if on a mission. I really knew nothing of ants, but was intrigued as to where they were going. I went inside to get a magnifying glass to see them closer up and knelt down on the floor. They seemed to run around for a while as if they were looking for something, they would turn around and go over the same path and I wondered if they were they looking for food or their home. One ant looked as if it was carrying another ant on its back and another looked like it was carrying one in its mouth, mmmm a baby ant perhaps. The one carrying the larger ant on its back dropped it and was running all around this unmoving ant for ages and I wondered if the ant he had dropped had died and it was running around grieving or just because it couldn't carry it anymore and didn't know what to do. It seemed a very long time until it went off in one direction. I followed it all the time with my magnifying glass and then it returned to the 'dead' ant with another ant. They both started running around it until they went off, out of sight, leaving the dead ant there. I had just eaten a biscuit and one ant picked up a tiny piece of crumb. It carried the crumb around for ages trying to find somewhere to hide it, I think, or perhaps it was taking it home to its little baby ants. The poor ant kept trying to carry the crumb of biscuit, but then finally put it down for a rest. Along came another ant from a different place and took the crumb away from the one that had carried it around, even after all that work it had put in. Although, I liked to be in the courtyard during the day, I was scared of going out there in the dark, especially as a bat had hit me on the head the first night, but not only that, the buildings looked even older and I felt the place come alive with ghosts. I stood up and stamped on the ant that pinched the crumb and went inside to be greeted by Gyp wanting to go for a walk.

Chapter Fourteen

There were some beautiful dogs that came into The Goat's Head with their owners; one man had a dog that looked just like 'Lassie', from the television series in the sixties. We had two dogs when we moved into The Goat, a small mongrel, Gypsy, that we had had for six years and a little dachshund called Misty. Gypsy was Gypsy by name and Gypsy by nature. She was always roaming off somewhere and just before we left The Shoulder of Mutton, she had had six puppies and I had sat up with her all night. They were beautiful pups and in no time at all we managed to find good homes for them. I was looking out of the window one day, annoyed to find she was out again, and saw her lowering herself to allow the smallest Jack Russell to mount her. I rushed outside, but it was too late and we found out later that she was having pups again, another six in fact. The trouble is, when a dog has pups, it's very hard to let them go, because she has to feed them for the first six weeks and I was hanging on to make sure that they had good homes to go to. In the meantime Chris had decided he wanted a 'Man' type dog, that he could go shooting with;

I'm all right going shooting with THEM, everyone will laugh at me. I want a proper dog, a man's dog.

But we already have eight dogs in there. Can't you wait while I find homes for them?

But no, Chris wanted a dog and he wanted one now. He came back the day after with a Doberman, a male dog that had balls hanging between its legs that could be seen quite clearly from the back and when he walked his balls moved and looked bigger still. They were ugly and it looked like he was walking with his legs open to make room for them.

What are we going to do with his balls, Chris? They look disgusting. Can't they be lifted or something? Do they have to be on show and what if he licks them? I've heard of that before and I wouldn't be able to eat if he were in the same room.

It's a dog, not a bitch, and that's how they are.

Well couldn't you have bought a bitch or a dog with long hair to cover its balls?

The dog sensed we were discussing him and let out a big sigh. He was only young and we named him Caesar. The people who had raised him had let him lie on the settee, so he just climbed up and stretched out. I was furious;

Get down off there Caesar, this minute.

Chris tried to get him off the settee, but he wouldn't budge. He just snarled at us.

It's because he's used to it. The owners had a blanket on the settee for the dogs and he was on the settee when I walked in the room.

Used to it or not, he is not lying on the settee.

The dog looked at me and we stared eye to eye before I eventually looked away because he wasn't going to give in first. I put on a very strong voice;

Down Caesar, down off there. Now Caesar, I mean it.

He stared right into my eyes again as I went to pull him off and gave a deep growl. I shot back.

Chris, I am not putting up with this. I am not sharing a settee with that bloody dog. Do something.

It took a while to persuade the dog to get off the settee and he marched out of the room. Chris said we could train him because he was only six months old.

Six months? That means he has had six months of doing what he wants. He has to go back, Chris.

I stormed off to the bedroom only to find him stretched out on the bed and before I said anything, he growled at me. He hated me.

It took quite a lot of work to stop him sleeping on the furniture, through bribing him and buying him a large, cosy bed of his own. Even worse however, within a short space of time we found he just farted all of the time and they were both noisy and smelly.

So, now we had nine dogs. Then one evening a man brought a lovely greyhound into the pub. I immediately went over to the dog and stroked her because she looked so sad and, as I gently bent down to her, she looked at me in such a sweet way.

Oh she's lovely. Is she yours?

Well, she was. I'm just about to take her to top of moors to shoot her.

Shoot her! But why, what has she done?

She's a greyhound. She races and makes me money. Well, she used to, but now she's stopped winning, so she's no good to me and no one would want a greyhound for a pet.

Well I would. How could you shoot her? She's lovely.

You can have her then, save me a job.

Her name was Tess and now we had ten dogs.

Chris never took much to dogs, even the Doberman that he had wanted to take shooting, and he never had, but he hated the little dachshund, mostly because she wouldn't go out in the rain and she always did her business inside. In fact, sometimes she would go outside and still do her business inside. We would have to clear up after her daily, or should I say, I had to clear up. Once when Chris walked into the kitchen in his bare feet, he stood on some poo and it squelched up through all of his toes. He went mad, shouting, hopping and swearing, chasing her into the lounge. Misty came running to me and I hid her behind the settee where she stayed quietly until he went for a shower, I laughed my head off until I realised I had to clean it up by following his footmarks. It was bad enough cleaning it from one spot, but now there was a trail of poo all along the route from the lounge to the kitchen and then to the bathroom. Chris did not clean dog mess up.

A few of the pups had gone to new homes now and I thought it was time to take Caesar for a walk to the park. I must have looked a sight. He pulled like hell, on the lead, while I held on for all my life with my heels digging into the ground and my body bent backwards trying to hold him back. A bus passed by and I knew that someone from the pub would have been on that bus. I finally managed to get him into the park and let him run around, as I had always done with the other two dogs and then I would clean up after them. The stupid dog would not come back. He ran away every time I got near to him. I pretended that I didn't care and turned my back. He would then nudge me and run off again. This went on for an hour. I didn't dare leave him there, but I couldn't catch him and neither could I get help from anyone because I couldn't get in touch. I think that eventually he tired himself out and came up to me;

Piss off, you horrible creature. You can wait for me now.

I ignored him and he kept nudging me and sitting down until I forgave him.

Chris was waiting outside the front door;

Where have you been? You've been gone ages. Did you go up to the wood?

No, I've been trying to catch your stupid, undisciplined, nasty natured dog for an hour. You can take him next time.

The thing was, I was getting to like Caesar. He was behaving a bit better inside now and had stopped bullying the other dogs, who were so terrified of him that I had had to let Gyp and the pups sleep in another room, where we kept the dryer and ironing board. Soon the pups had all gone, so now we had just the four dogs. The greyhound was such a sweet dog and still very young. How could they do this to dogs just because they had stopped earning money? I was out with her one day in the courtyard. She was a really well behaved dog, but when I rubbed her ears, she winced back and yelped, I knew she was in pain, I calmly pulled her towards me to take a look and a horrible thing was wriggling half in and half out of her skin near her ear. I immediately bundled her into the car and took her down into town to the vet who said it was a 'tick'. I had never heard of a 'tick' before but apparently they come from sheep and deer. Apart from being blood suckers, once a tick latches onto the skin, it not only sucks the blood, it also regurgitates some of its stomach contents into the site of the bite, causing severe infection. The vet went on to say;

Humans can get them as well as dogs and other animals. They can cause Lyme disease and the symptoms are very similar to influenza. It starts with a rash at the location of the bite and a few days later, you will feel tiredness, fever, headache, muscle and joint pain and swollen lymph nodes.

No wonder the poor dog had trouble running.

The vet took the horrible parasite out and gave Tess some pills for the infection and asked how old she was. I explained to him what had happened.

This greyhound would have cost a lot of money; she has a stamp here in her ear. She's an Irish greyhound.

On the way home I was wondering how many people thought they had a dose of flu when all the time there was a horrible parasite sucking away at their blood and putting toxins into their body.

It was like having a different dog after only two days. I took Tess to the park and she shot round the field in seconds. I have never known anything move so fast in all my life, she was so full of energy and even more affectionate than ever. However, I did realise that Tess needed more exercise than I could give her and I didn't know what to do. There was no way I was going to say anything about the tick to the man who brought her in, he might have wanted her back now it was gone and Tess was able to run at that speed. Tess would come down to the bar during the week when it was quiet and just lay peacefully where she could see us. Once when a couple that we knew very well came in, they started to stroke her and thought she was lovely. I told them of the situation and they said that they lived in a place that was ideal for dogs, which I already knew, and that they also had time to give her the exercise that she so badly needed. I knew they were a genuine couple and, although I was reluctant to let her go, I knew she would be well cared for with them and that I would still be able to see her. Tess came into the pub often after leaving us and I was pleased to see that the couple absolutely adored her.

Chris decided to take Caesar for a walk one evening after the pub closed. I had already been out with him, but as I would not let him off his lead anymore, Chris insisted that he needed a good run.

I'll take him then and let him have a good run. He's a lot better behaved now, so we won't be long.

If you let him off the lead, you won't get him back on.

Course I will.

OK then. I'm going up to bed now.

I went to bed but after about an hour he still wasn't back. I looked out of the window and could hear him whistling for the dog and I knew what had happened. I got dressed again and walked down to the park. It was so dark that I couldn't see or hear anything at first and I couldn't see Chris anywhere. Then when my eyes adjusted, I saw a figure crouched down near the fence. It was Chris with his head in his hands and at first I thought that he was crying.

Why are you crouched down there?

That bloody dog will not come back and I've been trying for over an hour. He comes towards me as if he's come back to go home and then just runs away again.

I wasn't cruel enough to say I told you so. I said;

Well let's leave him out here all night. We haven't got a collar with his name on yet, so no one will know he's ours. They might take him home with a bit of luck.

I knew that I couldn't leave him there and didn't mean what I said, but I was very angry with the dog and not used to this kind of behaviour. However, there was no way that the dog was going to come back to us and we eventually went home without him. We had been in bed for about an hour or more when I heard him barking, still in the field. I couldn't leave him there any longer and got dressed again. I walked down to the park on my own, because when Chris went to bed, there was no way he was getting up again until morning. It was about two thirty in the morning by this time. I went into the park and straight away the dog ran up to me and sat while I put his lead on and from that day on he came back at the first call. Unfortunately, Chris never did take him out again and he never used him as a gun dog, but he was part of the family now.

The cupboard that the dogs slept in was like a large larder and was ideal for ironing clothes in. I was ironing one day when the Doberman start to sniff and scratch at the wall. In fact the plaster was so soft, that it was starting to come away as he fiercely clawed at it. After yelling at him to stop, I went over to see why he had been acting this way and as I looked through the tiny hole, I saw a staircase. The staircase had been blocked off and it went down into the courtyard without walking through the pub. Now at the bottom of the stairs, near to the back door, was a cupboard where we stored the crisps and nuts. It looked just like storage space, but the back had been boarded off at some point and was hiding the staircase. Chris had gone to the bank, and when he got back I went rushing downstairs to tell him of my 'find'.

Chris, Chris, I've found a secret staircase. I think it must be a quick getaway or hiding place. Come and have a look.

Chris said the pub probably had two staircases and couldn't see why it had to be something dramatic or sinister.

There were times when it was quiet in the bar and sometimes it was nice just to have a chat with the locals. I was about to refill a pint for a customer when he announced;

Well, I'm off home. See you tomorrow.

Home? But it's only 10.30. What's with you going home at this time?

Normally we had trouble getting some of the customers to go home and this was one of them.

John Wayne film on telly tonight.

What is it with John Wayne and men? Anyway, I made a duvet for him once.

Oh yeah, you made him a duvet. Did he like it?

I'm telling the truth. When I was fifteen, my first job was at McLintocks, a factory in Barnsley that made continental quilts and duvets. I had always believed that because they were called continental quilts they were imported, but actually they were invented and made in Barnsley by McLintocks in the 1860s and later sent abroad. Anyway, getting back to John Wayne, John Wayne was to coming to London for the premier of his new film, McLintocks. This was in 1963, my first year working there. We made a huge quilt. In fact, it was seven feet long and I took a part in making it. The quilt was presented to him by some of the staff who had worked there for a while and I heard that he was thrilled with it. When the film was shown at the Empire Cinema in Barnsley, we were all given two free tickets to see it. At that age I had no interest in cowboy films and gave the tickets to Mam and Dad. It was over forty years later that I actually watched the film. I had a signed photograph of him as well that one of the women brought back for me.

Anything to do with John Wayne is worth a fortune now. You ought to have saved that photo.

Oh yeah, like I could predict the future.

I'm off now and next time I watch McLintock I'll look out for your quilt.

I never realised how much history there was to the McLintocks factory until I came across a book when I lived in Barnsley. It brought back happy memories of working there.

Probably the best working days of my life, was spent working in McLintocks' factory. I started working there with a friend from school, Mary. One day we were kneeling in a corridor outside of the school hall, with our hands in a prayer position, when Mary whispered;

Have you got a job, to go to when we leave school?

No, we have two weeks yet. I was thinking of going to the shirt factory.

Me mam's taking me today for an interview at McLintocks. Would you like to come? They allow us time off to go for work interviews.

I remember that day as if it was yesterday. The reason we were kneeling in the corridor with our hands in the prayer position, whispering, was because we had forgotten our berets. There was a small chapel in the school which opened up and extended the school hall on Wednesday mornings when Mass was given. We would kneel for what seemed like hours, our backs and knees hurting like mad. If you had forgotten your beret, then you weren't allowed inside the hall, but had to kneel just outside the entrance door in the corridor. I had to do this often and it was just as uncomfortable. At first, we were sent home to get our berets, but it didn't take long for the teachers to realise we had hidden them in our satchels just to get out of school for a while and to get out of going to Mass. The floors were very hard on the knees and kneeling in an upright position for all that time hurt your back and you weren't allowed to slouch back on your knees. My brother Patrick went to the same school after I left and he told me that he was always fainting in school Mass. The teachers would take him outside, sit him in a chair and leave him on his own until after Mass had finished.

Girls had to cover their heads with a beret at school, but for Mass on Sunday, most women wore a scarf or a lace cloth over their heads that looked like something off a sideboard. Men had to take their hats off, something I can't fathom out to this day. I was always forgetting my beret, which along with wearing a tie, was part of the school uniform. I sometimes got the cane for this, and physical punishment, such as caning, happened almost every day. We were often caned for talking in class or chewing gum. At first, you were told to put the gum in the bin, but beechnut chewing gum, a popular brand then, was tuppence a packet, so we were reluctant to waste it. We would tear a bit off, hiding the rest on the roof of our mouths. Sometimes you would start to chew it again later and if you were seen by the teacher you were caned.

On the day of the interview after the morning Mass, we were given the permission to go home and get changed for the interview, so I walked across the fields with Mary to her house. It was such a cold day and I only had a blazer to keep the wind from biting. Mary's mother took us for the interview and I remember she let me borrow a really nice warm yellow coat to go in. I was just fifteen at the time and didn't really know anything about working life then, in fact I was so naive and said things sometimes without thinking. The manageress was lovely as she explained what we would be doing and finished off by saying it was forty four hours, so I stupidly said, "a day"? She didn't embarrass me, but smiled then told us we had the job.

I never enjoyed my school days, mostly because being the eldest meant that I had to spend a lot of time at home helping me mam and I was constantly in trouble with the teachers for being absent. I very rarely did a full week in school, and left school with very little education. I don't know which school I hated the most, infants and junior school where the teachers were nuns or the senior school that was run by ordinary teachers, but I was still very nervous of leaving. It was now time to start work and the working hours were quite long then, but I felt content from the very first day. I had to wear my school skirt, white blouse and cardigan for the first few weeks until I received my first pay packet and could buy an overall. As usual, I took egg sandwiches for lunch. Not scrambled eggs, but hard boiled eggs chopped up and mashed with butter that Dad made before we both set of for work. We caught the same bus into town, where he would go to the building site that he was working on. McLintocks was very laid back and time meant nothing. There was never a rush to do anything; we were one big team, of all ages and I had many a laugh while working there. Time definitely seemed slower. For instance, after lunch we would go up to a local recreation ground and play on the swings. An hour lunch break seemed to last ages. We would walk into town sometimes or eat our sandwiches in a park, which was called Sparrow Park. It was opposite the factory and on a few occasions we went swimming, as the pool was situated only a few yards away. We were still children in every sense at fifteen, much younger than the fifteen year olds of today.

As I mentioned before, McLintocks was the birthplace of one of Barnsley's greatest inventions, the eiderdown or quilt, invented by James McLintocks. The quilt was patented by James McLintocks, a Barnsley businessman, in the 1860s. Eider down comes from the breast of the eider duck and the down filled quilts created tremendous warmth and were very light in weight. I remember to this day that it was four ounces that we had to weigh before putting it in the machine to blow into each panel of the duvet. Not only did James McLintock use feathers in quilts but also in clothes such as dressing gowns and jackets which would have been very warm in those damp and foggy days. I was amazed to find that he also had a display in the Crystal Palace to exhibit his wares. A number of times he held exhibitions in London and had many influential customers, including Queen Mary who was so impressed with the continental quilts, that she purchased one herself. McLintocks were the first to export continental quilts to the continent, yet I had always assumed that because they were called continental quilts they were invented abroad.

Because Nora's birthday fell four weeks after mine, she had to stay on at school until the summer break, whereas I left at Easter. I was so looking forward to her coming to work with me and immediately after she started work we were up to mischief. Lifts were new to us and we would ride up and down between the department floors, while people banged on the doors waiting to use them. We would wave through the little glass panel on the way up and down, to their annoyance. For the first few months I had worked on the ground floor level while training to use a sewing machine and I sat next to Mary. One day I sewed my finger in and it got stuck. The needle had gone in one side, bent in the middle and came out the other side. The mechanic released my finger from the machine and I went to hospital, which was within walking distance. They took the needle out and I had a tetanus jab and then went straight back to work. A few days after that Mary had her finger caught by the needle.

Soon, I was sent to work on the top floor where they made the duvets; the quilts were made on the floor below. There was only the one sewing machine on the top floor to sew the edges together after the feathers had gone into the duvets. This was where the cushion pads were filled. It was also the room where Nora worked. Because there wasn't always that much sewing to do, I was taught to use the feather machine for blowing feathers into the duvets and cushions. The feathers were turned around by blades inside a hopper then passed through a tunnel onto a big table where the duvet was laid and the feathers were blown in each panel. How Nora and I lived past our childhood and early teens, I don't know. We used to do such dangerous things. Once Nora hid from me for a joke, I looked everywhere for her and was about to switch my machine on when I heard her giggling. She had climbed into the hopper. Had I not heard her giggling and switched the machine on, she could have been sliced up or electrocuted and I shudder to think of the consequences.

The feathers used to stick in our hair because we refused to wear a head cover and they must have looked like head lice when we walked down to the bus station. It was easy enough to comb the feathers out, but not the white bits that clung to your hair. But then, we didn't care what people thought. To keep the dust of the feathers down, every night we had to sprinkled sand on the floor and sweep up. The sand was kept in a little building outside of the factory. There was no electricity in there, so in the winter time, when it was getting dark, we were allowed to go in twos. One evening Nora had noticed some wooden stairs further into the building and we went up to find out what was up there. There was a little window, which shed a bit of light, but not much, and it was very dusty and eerie. We found all kinds of war time memorabilia, such as helmets, which we put on our heads and gas masks. We picked things up to examine them and tried to work out what things were for. We walked further into the room and jumped as our reflection lit up in an old cracked mirror. We laughed out loud, went round a corner of the room, pushing away the cobwebs, and then both Nora and I screamed the place down. A woman in an army uniform with a helmet on glowed in the darkness, smiling at us. We ran downstairs, falling over one another, across the yard and headed towards the lift inside. We were both practically hysterical. We told our supervisor who was quite concerned at how upset we were. She calmed us down a bit and then took us back to the outside building to have a look with a torch at where we had been. We reluctantly followed her up the creaky stairs and with the torch we could see a mannequin in full army gear, smiling. In fact, there were a few dressmaking dummies, now we could see. I suppose at one time they must have made uniforms for the war and used mannequins to display them. We were given a good telling off for being nosey and we never did go up there again.

Sometimes we had to work in another room, making life jackets that were filled with a horrible fibre called kapok. This irritated our eyes and noses beyond belief and we had to wear a nylon scarf over our faces, tied to the back of the neck, which we hated. We all looked like bank robbers or something out of a horror film. We would sit around a big wooden table to stuff the life jackets with kapok and we played all sorts of guessing games, such as I Spy. We played the same guess for two days sometimes, until someone 'got it'. For two full days we went through everything beginning with S. It drove us all mad. Then, after two days, thinking it would go on the day after, I put my coat on to go home and realised that I had stained my overall. It hit me.

STAIN.

I yelled at the top of my voice, making them all jump and wonder what the hell I was on about.

Stain, it's the stain on my overall.

It certainly was.

Making the life jackets was never an easy job. We would push in the kapok with what we called a broddle and the scarves over our faces felt very restrictive and even today, if I smell a scarf of the same material, it brings back memories of feeling as though I am suffocating. Never the less, they were happy times. Apart from Nora, and myself, all the women, in this department, were much older, even older than my mother, who was only thirty five, but at fifteen you thought that was old then, and they would tell tales of their lives. One lady named Violet, who was my favourite person, told us she met her husband through a jam jar.

I worked in a jam factory and wrote down my name, age and address and put it under the paper on the jam jar lid. A young man was having breakfast when his mother noticed the bit of paper and passed it over to her son. He immediately wrote me a letter. We met outside the pictures a few days later, started going out together and married fours year later.

Nora and I looked at each other, went for a pen and some paper, wrote out our names and addresses and pushed them into the life jackets. We did the same thing when we had to make some flock mattresses for the forces. Unfortunately, we never heard anything from anyone.

We had settled in well now at The Goat's Head and I could explore further. At the back of the pub there was a country lane that led to a tower that could be seen for miles and a very steep climb it was too. The tower was owned by the local butcher and surrounding it was a large wooded area. This was a lovely walk. The wooded area was surrounded by hills and there were deep crevices, many were man-made as the stone was quarried for building the local houses and farm buildings. On reaching the top, it was possible to see all the way across Rombalds Moor, beyond to Ilkley Moor and, rising in the distance, on a clear day, you could see Simon's Seat on Barden Fell, high above Bolton Abbey.

I was told later that the Victorians used to gather in this woodland and special places were made for them to sit on the grass. It was quite easy to visualise this scene; picnics on white linen table clothes, blankets on the ground and baskets filled with food and wine. The families were dressed in all in their finery. The women wore heavy skirts supported by several petticoats made of stiffened silks and horsehair that we know as crinoline. They wore large white satin and lace hats, together with white lace gloves and parasols and, of course, they carried lace fans. Little girls would play, dressed in their pretty kilted skirts with hip length bodices tied up with deep sashes and matching bonnets. Boys wore culottes, long socks, and shiny shoes with big buckles. The men would probably have had top hats on, along with long, tailed coats and waistcoats. I would imagine that the Victorians never suffered from sun burn or skin cancer caused by too much sun. Apart from looking elegant, they were very well protected.

Surrounding the wood was a high stone wall and in one part of the wall there were some missing stones, making a hole that you could look through. Looking through the hole made the view seem like a picture or a postcard.

The view looked over to the horizon where the sun met the hills. You could also see the little park where I walked the dogs after closing time.

One sunny afternoon I took my usual walk up to the woods with my dogs and sat on the wall thinking and admiring the scenery in front of me. Walking back home, I saw the peacocks, amazing looking creatures that lived in the grounds of the tower. The peacock's tail contains spectacular designs and beauty because of the large feathers, bright, iridescent colours and intricate patterns. I carried on walking when one of them made the most horrible screaming sound that sent the dogs off running, yanking the leads out of my hand. The sound scared the living daylights out of me too. Apparently, this noise is a mating call, but I thought that the scream was enough to send its mates running in the opposite direction. It was more like the cry of the banshee.

The little park, or recreation ground as it was called, was at the side of the car park to our pub. Even though it was very dark, I walked there every night after the pub closed and some nights there would be another person there too. She was quite elderly and lived next to the park at the other side. When talking to her one night, she told me she was a local historian and I learned a lot from this dear lady. Sometimes it could be very late before I was able to take the dogs out, but rain or shine I went out and she would sometimes be there. We had been to a dinner and dance event one particular evening and got back very late. It was 2.30am, but she was there. I often wondered, as her side window overlooked the park, if she watched for me coming. This place was my relaxation after work, a place where I would sit on the swings, lay back and look at the sky or the stars if they were out. I wonder at times how I dared to venture into such a dark place on my own, but it was something I just did. I can't remember being scared, especially as the swings were near to the wall which separated the fields and hillside.

When my stepson, Russell, came to stay in the holidays, both he and my son, Christopher, would come with me late at night along with the dogs and they would push me high in the air on the swings and I screamed when they pushed too high. Along the side of the park, higher up, lived some sisters who were regulars customers of ours. They knew that I always took the dogs at that time of night and unknown to me had thought I was in danger and phoned the police, but we had gone home by the time they arrived apparently. One late night however, I heard a noise behind the wall of the rec, adjoining the field, and two policemen popped up scaring the life out of me. They didn't say why they were there. They were either waiting for someone or up to hanky panky.

Chapter Fifteen

Chris was still suffering from depression. I had hoped that moving pubs would have helped him out of it, but gradually he was getting worse. He had no motivation or enthusiasm and the once quick and witty person that had made me laugh was changing into someone that I hardly recognised. When Chris felt down, he would sulk and refuse to speak to me. This drove me mad and so, in the end, he went to the doctor. The doctor said he wanted him to go into hospital for a while, to which he agreed.

I went to see him in-between running the pub. It was handy the hospital being so close by. I visited him one Thursday when we had been doing the pools for nearly a year. We used the same numbers each week and the numbers were the birthday numbers and ages of Adrian, Christopher and Russell. He suddenly remembered that he hadn't filled them in;

I forgot to fill the pools coupon in. I didn't realise it was Thursday with being in this place. Can you do it? You know the numbers and someone will show you how to do it. It has to be in tomorrow morning.

I filled the numbers in, but because Russell had had a birthday two days before, I changed it to his age at that time, putting nine instead of eight. I checked the pools later and to my horror I realised that if I hadn't changed the number to nine, we would have won the jackpot. It sounds unreal, but it's true. However, we still won quite a bit of money from it, so things weren't too bad;

How are you feeling today, Chris?

Not bad. I'm ready for home now. I've been out jogging around the grounds of the hospital. The doctor said exercise was good for depression.

You certainly sound a lot better. You could always come to the woods with me after closing in the afternoon. I know it's quite a trek but the scenery is lovely from up there.

Chris liked to have an afternoon nap rather than go walking in the woods, but then I must say, standing at a bar every day and night can be monotonous and tiring. At least I had variety and fresh air daily when shopping for the pub lunches. Plus, at any opportunity, I would take the dogs up to the wood. I only worked behind the bar in the afternoon at weekends, as there were never that many customers during the week. I was always up and down the stairs serving lunches for an hour or so, but the customers that came in every day after lunch were the same men and they always stood at the bar and preferred Chris's company.

I'm glad you feel better now, Chris, because I have some good news for you. We won three thousand pounds on the pools.

Never. I can't believe it. Well that's cheered me up; I thought you might have more luck than me. Three thousand pounds, that's fantastic news.

I thought that was enough to tell him, for his health's sake.

We decided to buy our own disco equipment with the money. We had talked about having an Elvis Presley night because it was coming up to the tenth anniversary of his death and we thought we could let Adrian do it.

We were making plans for the Elvis night, having a few drinks after time, something we didn't do as much since moving there. If we did serve after time it would only be with a few customers and for a short while. It was about midnight when the phone rang. Chris answered and said it was someone called Michael that wanted to speak to me;

Hello;

How are yea, Margaret?

I immediately recognised my uncle's Irish voice.

I'm all right. How are you? It's late, is everything all right?

Yeah, I was waiting for you to close the bar. I thought you might be busy.

It had been years since I last saw him, in fact, it was in the seventies. He was phoning to ask if Darren, his son, could come over for the holidays. I said yes straight away;

But he's only young. Is he coming on his own?

Yeah, he's determined to come and see you. He's sixteen now.

When will he be here and how will I know him? He was only young when I last saw him.

In two days.

We had a chat and I arranged to pick Darren up from Leeds Station.

Chris, what if I don't recognise him or what if he doesn't recognise me? I'm getting worried.

How many young lads of that age will be getting off the train?

We waited for the train from Liverpool and there were loads of young lads, though only a few on their own, but then I saw this smiling face coming round the corner. I knew him immediately because he was the image of his Dad and he certainly remembered me. He was soon liked by the locals and straight away he went around the tables collecting the empty glasses, all the while smiling. He was lovely.

Later that night when we went upstairs, we sat up talking while Chris was cashing up.

What made you decide to come here? Not that I didn't want you to, but you were only a little child the last time I saw you.

Well to be honest, I loved the time at me Aunty Margaret's house when we all came over to England. Remember, I stayed at your house while all the rest of my family stayed at Paddy's and Joyce's house. Anyway, I promised myself that as soon as I was old enough, I would come and see you again. I have been saving money for a while now, but wasn't old enough to travel by myself. I almost had trouble anyway because they considered me too young at sixteen, but me da sorted it out.

I can't believe that I had made such an impression. I still remember you as you were then. In fact, I have a photo of you that I took just before you went home.

I was very surprised and flattered and so very happy to see him. We stayed up talking most of the night with Christopher and Adrian. We laughed at those days when he was last over in England; he was only about seven at the time. He told us that he babysat for someone;

You babysit? How long have you have been babysitting? You're still young enough to have a babysitter yourself.

Oh about four year now.

He failed to mention that his older siblings used to take him with them when they were babysitting for someone.

Christopher had two single beds in his bedroom, so there was no problem there, but I knew Mam and Dad were coming over so I had to make room for them. It would definitely not be in Adrian's room, there was not a piece of carpet to be seen in there. He had that much electrical stuff, an organ, two or three guitars, stereos, not to mention a disco with large speakers. The plug sockets bulged so much I'm surprised they didn't blow a fuse or worse, start a fire. Music was constantly playing in Adrian's room. I think he was sometimes trying to be louder than the juke box that was in the room below him. How he managed to study for his exams with the juke box going all the time, I'll never know. I was passing Adrian's door one day when he was out and his electric organ was playing, I opened the door and there was no-one in the room, I couldn't understand it and was convinced it was a ghost, but Adrian told me later that it could play on its own!

We made a makeshift bed in the lounge for me mam and dad and it was comfortable enough for them.

Obviously I was eager to show Darren around. We had already made plans to go out on Sunday to the Yorkshire Dales, but the first place we went to was the wood, with Christopher, and then later in the day we went to Cliffe Castle. Cliffe Castle Museum was originally the mansion of the local Victorian millionaire and textile manufacturer, Henry Butterfield. The grounds there were spectacular, with lawns surrounded by trees and although the house is a museum now with a wide variety of displays, we preferred to sit on the grass and look out over the views for a while before going back to the pub. Daren spotted Ilkley Moor in the distance and was fascinated that cars were travelling up there, so we arranged to go to Ilkley one day before he went home.

Mam and Dad finally arrived. It was funny really, because if they came by bus, which they did now, I used to sit by the window upstairs waiting for the bus to drop them off outside the pub, like an excited little girl. As soon as me mam walked through the door it was always;

Put kettle on, am gagging for a cuppa.

Mam loved her cups of tea, whereas Dad would always prefer a pint. I loved it when they came and missed them when they went home. I missed all my family, but I couldn't take time off to visit them in Barnsley and relied on them to come to see us.

The following Sunday we were all prepared to go to the Yorkshire Dales, straight after closing time which was at two o'clock on a Sunday afternoon and we had arranged for someone to open up for us in case we weren't back. The first place we were going to was Malham, which was not far from Steeton. Christopher had recently broke his leg and had a big plaster cast on it, but somehow we all managed to squeeze into the Ford Granada, all six of us. Adrian wanted to stay at home and practice for the Elvis night which was that evening and he was the DJ.

Malham was a lovely place for a day out and it was such a wonderful journey to get there. There was a stream that ran alongside the road as you drove into the village, passing only a few houses and farm buildings, until you reached two pubs, one on either side of a bridge over the stream. One of the pubs was posh and the other catered for walkers and climbers who seemed to be everywhere. Turning over the bridge, it was possible to drive to Gordale Scar and watch an impressive waterfall, which in a hard winter freezes and becomes a magnificent ice sculpture, as the freezing water cascades over the limestone boulders. If you were to travel straight through the village, you would take the moorland road to the next small town, called Settle, and as we travelled along this road, on our right hand side, there suddenly appeared a large limestone cliff face. Towering over a hundred feet in height and curving from one side of the valley to the other, this was the end of a glacier, formed in an ice age, millions of years ago and quite unbelievably the stream that runs down the valley, bubbles up and runs out of the bottom of the cliff face, as if by magic. Malham is one of my most favourite places and I have returned there many times over the years. We stood looking at the views; it was a strong but warm wind. Mam decided to do her Wuthering Heights 'Cathy' bit, running into the wind, arms outstretched, shouting for Heathcliffe before stopping to light a cigarette up. I laughed at her and said;

I don't think Cathy smoked, Mam.

No but she still deed befooar she wah thirty, dint she?

I was laughing at her running in the wind shouting for Heathcliffe and turned to find Christopher and Dad had disappeared;

Where have they gone? I can't see them.

Darren pointed to a large hill;

They went up to the top of that hill because Christopher said a sheep was in trouble.

He'll be in trouble when he gets back. He's already broke a tooth with that plaster cast on his leg.

Darren was puzzled by this;

How did he do that? Did he kick himself in the mouth er what?

No, he had difficulty getting down the slide in the rec and went down backwards instead, landing in a funny position, or so he said.

I couldn't believe how far Dad had got. It was a very steep hill, so Darren and I went running up to join them, leaving Chris and Mam to have a smoke. It was a steep hill and at the top you could see for miles while the wind whipped around our faces and we struggled to keep our balance. On our way home, we became stuck behind a herd of cows that we slowly followed for ages. It was so hot and stuffy in the car that we had all the windows open. I was talking to Darren and as he was looking at me to listen, a cow stuck its head through the window and mooed, Darren almost hit his head on the roof of the car, as he turned his head and was face to face with the cow. He had jumped so much that I'm surprised the cow didn't jump over the moon with the sound of the scream from Darren.

We got back to The Goat just in time to have something to eat and prepare for our Elvis night. I was amazed at how many people turned out for the night, the pub quickly filled up. Of course, as the night went on Karen became her usual mischievous self. She was teasing Darren and he was laughing all the time and running away from her. It was funny really because her husband, Mick, was using our camcorder for the night and when I watched it later, I was surprised to see Karen giving Darren a kiss. He was trying to struggle, but laughing at the same time. He was pushing her away, then she must have put her tongue in his mouth because he pulled back laughing and shouting, "Margaret, help me" at the top of his voice with such a surprised and stunned look on his face. Chris went to his rescue and Darren quickly ran upstairs to tell Christopher what had happened. As Chris was walking past Karen to get back behind the bar, she grabbed him by the balls. He hurried past, his hands in the air talking to the camera, saying;

It's not me Margaret. Look, my hands are here. I never touched her Margaret.

When closing time came we were left with a few regulars as usual. Chris had gone to bed early, leaving Adrian, Darren and a few locals. Adrian was minding the bar, while I sat down with the others. He was talking to a man at the bar that had some goat's milk with him and unknown to me, he had told Adrian it was good to drink after a glass of brandy. Brandy was not a drink Adrian had ever had before, after all, he was only sixteen and I certainly would not have let him drink it, however, as I was sat away from the bar, I had no idea what was happening and Adrian was never interested enough in alcohol for me to keep a watch on him. When everyone had gone home Darren and Christopher came with me to take the dogs out. We came back, locked up and went upstairs. I was walking to the bedroom when I heard Darren shouting Adrian's name out. I quickly ran to the bathroom where the shouting was coming from to see what was wrong. Adrian must have gone to the bathroom and passed out. We couldn't get him to answer, even though we were shouting and knocking on the door. Eventually Chris woke up and stormed towards the bathroom door. As Darren, Christopher and I took a few paces back; he kicked the door in, looked at Adrian and walked off without saying a word. Adrian's head was resting on the bathroom scales and I was really worried that he was unconscious, but we managed to bring him round and get him to his bed. We daren't leave him on his own, so we sat at the bottom of Adrian's bed for most of the night. It was so uncomfortable, but there wasn't space anywhere else where we could sit. Caesar was in the room with us as well and, as usual, he was farting all the while.

All of a sudden there was a groan from Adrian, he sat upright and projectile vomited with such force that it hit all of us in the face and also managed to hit the dog. It was like something out of the Exorcist film. The dog ran off in a flash and, for a second, I thought Darren was going to throw up from the awful smell of goat's milk and brandy. We cleaned up the mess and washed our faces and when we thought that Adrian was sleeping peacefully, we finally went to bed ourselves. The next morning Adrian was 'worse for wear', but his friends Carl and Vanessa came to visit him along with a few more friends in the evening, all of them giving him sympathy. Chris wasn't speaking to me because he blamed me for Adrian drinking and said that I was irresponsible. I was fuming and said,

"At least, I made sure that he was all right. You'd have just left him with the scales registering the weight of his head all night."

Not very long after that, Adrian came down with chicken pox. He was covered from head to foot in awful sores. Chicken pox is so much worse when you're older and he was very ill. It was good job he had them after the vomiting performance and not before, or he would have definitely looked the part for the Exorcist film, as weeping sores covered him, all over his face.

Darren was amazed at how good a pool player I was and was always boasting about me to other players. He was telling a man in the pool room about me one night while I was in the lounge side of the pub. The man had said that the day a woman beat him at pool; he would snap his cue in half. A challenge was set and I beat him quite easily really, leaving him with six balls on the table to the cheers of the crowd. He picked up his cue and walked out without saying a word. Not long after this happened, Christopher started going to a club that trained youngsters to play snooker and pool for competitions and he came runner up in an under sixteen competition in Northampton. His manager watched me play in a competition one evening and asked if I would like to be a county player and play for Keighley Town in a ladies league, which took place on the first Sunday of every month. I went to meet the rest of the team, who were what you could call very, 'street wise', but after a while when I got to know them, I really liked them all, although I wouldn't have liked to have got on the wrong side of them. At one match there was a dispute and one of the girls in our team threatened to put the opponent's head down the pocket of the pool table. Another time when we were playing, I was the last player and the match was on me to win as the score stood at three all. I potted all seven balls and was left with the black to win the match. I took a few deep breaths and bent to look along my cue. At the other end of my cue, I saw my team looking at me with tension on their faces. This was a grudge match, as the opposition was top of the league, and to lose to them would have been devastating after being so near. Seeing their faces like that made me burst out laughing and I had to compose myself again before taking the shot. Fortunately I won the game. The girls came rushing towards me and lifted me up, it was fantastic. On the coach ride home, we were all in high spirits. Some of them were drunk and, to my horror, started to 'moon' (showing their bare bottoms) at passing cars. Our driver was straining his neck to get a peek at them through the mirror and had to swerve to avoid hitting a bus.

As mentioned earlier, shooting was a big hobby of Chris's and he often went rabbit shooting in the early morning, coming back with things that I refused to cook. Early one morning, Chris said,

"Fancy going shooting with me this morning? When we get back we can have a big fry up for breakfast."

Chris, I hate guns and wouldn't even know how to hold one.

I was persuaded to go with him and have a go with the gun. I hated it and was glad he didn't catch anything that morning. He gave me the gun on the way back, teaching me how to hold it.

"Look up there and follow that bird" he shouted pointing to a single bird flying very high up in the air. I aimed the gun at the bird, knowing I wouldn't be able to shoot a moving target even if I wanted to. I did aim, I hit it, I killed it, a bird on its journey to find food for its family, flying along harmlessly and I took its life. I couldn't eat my breakfast for thinking about that poor bird. I would never touch a gun again as long as I lived.

Christopher, Darren and I got up very early one Sunday morning before Chris got up to go shooting. We sneaked out the front door very quietly with the intention of frightening the rabbits away, or anything that moved, to stop Chris from shooting them. Chris would normally get up and go out about seven, but we would be back by then. We went up to the woods and we never saw a thing, although we did enjoy the early morning dewy walk and Christopher was teaching us how to track animals. I was surprised to find that he knew so much about wildlife.

"We had better get back before Chris gets up. Come on lads."

We walked back down the hill towards home and as soon as I saw the door I knew we were locked out. I had used the Yale lock and not taken a key, and the back door was in the courtyard behind the ten foot gates. We tried to force the bars, which was impossible. We tried to stand on each other to reach the top but kept falling down. It was a Sunday morning and very quiet, but then one of our customers appeared and stopped to ask what we were doing. He was on his way to work and had walked across the road towards us, making us jump. He looked at the gate and opened it, it was never locked. We had spent at least half an hour trying to get in and I was so embarrassed. We were in the courtyard now, but still had to get in the back door which was also locked, I thought I was going to have to find a phone box and ring Chris. He would be fuming, as it was still very early and sometimes he changed his mind about going shooting, depending on how tired he was from the night before. I noticed the kitchen window was open at the top and the three of us went into the barn, looking for a ladder or something to get up there. Christopher could see a very rickety ladder in the old stables on a shelf that we couldn't reach. We managed somehow to help Christopher climb up to the shelf and throw the ladder down, but it only had half a dozen rungs left on it. We decided that we had no choice but to use it and agreed that Christopher should go up as he was the most daring. The missing rungs were a problem, of course, and I couldn't contain my laughter as we propped it up against the wall. Christopher managed to get to the top of the ladder, but the window was very small and he got stuck, so Darren had to climb up behind him with me holding the ladder at the bottom. I was about to give him a push when the back door opened. It was the cleaner who had keys for the pub and usually came early to get her job finished before opening. She had heard a commotion in the courtyard and came out to see what was happening, she didn't look as shocked as you would think really, so I walked quickly through the pub and up the stairs to the kitchen where I met Christopher sliding off the work surface after managing to get through the window. I turned around laughing and stood behind me was a not very amused Chris.

It was time for Darren to go home now and Christopher and I drove him to Leeds Station for the train to Liverpool. We were sad to see him go home. We had had such a great fortnight together with so much fun, and Christopher was going to miss him dreadfully. He had shared a room with Darren for two weeks and had been with him most of the time. Christopher was very quiet on that journey. We made sure Darren got on the right train, telling him to ring as soon as he arrived in Liverpool. I had been driving for years and had driven mini buses and an ambulance for the Social Services. I had gone from place to place, miles out in the countryside, driven on endless motorways and yet, I could not get out of Leeds. I kept driving around the ring road because I couldn't get off it, always ending up back in the city centre; I thought I would be there until everyone had gone home. Darren had been in Liverpool for ages before I got home and everyone assumed I had gone shopping. If ever I was late it was always assumed that I had gone shopping, I could be dead, kidnapped or could have run away, but everyone would think I was shopping.

We made arrangements to go to Ireland for four days with Mam and Dad and Adrian and Christopher. Mam and Dad had gone to stay for the week in Dublin, but we couldn't be away from the pub at weekends, at such short notice, so we followed later. We sat in the airport looking at the planes coming in to land and an Aer Lingus plane came down looking big and bright. We assumed we would be going on that one, but the plane we were to travel on was a little old red thing that made a lot of noise. Chris asked the steward if it had managed to pass its MOT this time.

It was so nice to see my grandmother and the rest of Dad's side of the family again. My grandmother was stood on the balcony of the Ballybough flats waiting for us to arrive and from where we were it was easy to see the excitement in her small frame, her white hair shining in the sun. We walked up the three flights of stairs and she greeted us all;

How are yis all? Come in and I'll be making yis a sup o tay.

We all trooped in through the door and had a cup of tea. It felt good to be back again. The last time I was there was when I was pregnant with Adrian and the time before that, I had come with my friend Sandra for a week.

My grandmother always called me Margarita, the mad one, ever since I stayed there with Sandra in the 1960s. We were seventeen at the time and she would follow us when we went out, hiding behind a huge umbrella. It was Sandra that first noticed her;

Margaret, I recognise those shoes. It's your grandma, I'm sure it is.

That's really strange, Sandra, because I've seen that umbrella before when we went into the City.

We went over to say hello and surprised her;

I was on me way te town. Are yis going in dere yerselves?

Sandra and I once went out for a night in the city. She was stood on the balcony with the neighbours waiting for us to come home and it was only ten o'clock. Grandmother, like Dad, had very soft low voice and I can't ever remember a time when she was angry or a time that she had raised her voice. She said very quietly, but with concern,

"Ryan has gone looking fer yis, as I was worried. It isn't safe to be in de city at night. Yis wouldn't know yer way around. Come in and I'll make yis a sup o tay."

Ryan was my grandfather's surname, his name was Michael Ryan, but it was the name that everyone, including Dad, and my grandmother called him. When we were young, he would take Teresa and myself to the pictures and fall asleep immediately on sitting down. Once a woman stood up to leave the cinema and she stood on his toe. He yelled out very loudly in the quietness;

Jaysus, Mary and Joseph, yis stood on me toe, missus.

When walking through the city, he didn't wait for the cars to stop. He would walk into the middle of the road and stop the traffic with a wave of his hand, so that Teresa and I could cross the road safely. After seeing him do that, I believed that he must have been important some time in his life and was used to giving commands because cars stopped in their tracks without the drivers yelling at him.

I suppose it was hard for my Grandmother to realise that I was grown up now and she was worried, understandably, when Sandra and I were out in a city as big as Dublin. My grandfather had warned us to stay away from a certain place, but he didn't say why we should. We walked along the side of the River Liffy and found ourselves in the very area he had told us to avoid. We soon found out it was a prostitute area and we ran for our lives. I realise now it was probably the area that the locals called 'The Monto' because it was on Montgomery Street and all the young women were leaning out of the windows.

We travelled home to England on the old cattle boat. We were the last ones on and had to sit on deck. We had no money left because we had had to pay some money before we got on the boat, which we hadn't accounted for as we had a return ticket. It must have been some sort of tax or something. When we arrived in Liverpool, we had missed the train connection because the boat was late docking and there wasn't another train until the morning after. We had to sleep in the waiting room with a few other people who had missed the train and the porter locked us in there for the night to stop tramps from coming in. We were starving by now and all we had were some sticks of rock that I had bought my brothers. Me mam and Sandra's mam must have been worried sick as to where we were. The boat had taken ten hours and with the train ride, we had gone twenty four hours without food. Apart from the breakfast at my grandmother's before we left Dublin, we had had nothing to eat until the following afternoon. Of course, we brought the dreaded fleas back with us. Although the flat was clean some people still used turf fires. Turf is what Irish people call peat, which is dug from the extensive peat bogs and dried so that it can be burned in place of coal. This is where the fleas came from. The hoppers, hopped from one flat to another. Sandra was bitten much worse than I was because I was used to them and she scratched herself all the way home. We were both shattered when we arrived home. We had sat on the deck and slept in a waiting room which only had a wooden bench to lie on. I was eagerly met by my two younger brothers and I opened the case to give them the little presents that I had brought back. I had bought them some bows and arrows but found when I was packing that they wouldn't fit in the case. The only options were to break them in two or leave them behind and I couldn't afford anything else. I passed them sheepishly to the boys and they both said more or less at the same time;

These a broc.

I know they are, but when I started to pack, I realised that they wouldn't fit in the suitcase so I had to snap them in two. Can't you put sellotape on them or tie them together?

They both burst into floods of tears. I tried both ways of mending them, but nothing could save the bows.

Both Sandra and I were absolutely shattered, but we still went out the same night we came home, just to tell our friends of our great adventure.

A few days after I arrived back home from my visit to Ireland with Sandra, Mam told me that my grandmother had written her a letter saying we were mad. Margarita the mad one she had said. My grandmother told me mam how we had once barricaded the bedroom door with all the furniture. The man next door used to shout abuse at his wife, and from the screaming, he was obviously beating her. We had thought that he might break in and kill us, so we put anything that we could move behind the door. When my grandmother tried bringing us a cup of tea next morning, she wondered what had happened. Another time we were taking photos of each other in a bikini sitting on the window sill with the window wide open, three floors up, just as my grandmother walked into the bedroom;

What de hell are yis playing at? Do yis know how big a drop it is down to de bottom er what?

The reason we had done that was because it had rained every day up until then, so we took the photos of each other to show to our friends, making out that they were taken on a beach because the sky was so blue in the background. Another time we had returned to the flat in long wigs with a big hat on and sunglasses and frightened my poor grandmother to death as we walked through the door.

The only real sunny day was when we went to the local beach at Dollymount and managed to get a few pictures of each other sun bathing. We lay back on towels soaking up the sun with our eyes closed, but we were surprised to see that the tide had come in very quickly and we somehow seemed to be surrounded by water, as if we were on an island. Even worse, the beach was full of jelly fish, they were everywhere. I can't remember a time when I had moved so fast. We had to wade through the water, carrying all our gear and watch for jelly fish as we jumped over one and then another.

I was happy to be in Dublin again after all those years. I looked around the flat and nothing had changed much since I was there with Sandra, apart from my grandfather who wasn't here now, he had died in 1974. I walked into the bedroom and laughed when I pictured Sandra and I sat on the window sill. After tea I took out the camcorder we had recently purchased. I filmed my grandmother as she chatted away to Dad and Mam; she looked at me in a strange way as I was filming and said;

What's dat yea have in yer hand?

It's a camera that records you, like they have for television.

A what? A Television Camera?

Similar, we can record you and show it to all the family back in England.

Oh Jaysus what will dey bring out next, Margarita de mad one? Mad yea are.

Say hello to everyone at home.

What, in dat?

Yeah, they will be able to hear you.

Jesus, Mary and Joseph.

She started to wave at the camera and shouted, "Hello, how are yeah".

You're looking really well, how are you?

Oh Jaysus, you wouldn't see a man, woman, choild, cat nor dog in dis place. Michael Ryan never comes to see me.

Grandmother would always say the same thing. Dad and my uncle, Michael, had different surnames as they had different fathers and she would always say Paddy Miller or Michael Ryan. Never once did she use their first name only, in all those years. Dad was living in England and so Michael was left to look after her and he was often at her flat. He looked after her well, but she would blame him for everything and it was just as well we all knew what she was like. I asked where the fridge was and she said;

Michael Ryan wouldn't let me buy a fridge.

This was said in such sad way and it was so funny. The reason that she didn't have a fridge was because her meals were brought in and apart from the milk, the fridge had nothing in it, so it would overheat. It was the same for Dad really. Michael told me that she complained that Paddy Miller never wrote to her even if she had received a letter the day before. I put this down to her having lived in the same house, shared with family and friends, for all those years and that she now felt lonely as most old tenement people did.

Oh before yea go Margarita; Mrs O'Connell wants to meet you.

Darren, who had gone to my grandmother's with us, went to her flat, to bring her and Mrs O'Connell walked in and I introduced myself.

Oh Jaysus, what de hell is dat you have dere?

We explained to her what a camcorder was and;

Oh Jaysus, Mary and Joseph, whatever will dey bring out next, Jaysus?

Mam and Dad started to speak to Mrs O'Connell and even though she was quite old, she told them that she still went out to work. Dad was surprised and asked;

Where a yis working?

The Bank of Ireland.

We were shocked; she just didn't look like someone that worked in a bank, so I asked if she worked as a teller.

Jaysus, what in God's name is a teller? I do de cleaning fer God's sakes, Jaysus, Mary and Joseph, what de hell is a teller?

We all started laughing, along with Mrs O'Conner. Both of these two wonderful people were from the old Ireland. Their accents were from the olden times, that I remember as a child and I am so glad that I have a recording of them for future generations to watch, as now, through television and travel, accents in Dublin have changed over the years. We said our goodbyes before leaving Dublin. My grandmother stood on the balcony and waved as we set off in the car and I wondered if I would see her again, but she lived to the ripe old age of eighty seven and I saw her twice more over the years. Indeed I saw her the year before she died and she never changed, she still had the Irish humour and wit up to the end.

The weather was good and gave us a much needed break. Michael drove us to the airport and we promised not to leave it too long before we saw each other again. I felt really sad on the plane home. I was going to miss Darren and the place was going to be quiet without his laughter.

Chapter Sixteen

When we arrived home, Peter, a young man who sometimes worked behind the bar, had done a really good job of looking after the pub for us. Peter was very trustworthy and I felt confident leaving him with the pub. In fact he would have made a good landlord. In time, I got back into the routine of being a landlady again, and it was not long before Jack brightened things up. He had already been barred from the pub opposite, along with a few others and he was homeless again. We let him stay on the settee for a couple of days as he had nowhere to go, but Chris made it clear that it was only for a few days whether he had found somewhere else or not. He left the pub after three nights and went back to his mother's house just up the road. There was never a dull or quiet time when he was around and he made me laugh so much with his expressions when being told off by someone.

One night, about one am, I went to bed while Chris was cashing up downstairs. I could hear music, so I looked out of the window and saw Jack laid on the wall that surrounded the car park, with a little radio.

What you doing Jack? It's after midnight.

Nowhere to sleep again Maggie so I'm sleeping here on this wall.

Jack, it's only a narrow wall. How can you sleep on a wall? You're not a bloody cat.

It's not that bad and it's a lovely warm night.

But you have no bedding or anything.

I might just listen to my radio all night and think of you, Maggie.

Jack you're out of your head.

After talking to him and laughing with him a while, I was about to say goodnight and close the window, but I hung over the edge of the window and leaning out I shouted;

Romeo, Romeo wherefore art thou Romeo?

Here I am Juliet, here I am.

I stood back in horror as Jack rushed forward and proceeded to climb the drainpipe. I yelled at him to get down before Chris heard him, but somehow he got stuck halfway up. The drainpipe came away from the wall and Jack went crashing to the floor.

I dived into bed fully dressed, pulling the covers up, thinking that Chris would come up to the bedroom to see where the noise had come from, but then I heard terrible shouting going off outside and I realised that he had gone outside instead. I jumped out of bed and tiptoed to the window, hiding behind the curtain. Jack was still on the ground in the road, unhurt from what I could see and Chris was yelling at him. Just then a taxi came around the corner and nearly ran into them both. The taxi skidded all over the road, the driver wound down the window and gave Chris a mouthful of abuse, thinking that he was the reason Jack was lying on the road. Chris finally came to bed and I pretended to be asleep. He lay back and sighed then scared me to death as he jumped out of bed again and raced over to the window. He stuck his head out and yelled down at Jack;

Jack, turn that bloody radio off.

All right, Chris. Good night, sweet dreams.

I could hear Chris cursing under his breath but I never made a peep. In fact, I dared not move until I knew that he was sleeping. Then I crept into the bathroom and changed into my night clothes. When I went back into the bedroom I was tempted to see what Jack was up to, but decided against it.

Jack came in the next afternoon with a bunch of flowers. We didn't ask where he got them from, God knows, but they weren't from a florist.

I can't recall where we were going one afternoon, it was somewhere just out of town to pick something up that Chris needed and as it was a pleasant journey, Jack came with us for the ride. This was after the incident of the drainpipe and Mam and Dad went with us too, sitting with Jack in the back. All of a sudden, we heard a loud bang and realised we had run over a big brick that had flown up under the car. Chris got out to look and said it had burst the petrol tank and to get out of the car quickly. Just as we got out, Jack put a cigarette in his mouth and was about to light up. Everyone screamed at him to stop. There was petrol all over the place, as we had only just filled the car up.

Later that week someone in the village took pity on Jack and let him stay in his caravan, so he didn't have to sleep outside anymore. This was good as he washed his feet in the sink, downstairs in the pub toilets, every night after closing and sometimes he accidently left the tap running. This angered Chris because we were on a water meter.

A week went by and Jack walked into the pub, looking smart in his suit as usual, a big smile on his face but also sporting a black eye. I thought it was best not to ask how he had got the black eye and made him a coffee and some toast, as it was only eleven o'clock.

Where's your caravan then Jack?

Just at the back of the pub, Maggie. It's on that bit of spare land and it's a smasher.

I'm glad you have somewhere to live. You can come here for your lunch.

You mean a free lunch, Maggie? You are so kind.

No, you'll have to pay like everyone else; I'm cheap enough as it is.

There's nowt cheap about you, Maggie.

I smiled at his cheeky wink and walked away to start preparing the lunches.

Jack had a couple of pints and said that he had to go somewhere and it was quite late in the evening when we next saw him. He said that he had been for an interview.

What sort of a job is it then, Jack?

It's sort of selling.

Yeah, selling what?

Selling mock burglar alarms. They look dead real and it stops people thinking of robbing you.

Well. I'm sure you'll do well Jack with your charm. You could sell sand to Blackpool.

I had heard from his brothers, that at one time, he was a really good sales person in men's designer wear and was often the salesman of the year. I was told that customers would sometimes go into the store for a shirt and come out with a suit as well.

Ah well I think I'll go off to bed now. See you in the morning for my breakfast.

In your dreams, Jack.

You're always in my dreams, Maggie.

A voice piped up behind. It was Chris.

Jack, piss off.

Jack smiled at him and said goodnight.

There were a few of the girls around the bar, later that night, when Jack had gone and we arranged to meet outside when I would be 'walking the dogs'.

We stalked around to the caravan and were surprised to see how big and posh it was; it was huge. Someone was certainly looking after Jack. We looked at each other and I nodded, then we started rocking the caravan as hard as we could, laughing like mischievous school girls. Then a voice came up behind us;

What you up to now, Maggie?

I turned round and it was Jack. I stared at him with my mouth open, as he said goodnight and went behind the caravan. We followed him and there stood the smallest caravan I had ever seen, hidden by the large caravan. We ran like the clappers in all directions, as now someone was moving about in there.

I went back inside. The dogs looked at me in a strange way because they hadn't been for their run and I slipped quietly upstairs and looked out the window to see if anyone was outside the pub. God knows what the people in the caravan thought, but I knew that Jack would not tell.

It wasn't long after that, that Jack moved out of the village without even saying goodbye but then that was Jack. The pub seemed much quieter without him. I missed him sitting there with his mischievous smile and sense of humour, even though Chris was glad to see the back of him. Don't know why.

Jack had quite a few brothers that came into The Goat, each with their own personality. One in particular, was as bad as Jack for flirting. In fact, in nearly all the camcorder filming that we did, he would be there in the background blowing kisses or looking at me up and down, smiling and winking, but it was all harmless fun which Chris just accepted.

If a man walked into the bar with a woman and asked for a pint of beer and half a lager, we always asked if the half was for the lady, as there were glasses for women. If the man was a regular that drank pints then we assumed the half was for the lady and therefore didn't ask. However, Jack's brother often came with new girlfriends. He walked through the door and asked for a pint and half a lager. As usual he was followed by a girl and I would always say to him in a sarcastic way;

Will this be for a lady, sir?

I knew that it was, but pretended to look round for a lady, which he always thought was funny.

Maggie this is for a very beautiful lady indeed.

I passed him the drinks and jokingly said;

I can't see one.

He paid me for the drinks and passed the half to me.

What's this for?

It's for you. I wanted to say thank you for giving my mother a lift back from the supermarket today.

Oh thank you, that's so nice of you, but what about a drink for the girl you brought in with you?

She just happened to walk in at the same time.

With that he gave that same smile that Jack always did and left the bar.

Not long after that a serious looking chap came in and asked for a glass of orange juice.

Can I have ice in there please and I would like fresh ice, not that frozen stuff.

Scuse me, but that ice is fresh every day I'll have you know.

I hadn't realised what he had said. We all burst out laughing and I never lived it down. Someone would ask "can I have fresh orange please". I would give them fresh orange and then they would ask how long since it had been peeled.

We finally went to Pendle. I was very excited about going there purely to find out a little more about the Lancashire witch trials in the 1600s. I was not expecting the scenery to be as beautiful as it was. Situated at the eastern edge of Lancashire, Pendle borders on the Yorkshire Dales and is close to the Forest of Bowland and the Ribble Valley. There was so much beautiful countryside surrounding us with its locks and reservoirs, trees and woodlands, and there was plenty of wildlife to be seen. This place was really amazing and Pendle Hill itself just towers above at the height of one thousand, eight hundred and twenty seven feet. We had brochures telling us the history of Pendle that I kept reading out loud, to the annoyance of everyone;

What about this then mam? The Quaker movement started off in Pendle when a man called George Fox had a vision at the top of Pendle Hill.

In 1652 George Fox had a vision that would transform his religious beliefs and lead to a new religion. He believed that everything and everyone was blessed with the light of God and this led to the formation of the Quaker Movement. George Fox had been compelled to climb Pendle Hill, and this he did with great difficulty because it was so steep and high. When he reached the top he could see, spread out before him, the whole of Lancashire and the places where people were living. It was then that George Fox was inspired by God to form the Society of Friends.

For the Quaker movement to have started here was fascinating, especially as Monkbretton, near to our first pub, The Woodmoor, was one of the first Quaker burial sites in the very early 1650s.

I wonder how they got to be called 'Quakers' instead of Society of Friends, which they used to be called?

Mam was either reading or doing cross words when she was at home and I was really impressed with her general knowledge. She already knew of George Fox and the Quaker movement and told me immediately how they came to be called Quakers;

It's something to do with trembling or 'quaking' when feeling moved by God to speak during a meeting.

Mam, you're like a walking encyclopaedia.

After having a good day in Pendle, we called at a shop that sold almost everything to do with witches. As you walked inside there was eerie music being played and an array of books. Hanging from the ceiling were little witches with the names of the witches who were hanged, I bought thirteen witches, a broomstick and books to take home. Outside of the shop, there stood three full sized witches that looked very realistic with their hooked noses, hunched backs and pointed chins and I stood in the middle of them for some photographs. When I showed them to our locals, they asked which one was me.

The Pendle witch trials of 1612 are among the most famous witch trials in England and resulted in the hanging of the largest number of witches on any single occasion. Throughout the sixteenth and seventeenth century there was widespread torture and even execution of witches, particularly on the continent of Europe. Almost five hundred so-called witches were hanged in England alone. It was King James I, at the start of the seventeenth century, who introduced the death penalty for witchcraft in England and the Pendle witches were amongst the first to be executed. James I was a staunch believer in the existence of witchcraft and it is possible that the local magistrate, Roger Nowell, who accused the Pendle witches, did so to gain favour with the King. After reading about the trial, I was convinced that the trial was a conspiracy. The poverty stricken people, the Demdikes and the Chattoxes, were two families that lived in Pendle at that time and were once close friends, but fell out constantly over money owed. Indeed, the two families concerned in these trials had been linked to witchcraft for over fifty years. Ann Whittle, whose family was nicknamed Chattox, was thought to have murdered two men, but she was never arrested for the crime. The two families were always arguing and accusing each other and when Bessie Chattox stole clothing from the Southern family, nicknamed Demdikes, leaving them nothing to wear, she was reported to the magistrate who started to question the Chattox family regarding witchcraft. Shortly afterwards Alizon Devise asked a peddler for a few pins and when he declined, she cursed him and he collapsed, suffering a stroke which left him paralysed. Little realising that she was admitting her guilt; Alizon apologised to the peddler for what she had done and the magistrate immediately arrested her for witchcraft. She quickly implicated her mother and grandmother, and as both families started to accuse each other, four of them were sent for trial at Lancaster Assizes and were locked in the dungeons of Lancaster Castle. The magistrate used the accusations, which were being tossed about by both families, to incarcerate thirteen suspected witches and on the 20th of August 1612, eleven of them were executed by public hanging, only two of them being found not guilty. Although torture wasn't used to try witches in England at the time of the trials, both parties were happy in the end to confess to the so called spells they had supposedly inflicted on humans and animals.

    I thought about the witches and the poor life they had led, begging, having to resort to stealing food because they were hungry, and standing in the one item of clothing that they owned. Perhaps they were ordinary people who lived at the edge of the village trying to make a living through healing using herbs and potions. Illness such as epilepsy, strokes and heart attacks may not have been fully understood then and the sight of a person that had a bent, misshapen body and ugly features who was cursing you, would be, I thought, enough to bring on an attack. One of our neighbours, when we were children, was terrified of gypsies and got into a really bad state when they called at our homes selling their wares. She would hide in the house before they saw her, if she had no money to buy from them, and blamed every bad deed that happened on the gypsies' curse. Me mam was almost as bad for not being able to turn them away in case they put a curse on her. Sometimes people can suffer from mass hysteria, feeding off each other's reactions and emotions, causing panic, perhaps even to the extent of causing people to believe they have seen things that were not there, like the witches' familiars. These so called witches pleaded guilty without the use of physical torture, but that's not to say mental torture wasn't used. Roger Nowell was obviously a clever man with words. Those poor exhausted people stood there with bent bodies and hunch backs caused by malnutrition, weak and fragile until they finally gave Nowell what he had hoped for. I often wonder what he had offered them in return for their confession.

I don't believe that there were any witches in Steeton. It would have been hard for them to travel in those days, unless, that is, they flew over on their broomsticks. I think Chris was right in saying the tools were there from previous farmers. Even so, it's surprising how many roofs in West Yorkshire and Lancashire have witch protectors sitting there. I thought of all the torture that went on over Europe, so called witches made to prove they were innocent by trials that no one would have been able to defend. The dunking stool was a favourite way of trying people. They were tied to a chair and tipped into water. If you drowned you were innocent, if not you were a witch and were burned at the stake. The 'tests' used on these innocent people are just too horrible to think about and it isn't any wonder that most of the accused confessed.

Chris had two marks on his chest beneath his nipples, which looked like an extra set of nipples. As an extra nipple was supposed to be for demons to suckle on, he would certainly have been accused of witchcraft in the past.

I was speaking to a gentleman that lived near Pendle one day at the bar and, of course, the subject soon got around to the witches there;

I thought it sad that those poor people had no-one to defend them at the trial and were really not able to understand what was happening. They must have been locked up for ages in terrible conditions before the trial. In fact, one of them died in the dungeons. I bet that Roger Nowell was pretending to be nice to them, telling them that if they admitted to being guilty, they would be let off.

Yeah, they were really poor people and they were probably local abortionists that lived away from prying eyes.

Abortionists? What in those days?

Oh, yeah, people have been having abortions for years you know; it's not a twentieth century thing.

I suppose so.

That's where the cauldron comes in. They would make fat from the foetus to make soap.

Wish I'd never asked now. Soap made from a foetus?

Well yeah, soap comes from animal fat doesn't it?

The day after I went into town and bought some fat free soap.

Chapter Seventeen

Quite a few of the elderly friends that I had made at The Goats Head, had allotments further down the road from us, and sometimes they brought in freshly picked tomatoes, that they had grown and mushrooms that they had gathered from their early morning walks. I was making my own pizzas now. I had had a full day with someone training me how to make them from scratch, Italian style, and I had bought a special oven, to bake them quickly. I used my friends' fresh tomatoes and mushrooms as a special topping. I had also met another elderly gentleman called Alan and a younger man named Carl who was only about five foot in height. What Carl didn't know about local history wasn't worth knowing. I also loved the passion that he had for the outdoor life and the good things of life. Both he and Alan had an allotment each and they went picking mushrooms or walked along the riverside or the canal, very early on Sunday mornings.

Can I come with you this Sunday?

Aye lass, but it's cold at the crack o dawn. You have to wrap up well and have proper shoes on or wellies.

I was up at the crack of dawn with Christopher, in my green wellies and wax jacket all set to go walking. I loved it when both men taught me about nature, talking about the history of each place, pointing out certain flowers and plants. Christopher was also a keen outdoor person and he would come with us. We walked miles and it was soon became a regular Sunday event. One Sunday, Carl suggested walking along the river for a change and he told us how the shape of the river had changed over the years, and at one point he said;

Just around the corner, a man and his two daughters drowned. They went over the little waterfall, their boat tipped over and they became fast in the undercurrent, it was such a tragic story.

I was shocked to hear this, as I had had recurring dreams of drowning for years. In my dream I was in a canoe with me dad and my sister Teresa. We were laughing and trailing our hands in the water. There were people walking by on the riverbank and families sitting on the grass and they would wave. The sun was shining and there was a feeling of pure happiness in my bones. Dad was a handsome man, I can see him clearly now in my mind, dark wavy hair, blue eyes and a certain smile that only he had. In my dream we were working our way towards what appeared to be a very small waterfall, coming up in the distance, and because Dad was strong we felt safe as we always did on our canoe trips, but as we turned the corner towards the waterfall, the boat somehow capsized and we all drowned. I remember looking for people to help us when we were splashing about, but being around a corner no one knew what had happened. No sound came from any of us. This is a dream I have had since childhood, always with the same details and when I have seen waterfalls on my journeys I always have a little shudder inside. I have never told anyone about this dream, not even my sister.

My other recurring dream started in my teens. In this dream I was sitting by a river on my own and even though there was a mist, the sun was trying hard to get through. I took off my shoes and was about to bathe my feet in the clear water, when I saw what I thought was a log floating towards me. I watched it float for a while and as it neared me I realised it was a body face down in the water. I turned the body over and it was me.

It felt very strange walking around the corner to where it had happened. My mouth went dry and I realised that I was shivering. I couldn't shake this feeling off but decided not to say anything and although I didn't recognise the river bank, after a while, we approached a small waterfall that really did fill me with dread but I soon cheered up as we continued on our way.

That morning I had taken the two dogs with me. I had warned Carl that the Doberman was a wilful dog, but he said he'd never been beaten by a dog yet and he would sort him out and train him to walk on a lead. Then Caesar spotted a rabbit and set off with Carl holding on for dear life. Carl fell on his front as the dog carried on running, pulling Carl through the mire. I was hysterical with laughter but I have to give Carl his due, he did not let go of the lead. We had many laughs that morning because of Caesar. We had to try and lift a dog that size over a style, as he struggled with us. It took four of us about twenty minutes to get him over the style. We never did take Caesar with us again; he had tried to chase anything living or that moved, including a herd of cows that quickly turned on him.

I remember many conversations with Carl. He was passionate about everything and one day he was complaining about how things had changed over the years. At that point Christopher came down and asked where the bin had gone from the kitchen. Without thinking, I answered;

I've thrown it away; it was always full of rubbish.

Now Carl was laughing at me. When he had quietened down he said;

It's reight abaht bins, they are all'ess full o rubbish. They gerron abaht these new diseases and what do they do? They bring bloody rubbish bins into the house along with shit houses. We had to go outside to the toilet when we wah young. Nar the toilets are inside the bloody houses, along wi dustbins.

I bumped into Carl a couple of years ago and he asked if I remembered jumping over the bar;

Yea jumped over that bar so fast. I've never seen anyone move as quick.

Oh God, Carl, don't remind me.

We were having a bit of trouble with a few youngsters one night and one of them swore at me inches from my face. As the gate to the bar had people drinking there, I jumped over the taproom bar and chased after him with a Guinness bottle in my hand. Later that night the pool room window was smashed. It was the original stained glass and would be expensive to replace. The window had been broken from the inside and there were plenty of people in the pool room, but no one would own up or tell me who had broken it. If it had been an accident the matter would have been dropped and they knew me well enough to know that, but the silence annoyed me and made me think the window had been purposely broken. It was nearly closing time, so I locked the front door and wouldn't let them out. I stood there holding the key in my hand and refused to let anyone go home.

Maggie let us go; I have to be up early in the morning.

No. Not until I find out who broke the window.

I was threatened and sworn at, but I would not give in. Eventually someone called the police and told them I was holding them against their will. The police banged on the door and I reluctantly let them in. They told me it was offence to keep the people there;

Yes and it's an offence to destroy someone else's property, so you find out what happened in there.

Let them go home and we'll sort it out tomorrow when you have calmed down.

No one owned up to it and we had the window replaced. Later we laughed at my stubbornness at refusing to let them go home that night and how Chris was telling me to let it drop and open the door.

Public houses can go months without trouble, but every so often, particularly on Bank Holidays or at weekends when a large amount of alcohol has been consumed, a heated discussion can lead to a fight and it wasn't long before we had trouble again. It was when my brother, Tony and his wife and two kids came to stay. Chris was having an argument with someone who had previously been barred from the pub and it got out of hand and they started to fight. All of a sudden it seemed that everyone was involved. Most of them were defending Chris, but because my brother was a stranger, this made him public enemy number one. Some believed that he was the one that had attacked Chris, but then as with most fights in pubs, people join in without knowing why. There were quite a few people having a go at Tony now and he was being attacked from all over, but my brother was a six foot karate expert who had been practising karate for years. He stood his ground and sent his attackers flying all over the place. Someone grabbed him from behind and he lifted him into the air and pulled him straight over his shoulder. My sister-in-law, Sharon, was also a karate expert and joined in. The fight soon finished and Tony never got so much as a scratch, never mind a black eye as some did and, as usual, we laughed it all off. The funny side of this is that Sharon complained because she had just bought him the jumper that he was wearing and the stitching on the shoulder came undone, causing a hole. When they went back to Barnsley, she took the jumper back to the store and complained about it and got a refund. A week later when she was in the store, she saw the jumper up for sale at a very low price, so she bought it again and stitched it up.

Occasionally, men would fall out with each other and it sometimes ended up with them fighting. We usually left them to it knowing that they would be friends shortly after, but one particular night about ten o'clock, two of our regulars came bursting through the door arguing and yelling at each other. I served them a drink, but they were still at each other's throats. I was told by Des that they had been kicked out of the pub opposite for fighting each other. I thought it was funny that they had come to another pub together to finish the fight off. The argument started to get very heated and the next minute, the two men were fighting on the floor. It was so laughable. One was yelling;

You're hurting me.

They stopped fighting to have a drink, and then started again and after they had finished, one of the men started to argue about how he had been hurt, I couldn't resist;

You were fighting; you're supposed to hurt each other, that is the whole point.

Yeah, but he really hurt me.

And so the argument started again about who was hurt the most.

Things went back to normal, as they always do in a public house. We were going out for a meal with another couple, who were also licensees, and I wanted to look my best. I had bought a new outfit which looked lovely and showed off my figure. I dried my hair into a bouncy style, took time with my makeup and was all ready to go downstairs, feeling really pleased with myself. Just as I was leaving the bedroom, I thought I would put some of Alison's hair spray on my hair. I put my head forward and gave it a really good spray, as I had seen Alison do. We would be out all evening and then either go to their pub for a drink or they would come to ours. The perfume from the spray smelt nice and hairspray was something I very rarely used. I 'fluffed' my hair up with my hands to give it body and went downstairs full of confidence.

To say everyone looked shocked at my appearance was an understatement. It was early in the evening and there were quite a few locals already at the bar. Everyone was looking at me; some of the men stopped drinking and stood with open mouths. I confidently walked towards the bar feeling pleased that my efforts were receiving so much attention. I went behind the bar to pour myself a glass of wine and caught sight of my reflection in the mirror behind the bar. My hair was completely white. I ran from the bar, pushing my way through the customers and dashed upstairs thinking it must a hormone problem. After all I had heard that a person's hair could turn white in their sleep. My great grandmother lost all her hair in her sleep when she was very young, after seeing her little sister run over by a car, and had had to wear a wig all her life. I remember being frightened of her once when she slept at our house because she took the wig off and looked like an alien that I had seen on Flash Gordon. Had I had a shock recently?

I ran upstairs to the mirror, devastated. My hair was snow white, and I looked like an old woman. I laid on the bed bawling my eyes out. Black mascara ran all over the pillow and all sorts of things came into my head. Of course, we'd have to leave the pub trade. I would never be able to leave the house looking like this. The doctor's surgery was closed until Monday and there was no way I was going to casualty looking like this. Chris walked through the door to see my mascara running down my face and leaving me looking like a sad panda. He looked round the room struggling for words, as shocked as I was. He stood there a while before picking up the aerosol can and asking;

Did you use this hairspray?

I nodded without looking up, thinking that he was thinking the same thing as me, that I had had a reaction to it, after all I did have sensitive skin. He had that sort of smile on his face that he always had when I had done something stupid. He walked over to the bed and held the can right in front of my eyes. Deodorant it read. I was confused until I looked on the shelf and saw a pink aerosol, containing hairspray. Two pink aerosols had stood next to each other, the same shape and height.

After a quick shower, an even faster makeup attempt, to cover my puffed eyes and a session with the hot brush, I went downstairs to be greeted by everyone's laughter. If I had felt my hair or looked closer in the mirror, I would have realised it was white powder. So much for vanity!

We were turning the light out after everyone had gone home when Chris suddenly looked up;

Margaret, I've just seen a......

Before he could finish, Caesar and Gyp started to growl. Their hair stood on end and they tried to get out of the room. Chris stood staring towards the stage that we had for entertainment. He turned to me and said;

I've just seen a lady walk across the stage, in a wide, bushy skirt and old fashioned long sleeved blouse and something like a mop cap. I couldn't see her feet, but she was holding an oil lamp. She was there for a few seconds, before I realised what I had seen, then she turned her head and smiled at me.

The air had turned so cold in the room, that something had to have happened. I supposed the reason that she was at the level she was, was because the stage wouldn't have been there when she was alive. I was annoyed because Chris had seen her and I hadn't, but I certainly felt something. I turned to Chris and said;

Do you think she might have been locked up in a priest hole?

Oh for God's sake, you and your priest holes. No, she looked like a servant.

Chris wasn't into priest holes and after all the knocking down I had done, this was a touchy subject anyway. As I walked away I muttered;

Well, servants pray you know.

Being licensees was hard on our relationship, as we were together twenty four hours a day even though most of the time there were other people around. Besides those who worked in the bar, there were draymen, reps, and people to empty the bandit and juke box machines, or make deliveries, plus of course, the cleaner. Unfortunately, tensions would get bottled up and one small argument easily dragged up something else that had been put on hold. Unlike the Woodmoor where there was a private room behind the bar to air our disagreements, the last two pubs had nowhere to talk in private. We were starting to argue more often now and Chris could sulk for England. We had fallen out over something one night and he refused to speak to me, but he was always smiling and laughing with everyone else while cutting me off. One evening, I was getting more irate by the minute when I saw him collecting glasses and chatting to the customers then walking behind the bar and ignoring me. When he went out to collect the ashtrays in, I calmly walked over and emptied a very large, full ashtray of cigarette ash, along with crisp papers, onto his head in front of the remaining customers. I froze for a while thinking he would kill me now, as his hair was very important to Chris. He would wash and blow it dry twice a day before going down to the bar. For a moment, probably only a second or two, time stood still, but Chris simply carried on collecting ashtrays with ash and tab ends on his head. I felt like screaming with frustration because he still didn't say anything to me. I went upstairs to put my coat on and took the dogs out. There was no moon that night, and it was much darker than usual. I sat on the swing looking up at the stars while muttering under my breath and stayed there a little longer than usual. When I got back to the pub, the front door was closed; he had shut me out, although he hadn't locked it. I could have been murdered and laid there all night, because when Chris was in a sulk, I ceased to exist. He had turned the lights off in the bar area, but left a small one on in the corridor, so at least I could see where I was going. Chris not waiting up for me made me even angrier, so I thought I would sit at the bar and drink a few whiskies before going to bed and hoped that by then he would be asleep. I was so stubborn that I sat in the dark with just the little light when suddenly the room went icy cold and the dogs barked fiercely at something in the dark, towards the other end of the pub. I couldn't see anything because the room was all in darkness and it was a race between me and the cowardly dogs as we all tried to fit through the door to the stairs at the same time.

I used to love the swing that Christopher and Russell had made in the spare room and I often went in there to sit on the swing myself. When the sun shone through all of the windows, the witch like faces stared at me as they were bulging out in the wall. They had faces drawn onto them now, Christopher and Russell had pencilled them in. This made them look even more real and they seemed to stare at me. This place could be quite spooky at times.

This was to be the time when my spirituality grew and there were a lot of people who came in to the pub who were involved with spiritualism. There was Mick; he was a brilliant astrologer and we nicknamed him Cosmic. His friend Rob was a healer and a psychic, I had myself been able to 'cure' headaches for years simply by putting my hands on people's heads. In fact when Darren was over here, he suffered a lot from headaches and he used to say to me;

Give us some of that voodoo crap will yer, I have a headache.

I would rest my hands on his head and could feel the heat or 'energy' coming through. It had always worked.

Mick must have read hundreds of books on the subject of spiritualism and was always talking about Karma and Karmic law. He stood at the bar one night telling us about a spiritual guru named Satay Sai Baba;

Baba is a spiritual leader and miracle worker. Some say he is another Jesus Christ and he has a great following of people who have witnessed him materialise substances from his hand, such as food and flowers. He has been seen by hundreds to turn water into wine.

Can he mek beer anall? If so, ask him to pull a pint for me will yeah?

Shurrup Des.

He's also a great healer and it's said that he is the reincarnation of a saint. When Baba comes into your life, then your life will change.

Change in what way? You mean for the better?

Not always at first. It might mean going through a rough time, but if it's meant to be, it will be. In Karmic law, sometimes you have to go through bad times to reach the good ones in your life.

I don't want my life to change thank you, Mick.

Well if Baba comes into your life it will, you will have no choice.

One of the men listening said;

Baba, Baba, had he any wool? Warra load o shit. Gerrit? Baba, shit.

Shurrup. Go on then Mick, how does he come into your life?

Through dreams and when you've seen him once, then he'll keep coming back.

The next day, Mick came in with a photograph of this so called Baba Guru and I was amazed to see that he looked like an ordinary man with bushy hair and a round fat face. That night, I had a dream of the guru sitting on a huge white horse and smiling at me. I shouted "go away, I don't want to change my life". I woke myself up shouting and thrashing about. Chris was not amused that I had woke him up from a deep sleep;

What the hell's up with you? Go to sleep, it's only four o clock. I have to get up in the morning.

Chris always annoyed me with that, as if it was something special to get up in a morning. Everyone gets up in a morning and as for thrashing about, one night he was dreaming of Jack and arguing with him. He thrashed out and hit me in the eye. I had a black eye for days.

Where's that black eye come from Maggie? Don't tell me you walked into a door. You've been punched.

Chris was dreaming of hitting Jack and hit me instead, I'm glad he doesn't sleepwalk or he might have gone for his gun and shot me.

The customer started laughing at this and I said;

I'm serious, that gun of his is only in the next room. It's not funny.

Although I had used Tarot cards in the past, I had only really read them for people that I knew, but I was persuaded by these two men, Mick and Rob, to start again and to take it seriously and they recommended getting new cards that chose me rather than me choosing them. These are the same cards that I use today.

I did as they advised and bought some cards that drew me to them after looking at several packs, from a shop called 'Spooks' in Haworth. I started to familiarise myself with the new cards during any spare time that I had. Then one night while I was sleeping, the cards started coming to me, one by one, hovering over my body, about the full length of a human. A voice explained what each of the cards meant, but more frightening was that the devil, hanged man and the death card kept reappearing. I woke up in a sweat but the feeling of fear still remained and the room felt icy. I walked to the bathroom, which was on the other side of all the upstairs rooms, I washed my face, then went back to bed and fell asleep, but the same thing happened again. It happened again the next night. I was telling Rob, who also read the cards and did healing, about these night terrors and he told me to put the cards in a box with a bible and use a sage stick to cleanse the box and also the bedroom. He also advised me never to take them out of the box after drinking alcohol as this could draw earthbound spirits. After I took his advice things went back to normal and I was beginning to do readings for some of our customers. To this day I protect my cards in the same manner and treat them with respect.

I was also interested in a man called Edgar Cayce and started to buy books written by this great man. It was Mick who first introduced me to these books, when he gave me a book called 'Man of Miracles' and this was the book that really paved the way for what I do today, hypnotherapy and healing together.

Edgar Cayce was at that time classed as one of the world's greatest healers. He believed that this power came from God. Cayce, quite by accident, was able to induce himself into a deep hypnotic state and see inside a person's body to identify the cause of their ailments, using words that were not known to him. He was known to have 'read' fourteen thousand sets of symptoms over a period of forty four years.

It first began at the age of twenty one when he developed a gradual paralysis of the throat that was likely to lead to the loss of his voice. When the doctors said there was nothing they could do to find a cause for his condition, Cayce tried hypnosis, something he had tried earlier in his life when having difficulty learning his schoolwork. He entered into a deep, hypnotic trance and, in this state, he was able to diagnose the problem and repair the muscles to restore his voice.

Over the years as his healing went on, hundreds of people tried to prove that Cayce was a hoaxer, labelling him a charlatan, but when sceptical medical investigators studied his thirty thousand case records, they arrived at an astounding conclusion; more than ninety per cent were accurate. Doctors throughout the world would send their 'incurables' to him and even asked him to diagnose people that Cayce had never seen.

The headlines of the New York Times printed in 1910, read;

"Illiterate man becomes doctor when hypnotised…strange power shown by Edgar Cayce puzzles physicians".

Called 'The Sleeping Prophet', Edgar Cayce was also a clairvoyant and made hundreds of predictions in his lifetime, including the discovery of the Dead Sea Scrolls. The Dead Sea Scrolls comprise between eight hundred and twenty five and eight hundred and seventy documents, including texts from the Hebrew Bible. They were discovered sometime between 1947 and 1956 in eleven caves around the Wadi Qumran. Sadly they were found only a few years after his death in 1945. The texts are of great religious and historical significance, as they are practically the only known surviving biblical documents written before AD 100.

Cayce foretold many events that would happen in the world and the majority of the events did occur. He even foretold the date of his own funeral, years before he died at the age of sixty seven. Everything that Edgar Cayce achieved in his life interested me greatly, but what interested me the most were his 'readings' of Atlantis. He said that the people of Atlantis had constructed giant, laser-like crystals for power plants and that these were responsible for the second destruction of the land. According to Cayce, Atlantis was destroyed by volcanic and earthquake-like 'explosions' on three separate occasions. Each of these lasted over a period of months or perhaps even years. Cayce blamed the final destruction of Atlantis and the disintegration of its culture on greed and lust. But before the legendary land disappeared under the waves, Cayce claimed that there was an exodus of Atlanteans to ancient Egypt. He also believed the Great Flood of Noah to be a direct result of the sinking of the last huge remnants of Atlantis. Cayce maintained that Atlantis was an ancient civilization that was superior to our own and stated that its last surviving islands disappeared somewhere in the Atlantic Ocean some ten thousand years ago. Edgar Cayce claimed that the size of Atlantis was equal to that of Europe. He saw visions of this continent of the past going through three major periods of division; the first two occurred around 15,600 B.C., when the mainland was divided into islands. Cayce at times, would look into the past lives of those who came to him for information concerning their health and told a number of people that they had past lives in the legendary lost land of Atlantis. During the time of his readings, Cayce referred to Atlantis no fewer than seven hundred times over a span of twenty years, and so this was to be the perfect name for my hypnotherapy practice in later years:-Atlantis Hypnosis.

Edgar Cayce's view of astrology was based on the concept of reincarnation. Casey believed that it was not the positions of the planets that influenced the soul at birth, but that the soul chose the time in which it wished to be born. According to Cayce, some of us have had lives before our present one and bring our talents, abilities, and influences from those past lives. These influences, part of the universal law of cause and effect, are called "karma". Cayce also tells us that not only have we had previous lives, but that, between lifetimes, the soul has a life outside the physical world.

There were just the two of us in the bar when everyone had gone home and I turned to Chris and said;

My idea of how life began, then ending only to start again may well have been true. The people on the planet might all die, for some reason or another, but the planet will live on and a new species of life will evolve and this could have happened before. Cayce believed that Atlantis did exist, but that it was destroyed through power and greed and that it's starting to happen again.

What do you mean? In what way is it starting again?

In every way. We have people leaving the planet, travelling through space and coming back again. There's war all the time and nuclear power. Look at Chernobyl; we don't know the damage that has been done yet. Then there is the threat of huge volcanoes waiting to erupt and wipe us all out. There's also the dream of me sitting inside a planet looking down at the earth, waiting to be born. It could have easily happened. How could I have possibly known anything about reincarnation or different planets, I was only young when I first started having the dreams. I had barely learned the alphabet at school, never mind anything else. According to Edgar Cayce, we choose to be born as we are today.

I don't know. You could drive yourself nuts wondering where we came from or why we are here. I have always believed that there are other forms of life out there; we can't possibly be the only ones. There are some strange things out there that cannot be explained by science. Come on, time for bed, I've to get up in the morning.

I couldn't switch off that night. I wanted to talk about Edgar Cayce and Atlantis. I lay awake imagining myself being there, dressed in white, with the power to do all the things I wanted to do, only nice things, of course. I imagined it being a peaceful place with plants and flowers and wonderful bright colours. I imagined crystals everywhere and people that glowed with health and happiness. I imagined a slow, relaxed pace of life, with plenty of daylight. Of course, someone always has to spoil things by being greedy and power hungry.

My elderly friends, Jim and Peter, came in most nights and stood at the end of the bar, always in the same place, and along with Carl, Alan and Tony, they would have made ideal characters for Last of the Summer Wine. They were all on the mischievous side and loved life. Jim said one evening;

I can't believe you walk in that rec late at night. Anyone could be hiding in the bushes.

I'm OK, I look forward to walking at night and I have the dogs with me. I feel safe enough here in Steeton, but thanks for your concern Jim.

I did feel safe there and if I stayed out longer than usual, Chris would stand at the front door and whistle, if I didn't come back, then he would come looking for me. It was a particularly dark night when Jim had made that comment and, for the first time I did feel a little nervous at first, but once I set foot in the rec, I was all right. I was just about to make my way back through the little gate, in-between the bushes that surrounded the rec, when I saw two men walking quite quickly on the other side of the road. This caught my eye because of the way they walked, as if on a mission. When I came out of the darkness and onto the pathway I realised that it was Jim and Peter.

Hey up, where are you two off to? You're going the opposite way to where you live.

Strangely, and without looking up towards me, Jim replied;

Allotments.

It was not at all like them to be abrupt like that and the allotments, which were further down the road, would be completely in the dark, as they were in a field. I was thinking about this when I noticed Chris standing at the door about to whistle.

The next evening when Jim and Peter came in, Chris served them and, afterwards, I went over to ask what was wrong the night before;

What was up with you two last night? You wouldn't talk to me and why were you going to the allotments at that time of night? You're up to something, you two.

Well, we had planned to follow you last night and hide in the bushes to frighten you and make you jump, but as we were approaching the gate at the rec, I turned around to see if anyone was about and saw Chris standing outside The Goat, so we quickly crossed the road towards the allotments.

I was choking with laughter. So that's why they were walking quickly. It would have looked suspicious if they had turned back. They would have had to walk down towards the allotments and wait for us to go in before they turned back.

I'm sure that husband of yours knew what we had planned. He must have overheard us.

I think he probably did. He usually whistles me after about twenty to thirty minutes and he was stood outside when I got back.

I was getting dressed one morning and thought how dull the bedroom was and how it could do with a facelift. I mentioned this to Chris while we drank our coffee but he didn't think we should decorate because we were too busy with the pub;

Well I'll do it then, it only wants a coat of emulsion to brighten it up.

He didn't answer me and that made me more determined to do it myself. I went to town and bought the paint and started with the ceiling. For some reason, I was soon splattered in spots of paint even though I had been very careful. I had a coffee break and after that I went outside to put washing on the line and Mick asked how I had managed to get so splattered with paint;

Did you stir it first?

No.

I made some lunch for Chris and started to move some furniture, but couldn't lift it on my own. I went back down stairs to ask if he would help me, but he said he was busy.

But Chris, it will only take a minute with the two of us.

I'm busy.

There are only two people in and Mick will keep his eye on the bar, it's only eleven o'clock.

He wouldn't help and it was one of those jobs that you wished you hadn't started, but needed to finish. I was mad at myself for starting it and mad at Chris for not giving me a hand. I picked the brush up and started painting again. It was easier now that I had stirred it, but I couldn't lift anything on my own so I painted around the bed, around Chris's computer and around the wardrobes and even the bedside cabinet. I didn't move anything. I thought it all looked nice and fresh now.

I took my tins and paintbrushes downstairs to the barn and saw my bike, or what was left of it. All over the floor were bent spoons and tools.

Christopher! It seemed that Christopher, Russell and Christopher's friend James, had been 'borrowing' parts of my bike to mend their own bikes. All that was left was a skeleton.

Steeton was such a pretty place and it was a pleasure just going for the morning bread and vegetables. Early every morning I would walk across the green as the winter sun cast intricate patterns, formed by the shadows of the now leafless branches. It was also lovely during the summer months with different colours all around and the sun glinting through the trees. The butcher used to say I was like a pretty flamingo. He would say to me,

Just like the song says, "When she walks by, she brightens up the neighbourhood".

The village was much quieter now they had finished the new bypass, no more heavy wagons and traffic. The men that had worked on the bypass had used caravans to eat and sleep in during the time they were here and they used to come in for a drink in the evening. One of the workers was only a young boy and he loved to dance on disco nights. We often used the camcorder on disco nights. They were new at that time so it was a novelty to everyone, and we filmed them all having a good time. The next morning when I looked at the recording, I was surprised to see that every time the camera focused on the young boy, the film went fuzzy. It was a new camera that had cost over a thousand pounds and I was about to tell Chris it needed to go back to the shop, when the look on his face stopped me.

You know the young lad from the caravan site? He's dead. He put the heater on last night in his caravan because he was cold and was overcome with fumes.

The pub was in total shock. He was well liked and looked after by the older workers. It was so sad. We hired a coach and many of us went to Lancashire to attend his funeral.

Chapter Eighteen

We were stood at the bar when one of our regulars came through the door obviously excited at something. She went to Chris to be served and before he had time to pour her drink she said;

Chris, you'll never believe this, but a woman that I work with didn't come into work today which is really unusual for her. We were naturally worried and rang her house. Her husband said that she had left home at the usual time, so the family rang around her friends and they went looking for her. It was four hours later when she turned up at home and she didn't have a clue as to where she had been.

Could she have had a blackout?

Don't think so. She's fitter than all of us there. All she knows is that she woke up to find herself miles away from home and work, just there in the middle of a country road. Four hours missing and her car wouldn't start at first as if the battery was flat and then she said the car suddenly started again. Some say that she was abducted by aliens.

The next day there was talk of UFO sightings all over Yorkshire including in Skipton which is a ten minute car ride from Steeton and another on Harden Moor near Keighley, again only ten minutes away. Two uniformed police officers observed a single bright white light for three to four seconds on Harden Moor initially at ground level approximately four hundred to eight hundred yards from their vehicle. It was seen near some high voltage power lines, then the object dropped below both of the officers' vision when it entered a valley. Rumour quickly went around that this woman had been abducted by aliens and I did notice when reading magazines and sometimes newspapers that 1988 was a year when a lot of UFO sightings were reported, just in Yorkshire alone.

We had a phone call from Dublin to say Michael and Dina were coming over for a long weekend, so I informed Mam and Dad and they made arrangements to come over with my brother Tony, his wife Sharon and my nephew and niece. Thinking back now, I can't think where everyone slept, but we were used to people staying and always managed. It was lovely to see Michael and Dina again and I was soon planning where we could go on the Sunday.

The first night in the pub we had a big party. A few customers stayed behind, chatting until about midnight and I went upstairs to make some of my special pizzas that were popular in the pub. Adrian came down with his guitar and we had a singsong. Michael was a singer in Ireland and had even been on the television with famous people and had sung on a chat show with stars that included Brit Ekland. Dad loved to sing and was singing Irish songs whilst Mam competed with Yorkshire and Lancashire songs. Everybody joined in, but we were usually stuck for the words and I wondered how Michael and other singers remembered the words to all the songs they sang. Mam always seemed to wave her glass of whisky about when singing and I joked that she looked like Dean Martin. After starting to sing the first two lines of 'Lassie from Lancashire' mam gave up because she only knew those two lines. Then she started to sing 'My Girl's a Yorkshire girl' but she only knew the first two lines of that song as well so decided to sing Ilkley Moor baht 'at, which goes on and on. There's a long list of verses with a chorus in-between each verse of; On Ilkley Moor baht 'at.

Mam sang five verses;-

Wheeare esta bin since ah saw thee...

Tha's been a-cooartin' Mary Jane'...

Tha's bahn ter cop thi death o' cold...

Then we s'll eter bury thee...

Then t'wurrums'll come an' eyt thee up...

Mam stopped and said "what's the next verse", to which I replied;

Now't Mam, he's dead, buried, en bin etten up wi worms. What more do you want?

I always thought the wah mooar than that.

God, I hope not.

It wasn't until years later I found the words to this song and apparently there's another four verses;

Then t'ducks'll come an' eyt up t'wurrums...

Then we s'll come an' eyt up t'ducks...

Then we s'll all ev etten thee...

That's wheeare wi get us ooan back...

On Ilkley Mooar, baht 'at. Etc etc.

Dad sang an old Irish song, 'Did you ever go across the sea to Ireland?' Which we all joined in then and Michael sang some of his favourites songs that he sang on stage. Later in the evening on request, Michael sang one of Dad's favourites of all the Irish songs, 'Noreen Bawn'. It tells a sad story of a widow that lived happily with her daughter, who the neighbours called, 'The Irish colleen'. It had broken her mother's heart when Noreen emigrated to America. After years of waiting to hear from her, she turned up one morning at the door. Noreen's mother didn't recognise this beautiful young lady dressed in elegant clothes, on first sight, but recognised the purple spots upon her cheeks. The song goes on to say; 'There's a churchyard in Tirconnell, where a broken hearted mother's cries', "Poor Noreen, tis I'm lonesome since you're gone, 'twas the curse of emigration laid you low my Noreen Bawn.

There was silence in the room when he had finished singing the song. Michael had sung it so well and it almost made me cry as the song does every time I hear it played.

We cheered the atmosphere up again with singing jolly Irish songs. Dad and Michael stood together and sang some old rebel songs, 'Kevin Barry', and the 'Dying Rebel'. They reminded me of mere cats because they both stood so straight and tall when they sang, especially Dad. When he was singing he always stood with his chest out, his head held high and his arms by his side.

It was three thirty in the morning when we went to bed and I was still up at seven, cooking them all a full English breakfast. On Sunday, we all set off to Knarsbrough and to Mother Shiptons Cave. However, it was closed in the winter months, which was a shame. Mother Shipton was another so called witch with a hump back and long crooked nose. She was also a famous prophet. There are lots of books on her prophesies that many claim to have come true. She predicted that men would walk and talk under water and be able to travel through the sky. Mother Shipton lived in the sixteenth century in a cave and you could visit the cave and see a full length statue of her, however, the last time I went to visit, the statue had gone. There is also a famous wishing well there and thousands of tourists have claimed that their wishes made there, have come true, including me. You should never wish harm on anyone however, or it could come back to you and you should never wish for money either.

The pub seemed really quiet when everyone had gone home apart from me mam and dad, but not for long. It was soon full again with Adrian and Christopher's friends; we always had a full house one way or another.

Winter was definitely here now and although I don't think that Steeton was as cold as Haworth, it was very cold as the wind came over from the Dales.

"There's a dominos match tonight in Skipton, if you two fancy going out in this freezing weather."

Mam and Dad were now playing dominoes on an evening with some of the locals and there was always a good atmosphere when there was any kind of match on. We had darts teams, pool teams and quiz nights and whether they were played home or away, it was always a good night.

When the teams played at home, I would put food on for them at half time, just like everyone else did at their home nights; barbecued spare ribs were a favourite, along with ham sandwiches. For away matches, they would come in and meet up to travel together and then they would come back for the last pint.

It was bitterly cold so I expected them to say no, but they were happy to go and support the team. I suggested that they wrap up well as it was going to be a very frosty night, especially late on. They were the kind of people that stayed in during winter, preferring nights by the fire, so were not used to the night frost. They both put on their suede coats looking warm as toast when Chris walked into the room.

They're nice coats you two are wearing. They look very warm. We have some suede coats like that.

Mam and Dad looked at me and then we all looked at the floor. Chris burst into laughter when he realised they used to be our coats.

Well, they suit you two better than us. I always felt uncomfortable in mine.

We all laughed, although I knew he wouldn't be bothered that I had given the coats to my parents. Chris never wore his coat anyway because we had a car and I had never worn mine, not even once.

We rushed to the car and it was really cold. It took ages for the car to warm up and we were almost there before it did eventually get warm. The pub where the match was being held was opposite a large, public car park. This was good because we wouldn't have far to walk to the car after the match, when it was late in the evening and colder still. The landlady had put a stew on to warm us all up and we left about ten thirty to go back to The Goat, shouting goodnight to everyone. The cold, frosty air hit us as soon as we opened the pub door. We clutched our coats tightly round our bodies and headed for the car park which was behind a little wall. Instead of walking to the car park entrance I thought I would just jump over the wall to get to the car first and get the car heated up, as I was driving. I was almost at the car when I saw Dad go running past me at some speed, his arms flying outwards;

My God, Dad, where did you spring from?

Little did I know that Dad had decided to do the same as I had and jump over the wall. What he didn't know, however, was that the wall was higher at the other side and it had a downhill slope. He had jumped over the wall and found he couldn't stop himself from running down the slope. Not only was it steep, but it was very icy. His speed increased as he went sailing past me, trying not to fall. To me, it seemed to happen in slow motion, yet it happened so fast. He finally landed spread eagled across the bonnet of a car, which was funny enough, but on standing up the shape of his body was visible in the frost which had settled on the car. The front of his coat was white with frost, as he stood there looking like a naughty boy, not knowing what to do or say, just as Mam and Chris walked into the car park. Seeing my Dad's coat and then the car, it didn't take long for them to work out what had happened. Chris just doubled up in laughter; and I laughed my head off. Mam was Mam;

For God's sake, Paddy, what the bloody hell do you think you're playing at? How old are you?

I was just following Margaret.

He replied in his ever so soft Irish accent which made him seem even more innocent and vulnerable.

Yer all reight following her, she's mad. Yer could ev broc yer bloody neck.

I climbed in the car. We were all laughing, including my mother, who could yell at Dad one minute and laugh the next. They had a very good relationship that never failed to bring laughter into the house. I have often wondered what the driver thought when he saw his car, complete with the shape of a body on its bonnet.

Christmas soon arrived and both the afternoons and evenings were very busy, followed by New Years Eve and, of course, fancy dress. There were some pretty good outfits that year, but the best fancy dress I had ever seen was snow white and the seven dwarfs. The dwarfs followed snow white across the road from the pub opposite. They walked on their knees to make themselves look like dwarfs. The traffic stopped to let them pass and they entered our pub one after the other, singing Hi Ho, Hi Ho, it's off to work we go.

Even though I love the summer months, I also looked forward to the winter. The walks were so much nicer, the feel of crunching as you walked on the frosty grass and the ferns were crisp and white, like stars or snowflakes. Yes I loved the winter months living there.

March arrived with its cold winds, the sun teased as it appeared and then disappeared again, leaving it cold. A few weeks later, I was reading the paper and realised that St. Patrick's Day was coming up.

It's St Patrick's Day next week, Chris. Shall we have an Irish band on?

Might be a bit short notice, but I'll try.

Mam and Dad might come over; it's been a couple of months since they were last here, Christmas in fact.

We had a lot of Irish living in Steeton. In fact, there is probably more Irish living in West Yorkshire and Lancashire than anywhere else in England, apart from Liverpool. Families came over to work in the mills, especially families with a few daughters.

My parents arrived the day before St Patrick's Day and already Mam was warning Dad to go steady with the drink, although these days he spent St Patrick's nights at home. I made them a coffee and some lunch and we talked about the time in the 1950s when Dad used to meet up with his Irish mates straight from work on St Patrick's Day. I asked me mam if she remembered Dad coming home drunk in the 1950s.

I do! The neighbours thought it was funny when he came up the street singing Irish songs and me rushing out to push him inside.

Mam would make him go to bed and sleep it off. He wasn't allowed a cup of tea, so Teresa or I would sneak a cup of tea and some bread and jam up to him, but I found out later that she always knew about it and thought it was funny.

Remember that year when he couldn't go for a drink because it was a Saturday and he wasn't at work. He said he had to go into town for something, so you hid his shoes.

Yeah, ah knew what he wanted to go into town for.

Mam laughed as she recalled that he was so annoyed that he found some green paint in the washhouse and painted the doors outside green, to celebrate St Patrick's Day, wearing his slippers and the shamrock on his shirt that his mother sent him every year. Mam said;

The rent man came for t'rent en reported him te council. They came out to see us and made him paint it blue again.

Anyway it should be a good night tonight, I love Irish folk bands.

Dad did get drunk that night and when they went to bed; we heard a crash followed by;

Paddeeee, yer silly sod, yer nearly broc yer neck. Gerrin te bed fer God's sake.

Minutes later I heard laughter from me mam. Apparently Dad had tripped and slid on the carpet and he had the pattern from the carpet on his head. The next day he had a black eye, as he had bruised one side of his face.

There was still a lot of tension between me and Chris. Trade was not as good as it used to be, the weekends were much quieter and we were having trouble with underage drinkers from another small village tucked away amongst the hills. Some young girls, of fifteen, were coming in looking like eighteen year olds, young boys were getting drunk and smashing glass in bus stops and we were in trouble with the police. At the time there was talk of youngsters carrying ID cards which would have helped. There was no way of being able to guess the ages of some and the police were unsympathetic because of the bad behaviour of some of them after leaving The Goat. There was one particular girl that I had served that looked easily eighteen or older. I was told by someone that she was only fourteen. Chris and I were constantly falling out and by the end of the year, things just weren't the same. It was also the time when 'all day opening' for public houses came into force and unless you could afford extra staff for the few customers that came in during the day, which could mean paying more money out than was coming in. It was a very long and tiring day with no rest in-between sessions, plus there was no free time to do anything else. We decided it was time to leave not only The Goats Head but the pub trade itself.

I had many happy times during my life as a landlady and still have wonderful memories brought to life by the old camcorder recordings. Things in life change all the time, however, and over the last three months at The Goats Head, life had changed. Apart from the arguments we were now having, it isn't a healthy life being a publican. You tend to do more drinking than you normally would, the hours are very long and it is very hard work, not to mention that in those days the air would be thick with smoke and nicotine, which twice gave me terrible chest infections. I started to think of what Mick (Cosmic) had said about life changing when this certain guru came into your life. Perhaps it was only a coincidence, I don't know, but even though it was a sad time, I was looking forward to new adventures that I was sure would come. As Scarlet O'Hara said, "After all, tomorrow is another day".

It was time to call last orders for the very last time.

Glossary

Yorkshire

Arht	out	Esta bin	have you been
Abart	about	'er	her
Ah	I	Ez	has
Art	out	Eye	yes
Ant	haven't	Eter	have to
Ar	our	'Em	them
Al	I will	Ed	had
All'ass	always	En	and
Abart	about	Ev	have
Ageean	again	Eyt	eat
Annall	as well	Etten	eaten
Bum	bottom	Ent	haven't
Bi	be	Frum	from
Bin	been	Fo	for
Brok	broke	Gi	give
Bahn	bound	Goo	go
Coit	coat	Gonna	going
Cooartin'	courting	Goorra	got a
Cum	come	Gerrin	getting
Cop	get	Giz	give
Dunt	don't	Goo	go
Darn	down	Gorrata	got out of
Deeing	dying	Gorrall	got all
Dint	didn't	Gerra	get a
Dus that	do you	Gerring	getting
Ent	haven't	Gerron	get on
Eead	head	Hoo'am	home
'ere	here	Init	in it

Laiking arht	playing out	Warra	was a
Lass'll	lass will	Wi	with
Leeter	lighter	Wheeze	where
mi	me	Want	wasn't
med	made	Weeave	where have
mooar	more	Wiv	we have
Niva	never	Weshed	washed
Neer	near	Wheeare	where
Nowt	-nothing	Wun	one
Nowt	nothing	Waint	won't
Nar	now	Warrin	was in
Pots	pots	Wurrums'll	worms will
Poo'il	pool	Yonder	there
Roo'ad	road	Yev	you have
Purra	put a		
Rec	recreation	**Irish**	
Reight	right	Auld	old
Raand	around	Chiold	child
Roaring	crying	Dat	that
Sen	self	Dis	this
Somat	something	Dere	there
Shis	she's	De	the
Speyks	speaks	Dease	these
Sumdy	somebody	Fer	for
Teneet	tonight	Ideut	idiot
Thall	you will	Tay	tea
Teld	told	Ting	thing
Te	to the	Tree	three
Thus	those	Trew	threw
Tha	you	Tis	it is
Tharren	that one	Winda	window
Thad	you had	Wid	with
Theear	there	Yis	you
Thi	your	Three	tree
Thingy	thing	Thing	ting
Tuther	the other	Idiot	Ideut
Un	one		
On't	on the		
Owt	anything		
Ore	over		
Wat	what		
Wah	was